S0-FUM-966

Second Presbyterian Church

The History of Second Presbyterian Church
Staunton, Virginia

1875-2000

Katharine L. Brown

Published by Lot's Wife Publishing for
Second Presbyterian Church
Staunton, Virginia
2002

Copyright © 2002 Second Presbyterian Church

All rights reserved. No part of this book may be reproduced, stored in a retrieval system, or transmitted, in any form or by any means, electronic, mechanical, photocopying, recording, or otherwise, without the written permission of Second Presbyterian Church.

The book is set in Palatino type by Barbara Corse;
Layout and interior design by Nancy Sorrells

Lot's Wife Publishing
P.O. Box 1844
Staunton, VA 24402

Library of Congress Catalog Card Number 2002107621
ISBN 0967602785

Table of Contents

Foreword v

Acknowledgments vi

Presbyterian Origins 1

Presbyterians in the Valley 10

A New Congregation is Born 21

Early Years 31

The Scott Era and a New House of Worship 55

Times of Transition 81

Second Church in Depression and War 102

The Boom Years 127

The Decision 148

Challenge, Change, and Centennial 161

A Time of Testing 191

Living in the Present, Looking to the Future 215

Members, 2002 233

Name Index 238

Foreword

In 1875, ten years after the end of the Civil War, thirteen members of First Presbyterian Church in Staunton petitioned Lexington Presbytery to establish a Presbyterian presence on the west side of town. The new church was needed, they argued, to respond to the growth and changes taking place in the city and surrounding areas. Second Presbyterian Church was the result of their faith, vision, and hard work.

Back then, people walked to church, or rode on a horse or in a carriage. There was no majestic pipe organ in the sanctuary, no gas-fired heat for the winter, or air conditioning in the summer. Bulletins weren't produced on a photocopier so each worshiper could have one. Information, from worship plans to prayer concerns, was not readily available on the internet. In fact, in 1875, the telephone was still one year away from being introduced to the nation.

Perhaps it is hard for us to envision what life was like in Second Church at its inception. So much has happened, in our lives, in our community, and in the nation and world that our connection to our past blurs and fades. One of the fundamental parameters of our human existence is change. We are always growing and changing, even as the world around us does likewise. Even so, Jesus Christ – the focus of our faith – is the same, yesterday, today, and forever (Hebrews 13:8).

This book tells the story of Second Presbyterian Church, and the significant role it has played in the lives of many as they experienced the joys and sorrows of life. It chronicles 125 years worth of yesterdays, to help us better understand who and where we are today. As we recall the stories of faithful men and women who have helped make Second Church what it is, may we remember that we serve the same Jesus Christ who led them, and who will inspire and guide us into the future.

Daniel S. Williams
Pastor
July 2002

Acknowledgments

A history book may have a sole author's name on the title page, but it is always the product of the work of many persons in addition to the author.

This book is the realization of a dream of the 125th anniversary planners to have a fully researched and documented history of this congregation to supplement and expand upon those briefer ones done by Dr. W.N. Scott, by the 75th anniversary committee, and by Lucille Sanger for the centennial. Special credit is due to Evelyn Beard, the persevering force behind this idea, and her committee, including Betty Landes, Juanita Mullins, and D.W. Sensabaugh.

Many members shared recollections of their long association in this church. Some who were interviewed individually include Nellie Reeves, Betty Landes, Lucille Sanger, Gennivee Carey, Eunice Wenger, and Kenneth Sensabaugh. Many members gathered at a supper with the partners of Lot's Wife Publishing and shared their recollections. It would not be possible to name them all. They know who they are, and I hope they know how much I appreciate their memories and anecdotes that depicted this warm and loving community.

Bill Haessly shared helpful detailed technical information about the restoration of the Möller organ. Herman Adkinson's photos of the Crusader Class events gave insight into a thriving fellowship in the congregation and helped with the book's illustrations. The historians for the Women of the Church and later the Presbyterian Women kept wonderfully detailed records of women's work beginning about 1950.

Shenandoah Presbytery congregations are to be commended for their fine work in preserving archives and artifacts. Second Church members who have given and raised funds for their Historical Room, caring for its archives, and changing its exhibits deserve special credit for their faithful attention to preserving the past.

Charlotte Ralston, church secretary, was unfailingly cheerful and helpful in opening the Historical Room whenever I needed to use its records and for making the session and deacons minutes stored in the office vault available for research.

Greg Kellerman of Butler, Pennsylvania, was an intern with Lot's Wife Publishing while he was completing his master's degree in history at James Madison University. He read Staunton newspapers from 1875-1950 to locate articles about Second Church. Those provide many details of women's work, ministers' activities, and church architecture that are not in the church records. I am grateful to Professor Raymond Hyser of JMU for recognizing our work as a professional training opportunity and for finding in Greg an ideal student to aid with the research.

My thanks are due to Nancy Sorrells, Sue Simmons, and Dorothy Boyd-Rush, my partners in Lot's Wife Publishing, for their work with interviews, in preparing a 125th anniversary exhibit, in taking notes in church records, and with proofreading and indexing. Barbara Corse's patient skill in typesetting, layout, and scanning has made the attractive appearance of the book possible. My husband, Madison Brown, was unfailingly patient through the long process of producing this volume.

Evelyn Beard was the gracious coordinator of the project. She, Betty Landes, Juanita Mullins, and D.W. Sensabaugh read the manuscript. They caught errors and made helpful suggestions for improvement. The book is better for their thoughtful attention. For further errors that we all missed, I take responsibility, and hope they will not detract from the reader's enjoyment of the story of a dedicated community of Christians.

Katharine L. Brown
Staunton, Virginia, July 2002

Second Presbyterian as seen on a 1905 postcard.

Chapter One
Presbyterian Origins

Staunton's beautiful Second Presbyterian Church marks its beginning in 1875, but its roots stretch back centuries and are planted deep in the soil of the lowlands of Scotland and in the province of Ulster in the north of Ireland. Understanding this is important to understanding the story of this congregation in the historic old city in the Shenandoah Valley.

In Scotland, on the far northern fringe of Europe, Christianity arrived slowly and late, over several centuries. Roman soldiers may have brought it into the south of Scotland as they encountered the Picts, a Celtic people. The Scoti, who gave their name to the land, arrived in the west of Scotland from the north of Ireland, bringing Christianity to that area. In the fifth, sixth, and seventh centuries, many in Scotland became Christians.[1]

Viking and Norse invasions and tribal warring made Scotland a battleground in the eighth to eleventh centuries. In the eleventh and twelfth centuries, orders of monks were introduced into Scotland from the Continent of Europe. Over several centuries, monks gained control of most Scottish parishes, and monasteries grew richer in a land where poverty prevailed for the ordinary folk.[2]

By the sixteenth century, the Renaissance, capitalism, the commercial revolution, the discovery of the New World, and the emerging Protestant Reformation had brought vast changes to Europe that had an effect in far-off Scotland. Indeed, by 1500, Scotland could boast three universities: St. Andrews, Glasgow, and Aberdeen. Yet most Scots were impoverished tenants, living in mud and stone huts thatched with straw, on the estates of local lairds and gentry. They grew oats for their staple food, grew barley to make beer, and raised sheep for wool. Border raids by rough gangs who stole cattle and abducted young women were common occurrences in the Scottish Lowlands where the Presbyterian Church was born.[3]

The Protestant Reformation made swift gains in Europe through the teachings of the former German monk, Martin Luther, but Patrick Hamilton, the man who introduced Luther's idea in Scotland, was burned at the stake as a heretic. It was not Luther's reformation that shaped Scotland, but that of John Knox, a former Scottish Roman Catholic priest who fled to Geneva, Switzerland, in 1541 when Mary Tudor, "Bloody Mary," ruled in England. Knox became a follower of the French theologian, John Calvin. His writings in his *Institutes of the Christian Religion* stressed the absolute sovereignty of God, the centrality of a covenant relationship with God, and the idea of predestination.[4]

Knox returned to Scotland in 1559 to a land divided between Protestantism and Catholicism. Radical Protestants were destroying churches and smashing works of art as idols. Scotland's Parliament, controlled by Protestants in 1560, eliminated Roman Catholicism, denied the authority of the pope, and forbade the saying of mass. Instead, it adopted a Confession of Faith and a Book of Discipline that Knox helped write. Believing that they were restoring a Biblical purity to the church, this new denomination placed authority in the hands of "presbyters" or elders who were to be elected by a majority vote in each congregation, and who sat with the minister as a judicial body called the Session. Beyond this local level was a district meeting, or court of elders and ministers, called the presbytery. Thus the term

The French theologian, John Calvin, dominated the Swiss city of Geneva. He attracted many Protestants from England when Mary Tudor ("Blood Mary") ruled from 1552 to 1558. John Knox was among them. Calvin's understanding of the absolute sovereignty of God and of the covenant relationship did much to shape Knox's thinking.

"presbyterian" came to describe the new Scottish church. The synod on a regional level and a General Assembly for the nation completed the pyramid of representative courts that governed this new denomination. It was a very different way from the traditional Roman Catholic governing structure and from the reformed Anglican and Lutheran churches, all of which relied on bishops.[5]

The new Presbyterian Church eliminated many traditional practices such as the observance of the Christian festivals of Christmas, Easter, and All Hallows Eve (Halloween). The symbol of the cross was regarded with suspicion and removed from churches and graveyards. Changes occurred in worship, including the elimination of a liturgy and of the practice of kneeling for prayers. Knox denounced kneeling to receive communion as "popish," and the Presbyterians have received communion seated ever since.

In long and fiery sermons, Knox and his successors reminded Scots that they were a contemporary version of the Israelites in the Old Testament. The Presbyterian Church

John Knox, a fiery preacher and skilled politician, did much to bring Scotland to Protestantism. His role in writing the Confession of Faith and the first Book of Discipline helped to shape the Presbyterian Church.

gave to the Scottish people a fierce sense of morality, a social conscience, a fear of sexuality, and a passion for education. It won the devotion of the people, especially in the Lowlands, where it gained control over the behavior of its members through enforcement of penalties for infractions of the ten commandments, including adultery, blasphemy and fornication, as well as failure to attend worship on the Sabbath.[6]

When, in the seventeenth century, opportunities arose for many Lowlanders to abandon their small holdings and seek a better life for their families just a few miles away across the Irish Sea in the north of Ireland, thousands welcomed the move. They took their meager possessions, their energy and drive, and their Presbyterianism with them. Some were attracted to the independent settlements established in County Antrim and in County Down, the parts of Ulster closest to Scotland, by the wealthy Scottish families of Hamilton and Montgomery. Others were attracted to the official Plantation of Ulster established by King James VI of Scotland and I of England to claim the lands in the north and west of Ulster abandoned by the native Irish leaders in what became known as the "Flight of the Earls." This occurred in 1608, a few years after the armies of Queen Elizabeth I of England had defeated these last Irish opponents of English domination in Ireland. Counties Londonderry, Tyrone, Fermanagh, and Donegal were largely settled in this way with Scots mainly, but also with some English.[7]

The first Presbyterian minister in Ulster was Edward Brice in 1613 who had a congregation at Broadisland between Carrickfergus and Larne on the coast in Antrim. The Irish established church, although Anglican, was very broadminded in the early seventeenth century under the leadership of Archbishop James Ussher. A number of Presbyterian ministers served in parish churches in Ulster and received the tithes. Robert Blair in Bangor, James Hamilton in Ballywalter, and Robert Cunningham in Holywood were other Presbyterians who occupied pulpits in the established church.[8]

This broad policy changed in the 1630s when Charles I succeeded to the thrones of England and Scotland and wished to enforce conformity with a strong emphasis on bishops. His Lord Lieutenant, Thomas Wentworth, and new bishops of the established church set out to remove Presbyterian ministers from parish churches in Ulster. In Scotland, ardent Presbyterians signed the National Covenant, vowing to fight episcopalianism with their lives. In Ireland, Wentworth ordered that all Scots in Ulster over age sixteen denounce that covenant. This oath became known as the "Black Oath." Some ministers and their congregations decided to leave Ireland, to return to Scotland, or to sail to America on the *Eagle Wing*. This ship was blown back by a storm, and ended that effort.[9]

An uprising of the native Irish Catholics against the newcomer Protestants, especially the Presbyterians, took

Ulster is the northern province of Ireland. When counties were organized in Ireland under English rule, nine were formed in Ulster: Antrim, Down, Armagh, Londonderry, Tyrone, Fermanagh, Cavan, Monaghan, and Donegal. When Northern Ireland was created in the 1920s, the last three listed counties remained with the Irish Free State (now Republic of Ireland). Many of the colonial era settlers of the Valley of Virginia had their roots in Donegal, Tyrone, and Londonderry.

place in Ulster in 1641. Although many of the stories of atrocities may have been exaggerated, there is truth to others. It was a brutal age, especially over matters of religion. This was the time of the Thirty Years' War in Europe between Protestant states and Catholic states. This uprising ushered in nearly two decades of civil war in Ireland, England, and Scotland. It also brought the occasion for the organization of the first presbytery in Ireland. This occurred with the army of Major-General Robert Munro, who landed at Carrickfergus from Scotland in April 1642. Five ministers who were army chaplains and four elders formed that presbytery on June 10, 1642. After the war, three of the ministers stayed on to take congregations in Ulster. Petitions for ministers flooded the presbytery from settlements all over Ulster where Scottish Presbyterians wanted ministers of their own. Because Oliver Cromwell ruled in England and oversaw an attempt to replace the established episcopal form of the church with something more like Presbyterianism, it was a good opportunity to form organized Presbyterian congregations in Ulster. Many did so.[10]

The Restoration that put Charles II on the throne actually brought a period of toleration, even though he was a strong supporter of bishops. Although Presbyterian ministers in established parish churches who refused to use the *Book of Common Prayer* for services were removed, Presbyterian ministers of their own congregations were not bothered. The king even made a grant of money toward their support, called the *regium donum*, that helped support them in the same way that tithes supported the established church clergy.

When Charles II died in 1685, his brother James II succeeded to the throne. He had become a Roman Catholic. When his second wife, an Italian Catholic princess, produced a son, ardent Protestants in England who would not accept a Catholic ruler forced James to flee. In 1688 they invited William of Orange, married to James II's eldest daughter by his Protestant first wife, to take the throne as William III, ruling jointly with his wife, Mary. This ushered in a war, with Ireland as the battleground. The Presbyterians of Ulster strongly supported William III against James II's armies that were supported by King Louis XIV of France. They were proud of their role defending the Protestant cause in the Siege of Londonderry and in the Battle of Enniskillen, as well as at the Battle of the Boyne in 1690.

In the peace that followed William III's victory, Ulster Scots Presbyterians were disappointed that William permitted the Anglo-Irish Ascendancy in the south of Ireland to dominate, and with it the established Church of Ireland with its bishops. The Penal Acts passed by the Irish Parliament were designed mainly to put down the native Irish Catholics who had supported James II. However, some of them had a negative impact on Protestant Dissenters, particularly the Presbyterians of Ulster.

The most distressing of these acts to Presbyterians was the Test Act, passed in 1704 after William III had died and his sister-in-law Queen Anne came to the throne. By this act, office holding was restricted to those who took communion in the established church. Also, only members of that church could obtain degrees at Ireland's only university, Trinity College, Dublin. And, Presbyterians always objected to having to pay tithes to support the established church.[11]

In the next decade, when rising rents, poor harvests, and severe weather descended on Ulster, these economic conditions, coming on top of dissatisfaction with their status as dissenters, caused many Ulster Scots to reach the decision to leave Ireland and try their luck in the Middle Colonies in North America.

Chapter One Notes

[1] Fitzroy Maclean, *Scotland: A Concise History* (London: Thames and Hudson, 1993), 14-15.

[2] J.D. Mowat, *A Text-Book of Scottish Church History* (Edinburgh: Robert Grant & Sons, Ltd., 1939), 13-43.

[3] Richard Webster, *A History of the Presbyterian Church in America, from its Origin until the Year 1760, with Biographical Sketches of Its Early Ministers* (Philadelphia: Joseph M. Wilson, 1857), 70-78.

[4] Vergilius Ferm, *Pictorial History of Protestantism: A Panoramic View of Western Europe and the United States* (New York: Philosophical Library, 1957), 72-73, 132.

[5] Mowat, *Scottish Church History*, 88-93; Julius Lloyd, *Sketches of Church History in Scotland* (London: Society for the Promotion of Christian Knowledge, nd), 57-61.

[6] Peter Brooke, *Ulster Presbyterianism: The Historical Perspective, 1610-1970* (Dublin: Gill and Macmillan; New York: St. Martin's Press, 1987), 8-9.

[7] Jonathan Bardon, *A History of Ulster* (Belfast: The Blackstaff Press, 1992), 120-131; Rory Fitzpatrick, *God's Frontiersmen: The Scots-Irish Epic* (London: Weidenfeld and Nicolson, 1989), 16-31.

[8] Thomas Hamilton, *History of the Irish Presbyterian Church,* (Edinburgh : T. & T. Clark, nd), 36-41.

[9] Ibid, 132-134; Hamilton, 49-51.

[10] Ibid, 136-141; Hamilton, 60-68.

[11] Ibid, 157-173.

Chapter Two
Presbyterians in the Valley

A few Presbyterians had come to the North American colonies between 1670 and 1715, mainly scattered groups of Scots or Ulstermen who founded several small congregations in New Jersey, Pennsylvania, Delaware, Maryland, and Virginia. As early as 1682, Presbyterians on the Eastern Shore of Maryland were appealing to the Presbytery of the Laggan in County Donegal for a minister. The best known of the handful of early ministers in the colonies was Francis Makemie from Rathmelton, County Donegal. He settled in Accomack County, Virginia, in 1690, itinerated widely to preach to scattered groups of Presbyterians, and joined with several other settled ministers to organize America's first presbytery, the Presbytery of Philadelphia, in 1706.[1]

But it was not until 1717 that large numbers of Presbyterians from Ulster began settling in the Middle Colonies, then in another generation moving south into Virginia. Although church historians have often emphasized that religious freedom was one of the main reasons that these settlers came to America, in reality most came for economic reasons.

Pressured by English merchants and farmers, Parliament had placed severe restrictions on Irish exports of livestock and agricultural produce and on direct trade with the colonies. The Woollen Act of 1698 nearly destroyed the thriving woollen industry built up by Scots in Ulster. Although many moved into linen production after that, the very success of linen put additional pressure on land, causing rents to rise. The twenty-year and thirty-year leases that lured thousands of Scottish Presbyterians to Ulster after the Williamite Protestant victory of 1690 were expiring around 1720. When landlords raised rents sharply for renewal of leases, many Ulster Scots decided to immigrate to the colonies to become landowners there rather than remain tenants in Ireland. Harvests failed in 1725, 1726, and 1727, driving food prices beyond the reach of many, and convincing thousands to emigrate to America. Brutal winters in 1739, 1740, and 1741 brought hunger and disease approaching levels of the more famous potato famine of the 1840s. Again, thousands chose to sail for America.[2]

Although some went to New England, where the Calvinist theology of the established Congregationalist churches was similar to Presbyterianism, they did not find a warm welcome in Boston. It was in Pennsylvania, the colony founded by William Penn as a refuge for Quakers, that the Ulster Scots readily made themselves at home. Newcastle, Delaware and Philadelphia were their chief ports of entry. Surviving statistical records are not good, but observers' reports suggest that 1,000-3,000 arrived in those ports annually for much of the eighteenth century. A great many of these Ulster Scots Presbyterians came in family groups and acquired farm land, but large numbers of single young men and women came as indentured servants, with the promise of land when their term of service was over.[3]

The Quakers and Germans, who arrived earlier than the Scotch-Irish, had claimed the best lands in eastern Pennsylvania, so the Scotch-Irish moved to the Pennsylvania frontier areas. Their church was ready to greet them. The Synod of Pennsylvania organized in 1716 with three presbyteries: Long Island, Philadelphia, and New Castle. The swarm of immigrants soon outgrew the number of ministers available to serve congregations being formed. An important church for the frontier settlers was Donegal Church near the Susquehanna River in Lancaster County, Pennsylvania. It was founded about 1721, and in 1732 became the focal point of the new Donegal Presbytery. Their minister, James Anderson, was to play an important role in bringing Presbyterianism to Virginia.[4]

By the 1730s, land was becoming more difficult and more expensive to obtain in Pennsylvania. The most recent Scotch-Irish immigrants and the children of the earliest Scotch-Irish immigrants, who had reached adulthood, married, and wanted farms of their own, were attracted to the Virginia frontier. There, land was plentiful and cheap, and did not have an Indian threat. In the 1730s Governor Gooch, the Virginia government, and land developers were eager to encourage settlers who could extend the colony's line of settlement westward and also serve as a buffer between eastern Virginia and the Indians.

Virginia had an established Anglican church, much like that the Scotch-Irish Presbyterians had left behind in Ireland. Many of them wanted to be sure that they would be welcome in Virginia and that their form of worship would be tolerated. In 1738, Synod sent the minister, James Anderson, from Donegal Church to preach to Presbyterians settled in the Shenandoah Valley and to visit Governor Gooch with a letter from the synod requesting assurance of toleration.

Anderson helped set up a Christian Society, which was a congregation without elders, called the Triple Forks of the Shenandoah. This covered the area of the North, Middle, and South Rivers in present Augusta County. He preached the first recorded sermon in the Upper Valley at the home of John Lewis near present-day Staunton. All Presbyterianism in Augusta County and Staunton stems from this early effort. Anderson was also successful in gaining the governor's promise that Presbyterian ministers and meeting houses would be tolerated and able to worship, so long as they registered the ministers' names and the location of the places of worship.[5]

The first settled minister in Augusta County was the Reverend John Craig. He was a native of the parish of Donegore, County Antrim, Ireland and was educated at Glasgow University. His two congregations, Tinkling Spring in present Fishersville, and Augusta Stone in present Fort Defiance, were the first two organized congregations in the county. Craig traveled widely on horseback, even as far as present Roanoke, to preach to scattered Christian Societies and to baptize infants. Meeting houses sprang up in several of these locations, especially North Mountain and South Mountain, from which several permanent churches in Augusta and Rockbridge Counties developed.[6]

Presbyterianism has a great tendency to form factions over doctrinal differences, and often to spawn splinter denominations. Factionalism entered the Valley of Virginia and its infant Presbyterian congregations in the 1740s with the movement called the Great Awakening. This revival movement swept across Britain, Ireland, and all the American colonies in the years from 1730-1760, affecting every denomination in some way. The movement was especially strong among Scotch-Irish Presbyterians, where emotional meetings had roots in the Six-Mile Water Revival in County Antrim in the mid-seventeenth century.

The New Side or New Light revivalist faction in the colonial Presbyterian church held that emotional preaching by ministers who had a conversion experience was essential in order to lead hearers to a conviction of sin, repentance, and a conversion. The New Side also believed that ministers must be trained in the American colonies to serve the growing number of congregations. The Old Side resisted the emotionalism, and believed that ministers must hold a degree from a Scottish university. John Craig and his congregations adhered to the Old Side.

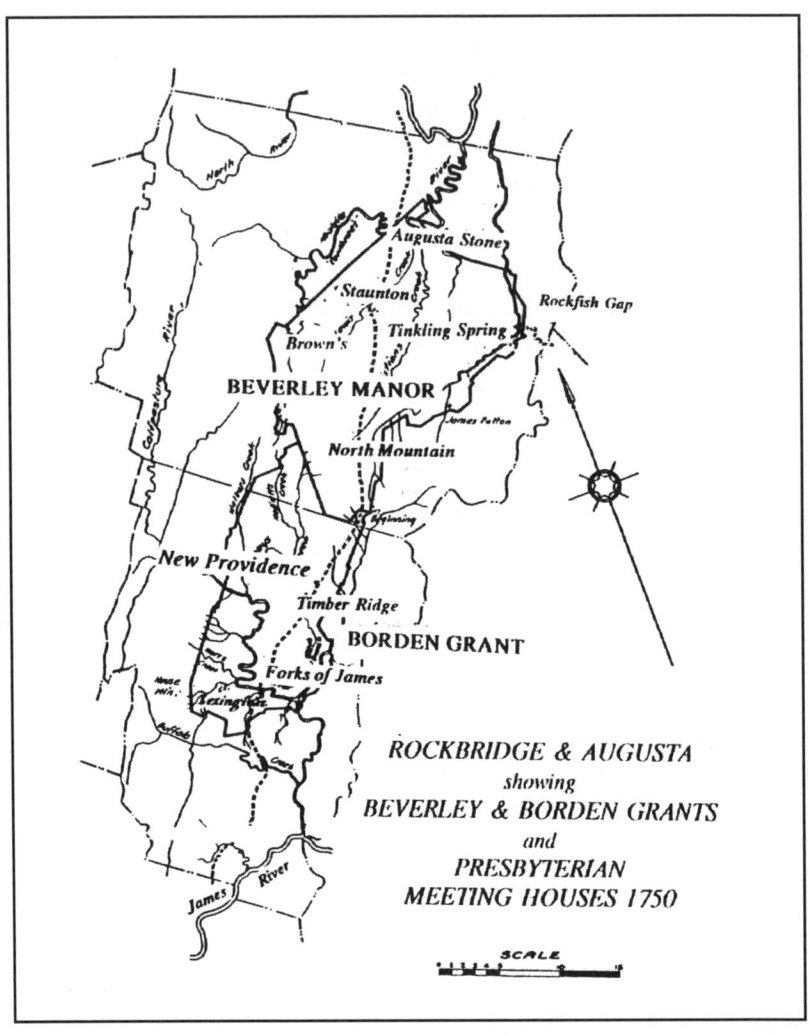

In the area covered by the Beverley Manor and Borden Grants in present-day Augusta and Rockbridge Counties, numerous Presbyterian congregations with meeting houses sprang up by 1760. These included Augusta Stone, Tinkling Spring, New Providence, North Mountain (soon divided into Bethel and Brown's, later Hebron), Forks of James (Monmouth), Timber Ridge, and the South Mountain meeting house that was a forerunner of Old Providence Associate Reformed Presbyterian Church.

Some of the settlers in the Valley were New Light sympathizers who welcomed itinerant revivalist ministers. John Blair, a young New Light preacher who visited the Valley in 1746 organized six congregations that soon became New Providence, Timber Ridge, and Monmouth Churches in present Rockbridge County, and Bethel and Rocky Spring in Augusta County. Presbyterian settlers in the north of present Augusta County and the south of present Rockingham County worshipped at Cook's Creek and Peaked Mountain Meetinghouses until Mossy Creek was formed in the late 1760s.[7]

When the members of North Mountain Meeting House split over the revival, some formed Bethel, and the conservative Old Side group left to form Brown's Meeting House (later Hebron Church) in the present Swoope area of Augusta County. When the Timber Ridge and New Providence congregations left the old South Mountain Meeting House to form their own New Side congregations, some of the conservative members stayed behind and sought supply ministers from a splinter group, the Associate Presbytery, or Seceders. They eventually formed Old Providence Associate Reformed Presbyterian Church. So several varieties of Presbyterianism were represented in the Upper Valley well before the American Revolution. The Old Side-New Side healed their rift by 1760, joined their separate synods into one, and in Virginia were united in Hanover Presbytery, formed in 1755 and covering the entire colony.[8]

All the Presbyterian congregations in the Upper Valley were in rural areas. Staunton, the county seat and principal town of the Upper Valley, had no Presbyterian church, although the majority of the town's residents were probably Presbyterians. They went by horseback or wagon on the Sabbath to worship at Tinkling Spring. Staunton's Presbyterians petitioned Hanover Presbytery in May 1765 for supply ministers and for permission to construct their own building in town. Presbytery did not approve that building, so Staunton's Presbyterians continued to travel to Tinkling Spring. After John Craig left that congregation to devote himself full time to Augusta Stone Church, Tinkling Spring had short-term supply ministers until 1776 when the Reverend James Waddell arrived from Lancaster County, Virginia, as a supply minister and remained until 1784. Waddell was an outstanding orator and a much-loved minister. He preached occasionally in Staunton, either in the courthouse or in the parish church on the site of present Trinity Episcopal Church. At the end of the American Revolution, the Presbyterians in Staunton, who were still a Christian Society, not an organized congregation, joined with Tinkling Spring to make out a call to Waddell as minister, but they never presented it, and he moved instead to Gordonsville in Orange County.[9]

Waddell's successor at Tinkling Spring was the Reverend John McCue, a graduate of Liberty Hall Academy (later Washington College, then Washington and Lee University), who had studied theology with Waddell. When the Presbyterian Church was strong enough in Virginia to divide into two presbyteries, McCue attended the first meeting of Lexington Presbytery at Timber Ridge Church in 1786. He supplied the Staunton congregation occasionally until 1799.[10]

In 1799, the Staunton Presbyterians acquired the services of the Reverend John Glendy, former minister of Maghera, County Londonderry, Ireland. Glendy had taken an active role in the revolutionary Society of United Irishmen in Ireland. After the failed Rebellion of 1798 against British rule in Ireland, Glendy had to flee the country. He settled in Augusta County, bought a farm, and became the stated supply at Bethel Church. While in that position, he also served the Staunton congregation. He preached an important oration in Staunton on George Washington's Birthday in 1800. Glendy also attracted the attention of Thomas Jefferson who invited him to address Congress. Glendy was called to a Baltimore Church, and left the Staunton congregation in 1803.[11]

In May 1804, the Staunton Christian Society requested that Lexington Presbytery provide it supplies. Presbytery appointed two ministers in Augusta County, the Reverend John Montgomery of Rocky Spring in the Deerfield Valley and the Reverend Benjamin Erwin of Mossy Creek, to organize the church, which then may have had only a couple dozen members, and elect elders. In August 1806, the Reverend William Calhoun became the first minister installed in Staunton, serving Brown's Meeting House (Hebron) also. He remained until 1826, and in 1818 oversaw the building of the first Presbyterian house of worship, a brick building described as "large and very decent."[12]

After Calhoun left to devote himself full time to Hebron, the Staunton church had several ministers who stayed only a few years: Joseph Smith, 1826-1832, John Steele, 1834-1837, Paul Stevenson, 1838-1844, and Robert Howison, 1844-1845. Staunton experienced considerable growth in those two decades, for it was in that span that the Western Lunatic Asylum and the Virginia School for the Deaf, Dumb, and Blind were located in the town. Two academies or seminaries for girls were also established in the town, the Virginia Female Institute in 1842 and the Augusta Female Seminary chartered in 1845. The latter school, under Presbyterian leadership, had leaders of the Staunton Presbyterian Church among its founders, and was located beside the church building. The congregation used one of the rooms in the school as its lecture hall.[13]

The Reverend Benjamin Mosby Smith was minister for nearly a decade, from 1845-1854. The first election of Deacons took place while Smith was minister. It was in this time that the Staunton Presbyterian Church built its first manse, a handsome Greek Revival structure. After Smith left to become a professor in the theological seminary at Hampden-Sydney College, the congregation in December 1854 called a young professor there as its next minister, the Reverend Joseph Ruggles Wilson. Although Wilson was in

The building where Staunton's Presbyterians worshipped until after the Civil War stood beside what is now the administration building of Mary Baldwin College. It was a Greek Revival structure typical of rural Presbyterian churches built in central and western Virginia in the first half of the nineteenth century.

Staunton less than three years, in that time both Augusta Female Seminary and the church were enlarged.[14] The minister's little son, Thomas Woodrow Wilson, who was born while the Wilsons lived in the manse, grew up to become President of Princeton University, Governor of New Jersey, and President of the United States.

The next minister, the Reverend William E. Baker, came in 1859 as stated supply, then was called as minister and installed in 1859. He remained until 1884, and saw the Staunton Presbyterian Church through the most difficult and tempestuous time in its entire history. He was the minister through the Civil War, when many of the men in the congregation served in the military, some returning wounded and maimed for life, others not returning at all.

He was the minister as Union armies marched through the town, inflicting considerable damage. It was Baker's job to help the congregation bind up its wounds after the war and look ahead to better times.

That the congregation did that successfully is testified to by the fact that just five years after the end of the war, Staunton Presbyterian Church had outgrown its classical revival church adjacent to Augusta Female Seminary. The congregation determined in 1870 to construct an entirely new church across Frederick Street in the Norman/Romanesque revival style then popular in Virginia. Similar church structures nearby include Falling Spring in Rockbridge County and Lee Chapel at Washington College in Lexington. The last service in the old church was on June 25, 1871, and the dedication of the new church took place in June 1872.

The church seemed poised to go from strength to strength at a time Staunton was experiencing great growth in population, an important expansion in building commercial and residential structures, and transportation growth with a new north-south railroad through the city. Yet, it was just at this point that some in the congregation determined to leave Staunton Presbyterian Church and form a new congregation in the city.

Chapter Two Notes

[1] James H. Smylie, "Francis Makemie: Tradition and Challenge," *Journal of Presbyterian History*, 61(1983):199-208; Webster, *A History of the Presbyterian Church in America*, 67, 90; Leonard Trinterud, *The Forming of an American Tradition: A Re-Examination of Colonial Presbyterianism* (Philadelphia: The Westminster Press, 1949), 25-30.

[2] R.L. Dickson, *Ulster Emigration to Colonial America 1718-1775* (Belfast: Ulster Historical Foundation, 1966), 6n, 7, 34-40. The notion that economic motivation was the chief driving force was first presented by Wayland Dunaway, *The Scotch-Irish of Colonial Pennsylvania* (Chapel Hill: University of North Carolina Press, 1944; reprinted Baltimore: Genealogical Publishing Co., Inc., 1979), 28. See also Guy Soulliard Klett, *Presbyterians in Colonial Pennsylvania* (Philadelphia, 1937), 18, 42-43, 52-53.

[3] Dickson, *Ulster Emigration*, 21-23; W. Desmond Baillie, et al., *History of Congregations in the Presbyterian Church in Ireland,1610-1982* (Belfast: Presbyte-

rian Historical Society of Ireland,1982), "Aghadowey," 1; Dunaway, *Scotch-Irish of Colonial Pennsylvania,* 34-37; Klett, *Presbyterians in Colonial Pennsylvania,* 30-35.

⁴Ernest Trice Thompson, *Presbyterians in the South, Volume One, 1607-1861* (Richmond, Va.: John Knox Press, 1963), 20-28; Howard McKnight Wilson, *The Tinkling Spring: Headwaters of Freedom* (Fishersville,Va.: The Tinkling Spring and Hermitage Presbyterian Churches, 1954), 36-37; Richard K. McMaster, *Donegal Presbyterians: A Scots-Irish Congregation in Pennsylvania* (Morgantown, Pa.: Printed for The Donegal Society by Masthof Press, 1995), 1-27.

⁵Wilson, *The Tinkling Spring,* 49-52, 62-63.

⁶Ibid., 64-66. From North Mountain both Bethel and Hebron churches were eventually formed, and from South Mountain came Timber Ridge and New Providence in Rockbridge County and Old Providence ARP Church in Augusta.

⁷Charles William Blair, *A History of Mossy Creek Presbyterian Church* (Bridgewater, Va.: Bridgewater Beacon Printing Co., 2000), 26-30.

⁸Katharine L. Brown, *New Providence Church, 1746-1996: A History* (Raphine, Va.: New Providence Church, 1996), 34-37; Nancy T. Sorrells, Katharine L. Brown, and J. Susanne Simmons, *The History of Old Providence Church, 1742-2001* (Staunton, Va.: Lot's Wife Publishing, 2001), 43-49, 51-55.

⁹Arista Hoge, *The First Presbyterian Church, Staunton, Virginia* (Staunton: Caldwell-Sites Company, 1908), 4-8.

¹⁰Ibid., 10.

¹¹Katharine L. Brown and Nancy T. Sorrells, "Presbyterian Pathways to Power: Networking Gentrification, and the Scotch-Irish Heritage among Virginia Presbyterian Ministers, 1760-1860" in *Atlantic Crossroads: Historical Connections between Scotland, Ulster and North America,* Patrick Fitzgerald and Steve Ickringill, editors, (Newtownards: Colourpoint, 2002). See also *One Hundred Fifty Years, 1803-1953* (Baltimore: Second Presbyterian Church of Baltimore, 1953), 7-12.

¹²Hoge, *First Presbyterian Church, Staunton,* 34.

¹³Ibid., 35-36; Howard McKnight Wilson, *Lexington Presbytery Heritage* (Verona, Va.: The McClure Press, 1971), 228.

¹⁴Hoge, *First Presbyterian Church, Staunton,* 36-37.

Chapter Three
A New Congregation is Born

The founding of a new church is an act of faith and an exciting event for a denomination and for the pioneering persons who formed the congregation. The birth of Second Presbyterian Church in Staunton was no exception to that rule.

It is difficult to know just when some members of the Staunton Presbyterian Church began to talk among themselves of forming a new congregation. It is certain that they had discussed and formulated their plan between the spring meeting of presbytery in April and August 1875, for they were prepared to present their case to Presbytery at its fall meeting in September. They even had a minister in mind to call, and could promise a salary of $700 a year for him.

The April 1875 meeting of Lexington Presbytery had learned from one of its ministers that two young Irish graduates of the Free Church College in Edinburgh, Scotland, proposed to come to America if Lexington Presbytery would accept them. The young men arrived in June of 1875, passed their trials before Presbytery, and were licensed as probationers. The Staunton group that was planning the new congregation had its eye on one of them, MacDuff Simpson of the Presbytery of Dublin, Ireland. In the meanwhile, Loch Willow congregation in Churchville also eyed the young man and issued a call for him when Presbytery met.[1]

At its meeting on September 15, 1875, Lexington

Presbytery received a petition from thirteen persons asking for the formation of a second Presbyterian Church in Staunton. Those names were James Bumgardner, Thomas S. Doyle, M. Harvey Effinger, Mrs. Margaret Effinger, Holmes Erwin, G.D. Everett, Jed Hotchkiss, Mrs. Sarah Hotchkiss, Miss Nellie Hotchkiss, William A. Hudson, Charles D. McCoy, Mary McDonough McCoy and Charles W.S. Turner.[2] Nine of these persons went on to become charter members of the church. Jed Hotchkiss attended the Presbytery meeting representing the group and speaking on behalf of the petition. His prominence as an educator, but especially as mapmaker for Confederate General Thomas "Stonewall" Jackson, guaranteed that he would receive a respectful hearing by ministers and laymen alike.

The petitioners presented five points to justify the need for a new church. First they claimed that the population of Staunton had doubled since 1866, and secondly that many of the newcomers were Presbyterians, whom the present (new) church building could not accommodate in its pews. In the third place, the petitioners said that the current pastor (Baker) was "most efficient" but that there was more work to be done than one man could handle. Their fourth reason was that a new church would "advance the cause of Christ and the interests of Presbyterianism in our midst." Finally, the petitioners claimed that "our work in this new field will be conducive to our personal religion and piety."[3]

Discussion of the issue was lively and lengthy resulting in a committee to inquire into "the expediency of such an organization" and report to a meeting of Presbytery in Staunton on October 19. That committee consisted of three ministers: Givens B. Strickler of Tinkling Spring, Ebenezer D. Junkin of New Providence, and James Murray of Bethel, and elders David S. Bell of Tinkling Spring, William M. Tate of Bethel, and George G. Grattan of Harrisonburg.[4]

The underlying circumstances behind the petition's five points that caused those thirteen members of First Presbyterian Church in Staunton to want to leave that congregation and start a new one remain unclear. There are many typical reasons for which new congregations are formed. One of these is growth of the congregation, causing crowding of the facilities. This can suggest it would be better to start a second church than to expand the old one. This could not have been the reason in this case, for the congregation of Staunton's Presbyterian Church had recently completed the construction of the large building which still houses that congregation. On June 11, 1872, the *Staunton Spectator* reported that on the Sabbath just past took place "the dedication of that large and splendid church, in the afternoon the thanksgiving services in connection therewith, and in the evening the anniversary celebration of the Sabbath School of that congregation."[5] When the committee that wished to form the new church presented lack of space as one of their reasons, presbytery investigated the charge and rejected it.

Another reason for division in a congregation could be dissatisfaction of some members with the pastor. This does not seem to have been the case with the Reverend William E. Baker, pastor of Staunton's Presbyterian Church since 1857. However, Baker thought that the petition was "regarded by the public as a demonstration unfriendly to himself," as he expressed it in a letter to his congregation. Baker was sufficiently upset over the petition to submit his resignation and to have his Session call a congregational meeting on October 8, 1875, to vote on the question of asking presbytery to dissolve the pastoral relationship at its called meeting on October 19.

The leaders of the petitioners' group were Jed Hotchkiss and Capt. Charles D. McCoy, Superintendent of the Virginia School for the Deaf, Dumb, and Blind. Correspondence took place between the Reverend Mr. Baker and Hotchkiss and McCoy at this time. Hotchkiss had apparently moved swiftly to assure his pastor that the petition was not intended in any way to be a negative reflection on him, or to "place him in a false position before the general public," as Baker believed. Baker for his part had written Hotchkiss on September 25 to assure him of his good feelings and respect for his Christian motives in the affair. Hotchkiss was out of town, so his wife sent the letter to Captain McCoy to answer. McCoy wrote Baker

> In our petition for a new Church we gave our honest reasons for the course we take. These reasons are, we think, cogent and they are supported by conscientious convictions, reached after deliberate and prayerful consideration. I am sure I speak not only for myself, but for every signer of that paper, when I say that there is nothing but the kindest feeling on our part towards you and every member of the congregation. And further, that no signed of the petition desires your resignation of your Pastorship.[6]

Two other petition signers, M. Harvey Effinger and T.S. Doyle, a member of the staff at the Virginia School for the Deaf, Dumb, and Blind, also wrote Baker. They indicated that they believed they had been "placed in a false position before the public" regarding their feelings toward Baker, and requested that the correspondence between Baker and Captain McCoy "be read to the congregation at the time your resignation is tendered." Thus the discussion made its way into the press which gives more details than church records do about the founding of Second Presbyterian Church, but no insight into the underlying reasons.

At the congregational meeting, General John Echols, an elder of the congregation, and one of Staunton's most respected citizens, delivered a stirring speech in support of Baker's ministry. Echols noted that "our friends who seek for a new church have confessed that they are actuated by no unfriendly feeling to our pastor." He commended their frank correspondence on the subject, but he personally thought that their actions would impair Baker's usefulness and manliness, and offered a resolution in support of the pastor and urging him not to resign. Others spoke to the resolution, including William Frazier, who had chaired the building committee for the recently dedicated new church. General Echols took the floor again and with all of his skill as a leading local attorney, gave an impassioned plea of support for the resolution upholding Baker's ministry. The newspaper reported that "many of the congregation were in tears."[7]

It was made perfectly clear at the meeting that the results of the vote "shall not prejudice the prayer of the petitioners before Presbytery." In other words, even if the congregation upheld Baker, the petitioners would still be free to place their case before Presbytery and, if approved, take action to form a new congregation. When the written secret ballots were counted, 340 voted in favor of the resolution of support and retention for Baker, eight voted no, and four more voted no on the final clause of the resolution, not its entirety.[8] It was a resounding victory for Baker, who remained the pastor until 1882.

The meeting was not a loss for the petitioners, however, for they were upheld in their intention to form a new congregation, if Presbytery granted permission. When the Reverend Mr. Strickler and his committee appointed to investigate the matter presented a full written report to presbytery on October 19, they disagreed with most of the points that Hotchkiss had presented in the petition in September. They said that many doubted the doubling of the Staunton population, but that in any case, there was no current census. They rejected the argument that the new church did not have pew space for all the Presbyterians in town, saying simply that some may not get as good a pew location as they wished. On the third, fourth, and fifth points, the committee believed that all could be accomplished by going through the normal channels of sponsoring a mission church under the wing of the existing church. In short, the committee recommended that the request of the petitioners be denied.

After the report, Baker spoke. He indicated that the plan for a new church had been developed when he was out of town on his vacation in Highland County the summer of 1875. He noted that he had a book he had filled with the names of and information about every Presbyterian in Staunton as evidence that he was well on top of pastoral developments. Further, he indicated that there were still forty of the 160 pews in the new church that were not rented, indicating ample space for worshippers. After hearing these views, Presbytery adjourned until the next day.[9]

There must have been considerable lobbying and pressure placed on committee members that night. When they met in the morning to consider the issue again, Hotchkiss spoke on behalf of the petition. He assured that the petitioners were not malcontents, had no evil intent, and did not wish to break up the old church. They believed that the Sunday School of 400 children at the church was all that could be handled, but that a second church could develop a Sunday School with an additional 300 children.

The Reverend James Murray of Bethel spoke against a new church, saying that no one could guarantee that the group could pay the $700 promised a minister, and that none but a single man could live on such a small amount anyhow. He was forced to concede his first point when M. Harvey Effinger promised his personal bond for the payment of the salary. When questioned by Major William Tate about Presbyterian families not in the church, Hotchkiss said that there were twenty to forty of them, but that the more important point than arguing individual families was that his statistics showed that the Presbyterian Church, over the course of the century since 1775, had fallen from first place to sixth place in Staunton and environs.[10]

Dr. David C. Irwin, pastor of Timber Ridge, spoke strongly on behalf of forming the new church. Finally the

Presbytery relented and gave its permission to form a new congregation. They also appointed a committee of the Reverend Robert C. Walker of Union Church near Churchville, the Reverend John W. Rosebro of Mossy Creek, and Elder David S. Bell of Tinkling Spring to work with the petitioners to determine a date for organization.[11]

On November 5, 1875, *The Vindicator* reported that "The Second Presbyterian Church of Staunton will be organized at Town Hall, which has been rented for a year, Sunday night week, the 14th inst."[12] The Reverend Mr. Baker at First Church told the newspaper that "while the movement for a new church had not met their approval, yet, now that it was a fact, the members of the new congregation should have their kindest wishes and prayers for their success; though in view of the many objects requiring its aid it was not likely the mother church could aid the new one pecuniarily."

The first worship service of the new congregation took place at the old Town Hall on W. Beverley Street, where the Masonic Building now stands, on November 14, 1875, with the Reverend Mr. Rosebro of Mossy Creek preaching.

The founding members were thirteen in number, but not the same thirteen as on the petition. The charter members were Thomas S. Doyle, who later became principal of VSDB, J. Frederick Effinger, Mrs. Margaret Effinger, Holmes Erwin, William C. Geiger, Jedediah Hotchkiss, his wife, Sarah Hotchkiss, their daughter, Nellie Hotchkiss, William A. Hudson, Charles D. McCoy, of VSDB, Charles W.S. Turner, Henry A. Walker and Mrs. Lucy D. Woods.[13] That initial congregation elected as its first officers Elder Charles D. McCoy and Deacons William A. Hudson and Henry A. Walker, a cashier at the National Valley Bank.

Hotchkiss is the founding member who was the best known at the time, and whose reputation time has done nothing to diminish. He was a northerner who had moved to Virginia in the antebellum years to operate academies at Mossy Creek and Loch Willow. He adopted Virginia's well-being as a primary interest of his life and gave himself to promoting its economic, religious, and educational welfare until his death in 1898.

After the war and his outstanding service as Jackson's mapmaker, Hotchkiss moved with his wife Sarah and their two daughters from Churchville to Staunton. He taught as a Professor of Natural Sciences for Mary Julia Baldwin when she reopened her seminary. He also did surveying and mapmaking for the law firms of Echols, Bell and Catlett. In 1867, he helped found the Augusta County Fair. He became a close friend of Dr. Barnas Sears when that important northern educator moved to Staunton with the Peabody Fund. When Virginia created its first public school system under William Henry Ruffner of Washington College, Hotchkiss became the first superintendent of Augusta County Schools. Robert E. Lee as President of Washington College had created a Board of Survey with Hotchkiss as its topographical engineer. The group hoped to publish maps of many counties, but Hotchkiss's 1870 map of Augusta County is the only one, for Lee died and his support for the project died with him.[14]

Those accomplishments alone were sufficient to earn Hotchkiss distinction, but he moved on to areas of economic growth and development, seeking always to find ways to bring Virginia into the growing international mineral, transportation, and industrialization picture. Understanding that capital was sorely needed in the defeated former Confederate state, Hotchkiss made trips to England in 1872 and in the fall of 1874 until the spring of 1875 to try to interest wealthy British citizens in Virginia investments. His involvement in this work may help to explain why he was not one of the original elders of Second Presbyterian Church, even though he was one of the most ardent of the spokesmen for the creation of the new congregation. His own financial affairs were often difficult and plagued with debt, so that he was in no position to bestow wealth upon the struggling

Jed Hotchkiss, born in Windsor, New York in 1828, was the most prominent of the founders of Second Church. He was an original Fellow of the Geographical Society, a member of the American Philosophical Society, the Scotch-Irish Society, the American Association for the Advancement of Science, the American Institute of Mining Engineers, and in 1893 was Judge of Mines and Mining at the Chicago World's Fair. He died in Staunton on January 17, 1899, and is buried at Thornrose Cemetery.

young congregation either. As his work in urging mining in Virginia and West Virginia prospered, along with the journal he established in the 1880s, Hotchkiss built his mansion on East Beverley Street, "The Oaks" and was able to devote much more of his time to the temporal and spiritual affairs of his church as an elder and as Sunday School superintendent. [15]

Second Presbyterian Church was off to a sound start, but it was clear that there would be a period of struggle to build a congregation that could support a minister. Founding the church was a bold and courageous step, but the hard work of building a viable church still lay ahead.

Chapter Three Notes

[1] Minutes of Lexington Presbytery, 22 April, 1-2 June 1875.
[2] Minutes of Lexington Presbytery, 1 September 1875.
[3] [Lucille Sanger], *A History of the Second Presbyterian Church, Staunton, Virginia, 1875-1975* (Verona, Va.: McClure Printing Company, Inc., 1975), 1.
[4] Ibid. For identification of the ministers and elders, see Wilson, *Lexington Presbytery Heritage*, passim.
[5] Quoted in Frank Robbins Pancake, *A Historical Sketch of the First Presbyterian Church* (Richmond, Va.: Whittet & Shepperson, Printers, 1954), 18-19.
[6] "Presbyterian Congregation Meeting," *The Vindicator*, Friday, 8 October 1875. The text of the letter of Charles D. McCoy to the Rev. William E. Baker, 26 September 1875 is printed in full in this article.
[7] Ibid.
[8] Ibid.
[9] [Sanger], *A History of Second Presbyterian Church*, 3.
[10] Ibid., 4-5.
[11] Typed copy of an unpublished manuscript, "History of the Second Presbyterian Church, November 14, 1875- November 12, 1950," compiled by Elder A.M. Woodside and Mrs. Frank Dice. Congregational archives; Presbytery Minutes 19-20 October 1875. Sanger's account indicates it was not J.W. Walker, but J. Rice Bowman of Harrisonburg.
[12] "Organization of a Church," *The Vindicator*, 5 November 1875.
[13] Session Book, 1876-1898.
[14] Peter W. Roper, *Jedediah Hotchkiss: Rebel Mapmaker and Virginia Businessman* (Shippensburg, Pa.: White Mane Publishing Company, 1992), 86-95, 104.
[15] Ibid., 122-128.

Chapter Four
Early Years

The first recorded Session meeting for Second Presbyterian Church took place on January 25, 1876, at the Deaf, Dumb, and Blind Institute, where Elder Charles D. McCoy had his office. Deacon Henry Walker was appointed treasurer. The first person whom the Session admitted to the congregation on examination was Mrs. M.M. McCoy, wife of the elder. The Session also received several members on certificate from other churches: Mr. and Mrs. William Jordan from Tinkling Spring, a married woman from the Loudoun Circuit of the Methodist Church, another from a Congregational Church in Boston, and an unmarried woman from a Presbyterian church in Kentucky. Six members of First Presbyterian in Staunton transferred their memberships, four women and two men.[1]

In 1876, the trustees purchased the lot at the northwest corner of Lewis and West Frederick Streets from John B. Baldwin for $3,000. Baldwin, a member of the House of Delegates, and one of Staunton's most prominent figures, owned the entire block and was building a mansion for himself on the area now occupied by the telephone building (Verizon in 2002). Baldwin Street, that runs the two blocks between Central Avenue and Institute Street behind the Church, was named for him. In 1887, his widow, Susan M. Baldwin, made over the deed to the church's trustees. As an elder, Hugh W. Henry had lent the church the $1,000 needed to complete the payment for the lot.[2]

Work on the church building took place in 1876. It was constructed of red brick in the Gothic Revival style of Trinity Episcopal Church, just a block away. Entrance to the building was through the bell tower at the corner. Unfortunately, the names of the designer and contractor for the structure are not known.

In 1876, the year that Americans celebrated the Centennial of Independence, construction work took place on a house of worship for the new congregation on the corner of Frederick and Lewis Streets. This neighborhood, near the Virginia Female Institute (Stuart Hall), was an expanding part of town with handsome new brick houses in the Italianate style being constructed.

A look at the persons admitted to the congregation on certificate from other churches in Second Presbyterian's first two years shows them coming from rural Virginia congregations such as Mt. Carmel and Hebron in Augusta County, Amelia Presbyterian, Pisgah in Highland County, Mountain Union in Botetourt County, and from Martinsburg, West Virginia, and Third Church in Richmond.[3] This proves

Hotchkiss's contention that there were new people in the community to whom the church would appeal. Here we can also see the beginning of the identification of Second Church as the "country church in town."

Thomas Colgate Morton and his wife transferred to Second from Mountain Union Church in March of 1876, and became quickly involved in the life of the congregation. Morton was immediately named superintendent of the newly-formed Sunday School, but resigned that post in April 1877.[4]

Although few records have survived to tell us what early worship services were like, we know that the congregation had organ and vocal music from the beginning. Nellie Hotchkiss, daughter of founding member Jed Hotchkiss, served as volunteer organist for the first six months. In March 1876, the Session employed Cora Turner "to perform on the organ & direct the music."[5] The Sunday School had an organ, for which purchase someone had donated thirty dollars. That instrument, with seven stops, was ordered from

The first pastor, MacDuff Simpson, 1875-1877, a native of Ireland, had been educated in Scotland.

James Edward Booker, the second pastor, 1878-1885, had studied in Germany.

a Richmond manufacturer and arrived in time for use on Sunday, December 10, 1875.[6]

In August 1877, the predictions of Major Tate about the difficulty of supporting a pastor in the presbytery debates over forming the church came true. Young Macduff Simpson informed the Session "that it had been evident for some time that he could no longer live on the salary paid him" and that he would have to accept a call he had received from a Philadelphia church unless they could offer him a raise. The congregation declined to do so, and in September Simpson asked Session to call a congregational meeting to ask presbytery to dissolve the pastoral relationship.[7]

The Reverend W.T. Richardson served as supply until a minister could be called. The Session originally looked at the Reverend Saul H. Chester of North Carolina as a pastor. A congregational meeting was called for Friday, November 2, 1877, but nothing came of that effort. It was another ten months before the Reverend James Edward Booker accepted the call and took up his post on September 18, 1878.[8]

Booker, who was born in Charlotte Court House in 1850, was a graduate of Hampden-Sydney College in 1870. Before he entered Union Theological Seminary, he had the unusual experience of studying at the post-graduate level in Germany, first at the university in Göttingen for a year and then at Leipzig for a year. He would have been a fluent German speaker. Second Church was his first pastorate. It would be interesting to know if any German immigrants were attracted to join the congregation because the pastor could speak their language.[9]

The first time that the Session operated as a court occurred in 1880 when one of the deacons was brought before it on the charge that the pastor had found him drunk. Booker visited and counseled with him and believed the man had sincerely repented. Session meted out the punishment of excommunication for six months, and the man asked the prayers of the congregation.[10] Unfortunately, he had further difficulty, and in 1882 the Session summoned him to explain why he had not attended church since November 1880 and to answer further charges of intemperance.[11] In 1886, the suspended deacon wrote to the pastor and Session asking to be reinstated, but saying that his crippled condition prevented him from appearing in person. Session decided that his repentance was sincere, and that he had met all the requirements of the Book of Discipline, Chapter XI, Paragraph 127 and 128, and reinstated him as a deacon.[12]

In February 1881, the Session admitted eleven new members, some by examination, and others by transfer from Charles Town, West Virginia; Fayetteville, Pennsylvania; Fauquier County, and from Augusta Stone, Windy Cove, and Waynesboro churches. It was also at this time that two men who would play a strong leadership role in the next decade were elected elders, Hotchkiss and Captain Thomas Colgate Morton. In the following year, the congregation elected new trustees, as the original ones had died or moved away. Those chosen were Hotchkiss, Morton, Captain C.A. Holt, J. Fred Effinger, and J.M. Lickliter.[13] The annual budget was $2,129.69. Of that, $725 went for the pastor's salary and $1,326.41 for congregational activities, including building upkeep and debt. The poor of the congregation received $22, the Sunday School library $24.45, the Sustenation Fund of the Synod received $21 and foreign missions $5.[14]

In 1885, just three years later, the congregational building outlays had declined sharply, and the amounts devoted to other needs had increased significantly. Booker's salary, for example, had risen to $1,250 and foreign missions had gone up to $34. Also, the amount contributed to the Sustenation Fund more than doubled, other benevolent objects received $143.55 and a modest contribution of $1.75 was made to a school for African-Americans, the Tuscaloosa Institute.[15]

Booker received a call to First Presbyterian in Charleston, West Virginia, so the congregation agreed to unite in a request to presbytery to dissolve the pastoral tie. Presbytery did so in April 1885. A congregational meeting on May 10, 1885, resolved to appoint a committee to solicit subscriptions for a pastor's salary and report back in five days. The committee reported $800 in subscriptions, but told the congregation that only $700 of that was likely to be paid. This amount was far short of what was needed to pay a pastor. Second Church had reached a crisis point in its short life. Sometime after the congregational meeting, the committee met with the Session of First Church. That church's Session adopted the following resolution:

> Resolved. That in our judgement the interest of Presbyterianism in this City requires that the organization of 2nd Church be sustained and that as it seems unable without help to support a Pastor, therefore the members of this Church are advised and recommended to assist it by individual subscriptions to the salary of a Pastor to 2nd Church.[16]

There were clearly touchy issues involved here. Second

Church was undoubtedly grateful for the positive attitude of First Church and the endorsement of contributions for a pastor's salary, but it must also have been embarrassing for Second Church to have such difficulty raising the needed funds. There also must have been some hard personal feelings at this time, for one of the church founders and leaders, Henry A. Walker, resigned as deacon and as Superintendent of the Sunday School, and asked for a letter of dismission to First Church.[17]

The strong efforts behind the scenes to raise a respectable salary and to find a good candidate succeeded. Word went out from the pulpit and in the newspaper that there would be a congregational meeting on Sunday, June 14. At that meeting, the subscription committee was happy to report that $1,720 had been subscribed for a pastor's salary. The congregation voted unanimously at that meeting to elect Dr. Herbert Henry Hawes of Farmville, Virginia, as pastor. Elders Hotchkiss and Lickliter were to present the call.[18]

The first two pastors, Simpson and Booker, had been very young men at the beginning of their ministerial careers. Hawes was a more experienced minister who had been born in Lunenburg County in 1834 and educated in the north at Princeton Seminary and New Brunswick Theological Seminary. He had been licensed by New Brunswick Presbytery in April 1861, just as the Civil War broke out, so he quickly returned to his native state. He had served briefly at Mount Horeb Church near Grottoes right after the war so was known to Staunton and Augusta County people, but for the previous fourteen years he had been pastor of the church in Farmville. Hawes was a thinker and writer, and in the course of his career published half a dozen books of theology and Biblical studies.[19]

Hawes was installed on August 23, 1885. At his first Session meeting a week later, his large family was received on certificate: his wife, Hattie, his daughters Alice, Louise, Mary Virginia, his son Samuel, and probably a younger son,

Dr. Herbert Henry Hawes, the third pastor, 1885-1891, was an experienced minister who had been educated in the north before the Civil War.

Herbert B. Hawes, "a baptized non-communicant."[20] There is no indication of where this large family lived when they first came to Staunton, for the church did not have a manse for them. We only know that the church rented a house for $240 per year.[21] Hawes must have indicated to Session the necessity for a manse, for in 1888, the congregation purchased a handsome brick Italianate house two doors west of the church at 207 Frederick Street, as well as the lot to its west. Later that year, the congregation sold the lot to B. F. Hughes for $2,000, directing that the proceeds from the sale be applied to payment of the debt on the parsonage purchase.[22]

The congregation grew under Hawes's care. The institution of an annual statistical report and questionnaire on the spiritual health of the congregation by the Lexington Presbytery each spring offers an opportunity to measure that growth.

In 1886, seventeen communicants were added by examination and twenty-six on certificate, to bring the total to 111. There were also twenty-seven baptized non communicants and ninety students in the Sunday School. The next year there were eighteen added on examination, thirty-five on transfer for a total of 130 communicants and forty baptized noncommunicants, but there were only fifty-three students in the Sunday School. In 1888, fourteen were admitted by examination, nineteen by certificate for a total of 145 communicants and twenty-nine baptized noncommunicants. In 1889, the number of communicants was 150, and in 1890 it reached 181, and in 1891 the number was 194. The communicant strength had nearly doubled in Hawes's time as pastor.[23]

The financial health of Second Church did not, however, keep up with the membership growth. The decade of the 1880s and into the 1890s was one of constant financial struggle for the Session and congregation. In the 1886 report to presbytery, the Session notes, "It was decided by the Session that for this year, at least, every energy of the Church should be given to liquidation of our church debt which is a great hindrance to our progress. Our pecuniary strength is such that we cannot do this, and contribute to other objects at the same time. This debt and our church expenses demand all the means within our reach."[24] Consequently, that year, Second Church gave nothing at all to sustenation, evangelism, foreign missions, education, publications, or to the Tuscaloosa Institute. A congregational meeting called in September of 1886 reminded the members that there was an operating deficit of $250, and the unpaid pledges, if collected, could only cover $150 of it. The visiting moderator, the Reverend John W. Pratt, in addressing the question of debt on the church lot, warned the congregation of the dangers that weak churches burdened with debt faced, and recommended a weekly collection plan.[25]

By 1887, the congregation was able once more to make very modest contributions to the presbytery funds: sustenation, evangelism, education, publication, and the institute, but still nothing for foreign missions. On Christmas day that year, Hawes announced to the congregation that the last of the debt on the church lot had been paid, and a service "of thankfulness & praise to God for His guidance & help" was held.[26] By July 1888, the congregation was in financial trouble again, as the pastor's salary was in arrears. At a congregational meeting, $100 was subscribed toward it. The deacons were directed to check on current subscriptions and canvass for additional pledges. This effort must have succeeded, for two months later, the congregation was making arrangements for the purchase of a manse and the sale of its adjacent lot. The manse cost $1,835, but the sale of the lot for $500 reduced the manse debt to $1,335.[27] Again in 1890 the pastor's salary was in arrears by $195, or more than ten percent.[28]

Session faced a difficult discipline problem in 1887, and sought the advice of Lexington Presbytery in a memorial. "What should be done when a member or an officer of the church has committed an offence worthy, beyond question, of judicial process, but has removed to some place unknown, and there are no means by which information concerning him can be obtained, and Session has no way of holding communication with him?" The problem facing Session was that one of the deacons had fled town, and that his disappearance was full of "wilful Sin, reproach, and scandall [sic], he having abandoned his wife and children and been guilty of deception and other crimes." Session decided, probably on advice from presbytery, to strike his name from the rolls, and to read the action from the pulpit at the Sunday worship service.[29]

The annual reports to presbytery offer insight into the Sunday School. It generally had about ten teachers and fifty to sixty students. The Shorter Catechism was a regular part of the curriculum, but not the Confession of Faith or the Forms of Government. The Bible was the only other book of instruction, but the children were not required to memorize passages of it, as the teachers had found it very difficult to get them to do so. Of the two publications of the Presbyterian Church for children, *The Earnest Worker* and *The*

Children's Friend, the Sunday School at Second Church subscribed to the former. By 1891, the Sunday School was using the International Lesson Series on Scripture Lessons, and passing out a weekly leaflet to the children. The Reverend Mr. Hawes, the minister, regularly visited the Sunday School classes, but did not preach special sermons to them. The older children attended the regular worship services of the congregation.[30]

There is a hint in Session minutes that some members were tiring of Hawes. The annual reports indicated that he was faithful, but one noted that attendance was good at some services and poor at others. Session asked presbytery how to handle the problem that some members were attending services at another Presbyterian church, but not asking for letters of dismission. This could indicate that they did not like to attend services Hawes conducted. Hawes, for his part, had tired of the annual hassle to get the arrears paid on his salary, and on November 29, 1891, gave his letter of resignation to the Session. His reasons for leaving were two: to accept an offer to be an evangelist for the synod, and "The confirmation of a criticism, long felt, that this church though struggling most nobly under its burdens and difficulties, is not able to continue to me the needed amount for my salary. Believing in the love of my people, I must also believe they have done what they could. But the burden is too great."[31] At that time, the congregation owed Hawes $380, or about one-quarter of his annual salary. The pastor's salary of $1,720 was the equivalent of about $32,500 in the year 2001, meaning that the church owed him an equivalent of almost $7,200, a significant amount.[32] Hawes and his family moved to Bluefield, West Virginia, where he took up his evangelistic work.

Elder T.C. Morton chaired the effort to find a new pastor. When the Reverend William Cumming of Baltimore visited to preach in early January, the congregation liked him, and at a called meeting on January 31, 1892, elected him by

William Cumming organized the first youth group, the Christian Endeavor Society, at Second Church when he was the fourth pastor from 1892 to 1896.

a vote of 64-1 (later changed to unanimous) at a salary of $1,350, of which $1,000 was in cash and the remainder being the rental value of the manse. Cumming took up the post immediately, and was installed on March 13, 1892.[33]

Cumming, a native of Baltimore, had studied at the Johns Hopkins University and worked as a secretary (paid director) for a Y.M.C.A. before entering the Reformed Presbyterian Seminary in Pittsburgh. He transferred to Union Theological Seminary in Richmond, where he graduated in 1886. He had served briefly at two small churches in southwestern Virginia, then spent four years at Waverley Church in Baltimore before coming to Staunton.[34]

Cumming represented a new kind of minister who relied on a highly active organizational life in a congregation to carry out the work of the local church. The very month he was installed, he organized a Young People's Society of Christian Endeavor at Second Church with seven members and Harry Lewis as president. This extremely active group received two banners for regional achievement. Other organizations active at Second Church while Cumming was pastor were the Brotherhood of Andrew and Philip for men, the Ladies Aid Society, the Women's Missionary Society, the Junior Aid Society, the Junior Endeavor Society, and the Little Pilgrim Mission Band. In April 1893, the Session thanked the Ladies Aid for its gift of a second communion service.

The Session was very concerned with moral behavior. As America prepared for the Columbian Exposition, or World's Fair, in Chicago to celebrate the 400th anniversary of Columbus's discovery of the New World, Cumming asked the elders to sign a memorial to the Virginia legislature urging them to use every means possible to "prevent the desecration of the Sabbath during the Columbian Exposition." Session referred the matter to a congregational meeting, which authorized the elders to sign.[35]

This was also a time that the temperance movement against alcoholic beverages was gaining strength, and many Protestant churches began to consider the use of grape juice, rather than wine, for communion. Hotchkiss was the one who introduced the issue at Second Church. Not wishing to appear to depart from scriptural practice, Hotchkiss, in July 1892, introduced a motion to use "unfermented wine," a clever euphemism for grape juice, in the communion service. The motion passed the Session by a vote of 3-2, but on further discussion, the elders tabled it and continued using "fermented wine."[36]

The issue was one that Hotchkiss was not willing to leave alone. In June 1893, he offered resolutions stating that "profitless discussion has arisen whereby the church is disquieted" because of Session's close vote on the question of grape juice for communion. This time, Hotchkiss brought in the authority of the General Assembly of the Presbyterian Church, noting that it had upheld the use of wine for communion as scriptural, but had also declared that the use of unfermented grape juice would not render the communion ordinance invalid. Hotchkiss then pressed for the loophole, noting that some in the congregation had been "rescued from the curse of Intemperance" and that the use of wine in communion might "lead them into temptation." His resolution asked that a congregational meeting be called to vote on the issue. Here he must have felt quite confident that he had the votes lined up. Session agreed to the meeting. Hotchkiss knew the congregational mood, for the vote was eighteen for the use of "fermented grape juice" and seventy-six for the use of unfermented.[37]

Second Church adopted a new hymn book in 1893, *Hymns of the Ages.* As soon as the copies were available, the old hymnals, which had been given by Hotchkiss's daughter, Nellie Hotchkiss McCullough, were returned to her, so that they could be given to the destitute and new churches that their former pastor, the Reverend Mr. Hawes, ministered to in West Virginia.[38]

When the Session prepared its answers to presbytery's annual questionnaire in 1893, the Session wrote modestly of its work that the mood was positive, with attendance at services "very good," additions to communicants "very marked," the fidelity of minister and officers "excellent." The elders noted "three special outpourings [of the Spirit] during the year," and Christian deportment and growth in grace was "wonderful." The Session that year replied that family worship was" well observed and marked improvement." Also indicative of pleasure with Cumming was the fact that there were no arrears on the pastor's salary.[39]

In the fall of 1893, Second Church initiated a missionary project with a chapel on Sears Hill that was called Endeavor Chapel originally, because the little house of worship was built by the young people of the Christian Endeavor Society. By April 1894, there were thirteen teachers and 101 students attending the Sunday School there. Elder B.F. Hughes was its superintendent. Another development in this year that had brought many changes to the church was the sale of the manse at 207 Frederick Street and the purchase of the house adjacent to the church at 205 Frederick Street from Hugh W. Henry.[41]

First Church and Second Church began some cooperative work about this time. The Session of First Church invited leaders of both to confer on serving mission needs of the area. In January 1894, First Church invited Second Church and other city churches to participate in a revival meeting held by Dr. Guerrant. Second Church's Session determined that it should follow this by sponsoring a revival meeting as well, which Cumming himself led. Next the Session directed Cumming to engage the Rev. Joseph Al Vance of Baltimore for a revival in February.[42] Besides an interest in revivals, Second Church began to show an increased interest in mission work in the mid-1890s. In May 1895, the congregation joined with First Church in morning services at which Y.N. Yenem of Persia preached. A month later, Session authorized the Sunday School to take up a collection for work among Native Americans. The practice of observing a week in January as a week of prayer began in 1896.[43]

The Session endorsed an active campaign on the part of the Virginia Bible Society to build support in the Staunton area in the fall of 1894, with the elders attending a meeting of church leaders at the Y.M.C.A. on a Friday, and regular services at Second Church suspended on the Sabbath so that the congregation could join with others at a union service.[44]

This was a period of considerable activity by Session regarding several members against whom charges were referred for immoral and unchristian conduct and of intoxication in the streets.[45] One of the elders was brought before Session on charges of adultery, which he denied, but confessed to intoxication, and was suspended from his church duties for a period. A young woman in the congregation was cited to appear before Session for "living so as to bring scandal upon the church."[46] Cumming also pushed for a careful effort to review the membership list, to attempt to get those who had not been attending more involved, and to remove those who were no longer interested in an active connection with the congregation. Then in 1895, they published the roll. Membership that year reached 360, with an additional 324 children in Sunday School. Presbytery found the Session a bit too zealous in its administration of disciplinary action when it reviewed the minutes at its spring 1896 meeting, and questioned whether Session had always followed the Book of Discipline.[47]

The energetic pace of activity that Cumming initiated reached a fever pitch by June 1896, when he requested that Session call a congregational meeting to ask members to unite with him in requesting Lexington Presbytery to dissolve the pastoral relationship. His former church, Waverley in Baltimore, wanted him to return as pastor, and sent two elders to address the congregational meeting at Second Church. It was a lively meeting. The congregation opposed the dissolution, and sent three commissioners to Lexington Presbytery, Captain T.C. Morton, Harry M. Lewis, and Captain H.W. Henry, to represent its view. When presbytery met at Shemariah on June 19, 1896, it voted to dissolve the pastoral relationship effective the fourth Sabbath of July. Second Church accepted the decision in good grace, if sadly, and after passing a resolution commending Cumming as a "warm hearted Christian brother, able teacher, fearless preacher, efficient Pastor, loyal Presbytr" and noting especially his work in building up the church, it sent him off with hearty wishes for success.[48]

A committee set to work to find a replacement, and reported to a congregational meeting on August 23, 1896, its recommendation of the Reverend John Miller Wells of Buena Vista. The congregation voted 106 to 1 to elect him at the same salary as Cumming, $1,000, plus the use of the manse. Wells, a young man, was the first minister of this congregation born after the Civil War, the event that was the watershed experience that had shaped the lives of most of the members. He was a native of Mississippi. His educa-

John Miller Wells, the fifth pastor, 1896-1901, was installed on the twenty-first anniversary of the founding of the Second Church. He brought a new level of committee organization to the congregation.

tional background was different from that of most Virginia Presbyterian ministers. He received a master's degree from Southwestern Presbyterian University in 1889 before his theological training at Union Theological Seminary. Buena Vista was his first church, and it was probably while there that he began the graduate studies that led to his receiving a Doctor of Philosophy from Illinois Wesleyan University in 1899 while he was still pastor in Staunton.[49]

Wells was installed in November on the occasion of the twenty-first anniversary of the founding of Second Church, with A.M. Fraser, minister of First Church, preaching the sermon from Nehemiah 6:3 and former pastor J.E. Booker giving the charge to the people. When the anniversary of the church was celebrated the following week, Hotchkiss presented a lecture about the history of the church, its ministers, its membership growth and losses, and reminded that the congregation had contributed a total of $53,000 over that time.[50]

Under Wells's leadership, the Session organized the church into committees in order to be more efficient, and in order to involve more of the congregation in the work of the church. These went into effect in January 1897. Hezekiah Jordan chaired the Committee on Sabbath School Work with four women and one additional man. John W. Lovegrove, a clerk, chaired the Committee on Work for Young Men with nine men. Mrs. A.S. Woodhouse, wife of a printer, chaired the Committee on Visiting the Sick, along with eight other women. S. Brown Allen was Chairman of the Committee on Welcoming Strangers at Church, with eight other men. Nellie Hotchkiss McCullough, who, with her husband, S.T. McCullough, was living at "The Oaks," chaired the Committee on Visiting Strangers and Newcomers with seven other women to help.[51] The new committee structure seemed to show promising results. The committee for visiting the sick paid forty-six calls in one month. The Sunday School committee made sixteen visits in one month and secured ten new students.[52]

The celebration of the 250th anniversary of the adoption of the Westminster Standards or the Westminster Confession of Faith, the basic doctrinal statement of Presbyterianism, which First and Second Church had planned jointly with other local Presbyterian churches, took place from Thursday evening April 29 through Sunday evening May 2, 1897. Several visiting ministers were involved. The joint Sabbath service, held in Columbian Hall, attracted 2,000 persons from all Presbyterian churches in Augusta County. That afternoon, certificates were presented to 1,300 children who had perfectly recited the Shorter Catechism. An evening service with the renowned and popular Reverend Moses D. Hoge as preacher attracted another 2,000 worshippers.[53]

In the fall of 1897, Session had to deal with assorted problems in the administration of the Sunday School on Sears Hill. First, it was learned that the treasurer there had taken thirty dollars contributed for the school for his own use in 1895 and not repaid it. Then a petition from some of the parents complained about the superintendent. Session found no cause to remove Superintendent Preston A. Ross, but urged that he and the parents work more closely together.

In November 1897, the proposal was made for a third Presbyterian church in Staunton, to be comprised of some from the Olivet Chapel sponsored by First Church, some members of both existing churches, especially twenty-five Second Church members living on Sears Hill and of people at the Sunday School on Sears Hill. Several weeks later, Ross resigned his post, which Session accepted, but commended his work and urged him to remain on the job until a Session could be organized for the new Third Church.[54] On November 28, letters of dismission were granted to seven married couples, three single women, three married women, and three men to Third Church. In January 1898, the congregation of Second Church met to consider conveying the Sears Hill Sunday School property to Third Church. The congregation voted instead to offer it to the new congregation free of charge for a year. When the new congregation elected its officers, one elder, all three deacons, and two of the three trustees were former Second Church members.[55]

A bequest in the will of Miss Mary Julia Baldwin, head of Augusta Female Seminary (now Mary Baldwin College) and administered through the General Assembly of the Presbyterian Church in the United States came to Second Church in April 1898. Session instructed the trustees to pay this amount toward the indebtedness on the manse.[56]

With no more Sears Hill Sunday School to look after, Second Church started a new effort called Englewood Sunday School on April 3, 1898. R.W. White originated the school. T.J. Martin was named superintendent. Six teachers were enlisted to instruct the twenty students who had initially enrolled. The work at Englewood prospered, so that by April 1899, Session could report to presbytery that twelve conversions had taken place there, and nine of them joined Second Church.[57]

At the close of 1898, Second Church was saddened by

This record book shows officers of the Ladies Aid Society in 1898.

the loss of two important leaders. Captain Hugh W. Henry, an Elder, was dismissed to Spring Garden Church in Pittsylvania County. The Reverend Mr. Wells wrote him a letter commending his splendid Christian service, and saying that "in losing you I feel that I have lost my right arm in our Church work here." Captain Henry still kept Second Church and Pastor Wells in his heart, and the next year sent $200 (worth $4,085 in 2001)[58] for repairs and improvements on the manse that he had sold to the church.[59] The Session was thrust immediately into consideration of a resolution on the death of founding member and longtime elder and Sunday School Superintendent, Major Jed Hotchkiss.

The lengthy and flowery resolution compared Hotchkiss with the apostles, saying, "He had enthusiasm and zeal of a Peter, he was a Paul in the boldness and firmness of his convictions; as simple in his expressions, as eloquent in his language as a John; what an inspiration for us!"[60] Hotchkiss would no doubt have been disappointed at the vote of the Session in April to use fermented wine instead of unfermented, because they could not obtain the latter!

The Ladies Aid Society had been busy all year on a complete redecoration of the Session Room. The Session offered its deep appreciation and hearty thanks not only for that work, but also for the "unceasing efforts to advance & promote by every means at their command both the spiritual and material or temporal interest of the church."[61] Another women's organization active at this time was the Maria Pratt Missionary Society.

Session attended zealously to its responsibilities to uphold moral and spiritual standards in the congregation as the century drew to a close. One member was investigated for opening a bar in the Virginia Hotel in town. Two were examined and found to be of "unregenerate heart" and were removed from the communicant roll to the list of baptized noncommunicants. Another had to answer to reports about his character. Wells had made 535 pastoral calls in 1898 and probably expressed the need for help. He and the Session devised a plan for dividing the congregation into eight sections with each elder taking responsibility for some of the pastoral calling in his section. One of the subjects during the pastoral visit would be whether each family was observing family worship. This was a question presbytery tried each year to determine, and the answers from Second Church usually indicated that this was a weak point in the congregation.[62]

The congregation surely joined with the Wells family in prayers for the successful treatment of their little boy, Thomas, when Dr. Wells took him to Baltimore for medical

> To Dorsey Wilson, in recognition of his attendance at every meeting of the Sunday School of the Second Presbyterian Church during this year.
>
> Dec. 28th, 1897
>
> Jed. Hotchkiss
> Supt

Jed Hotchkiss inscribed this book the year before his death as an attendance award for a Sunday School student, Dorsey Wilson.

advice in April 1900. The local newspaper was able to report the following week that father and son were back home, and that the operation had been a success.[63]

On January 20, 1901, Wells asked Session to call a congregational meeting about the dissolution of the pastoral tie, as he had received a call to First Presbyterian Church, Wilmington, North Carolina. This was the pulpit long held by the Reverend Joseph Ruggles Wilson, former pastor of First Church and father of Staunton's native son, Woodrow Wilson, soon to be chosen President of Princeton. The Reverend B. Craig Patterson, missionary to China, presided over that meeting. The morning and evening services on Sunday, February 3 both marked the final sermons that Wells preached to his congregation.[64]

When Wells departed, Second Presbyterian Church was just a little past its quarter-century mark. In that short time, it had grown from its original thirteen members to a congregation of more than 360 communicants, some 75 noncommunicants, and a Sunday School of more than 200 scholars. In addition, the congregation had played a significant role in founding a mission Sunday School on Sears Hill that was hopeful of becoming an independent Third Presbyterian Church. The road to this growth had been rocky, especially in financial matters, but the congregation had persisted and met its financial obligations, built a handsome little brick church, and acquired a fine Italianate brick manse adjacent to it for the pastor. The growth was such that the Session and deacons had decided in May 1900, that massive renovations and enlargment of the church building were necessary.[65] Because the finances of the church were not strong, and the salary offered the pastor always low, ministers stayed only a short time. This was a drawback in a denomination known for long pastorates, for the congregation had five pastors in its twenty-six year lifespan. It was ready for a man who would stay with them long enough to develop growth, continuity, and strength.

Chapter Four Notes

[1] Second Presbyterian Church, First Session Book. 25 January 1876.
[2] Sanger, *A History of Second Presbyterian Church*, 7.
[3] Ibid., 29, 30 January, 5 March, 18 June, 12 November 1876; 10 June, 23 September 1877.
[4] Ibid., 19 April 1877.
[5] Ibid., 5 March 1876.
[6] Sanger, 21.
[7] Ibid., 19 August, 2 September 1877.
[8] Ibid., 13 October 1878.
[9] Sanger, 45.
[10] Session Minutes, 16 November 1880.
[11] Ibid., 18 April 1882.
[12] Ibid., 4 April 1886.
[13] Ibid., 7 February 1881; Congregation Meeting Minutes, 12 February 1882.
[14] Ibid., 18 April 1882
[15] Session Minutes, 5 April 1885.
[16] Congregation Meeting Minutes, 15 May 1885.
[17] Session Minutes, 31 May 1885.
[18] Congregational Meeting Minutes, 14 June 1885.
[19] Sanger, 46-47.

[20]Session Minutes, 30 August 1885.
[21]Ibid., 2 April 1888.
[22]Ibid., 30 September 1888; Sanger, 26.
[23]Ibid., 25 April 1886, 4 April 1887, 2 April 1888, 7 April 1889, 6 April 1890, 19 April 1891.
[24]Ibid., 25 April 1886.
[25]Congregational Meeting Minutes, 12 September 1886.
[26]Session Minutes, 25 December 1887.
[27]Ibid., 22 July 1888; 7 April 1889.
[28]Ibid., 6 April 1890.
[29]Ibid., 27 April, 5 June 1887.
[30]Ibid, 6 April 1890, 19 April 1891.
[31]H.H. Hawes to the Session, 29 November 1891. Filed with Session Minutes.
[32]The Inflation Calculator, www.westegg.com/inflation/infl.cgi.
[33]Minutes of Congregation Meeting, 31 January 1892. Session Minutes, 7 February, 13 March 1892.
[34]Sanger, 47.
[35]Session Minutes, Congregational Meeting Minutes, 21 February 1892.
[36]Session Minutes, 3 July 1892.
[37]Ibid., 4 June 1893.
[38]Ibid., 19 February 1893.
[39]Ibid., 2 April 1893.
[40]Ibid., 3 September 193, 8 April 1894.
[41]Ibid., 3 September, 14 September 1893.
[42]Ibid., 7, 14, 21, 28 January, 4 February 1894.
[43]Ibid., 12 May, 23 June, 22, 29 December 1895.
[44]Ibid., 16, 23 September 1894.
[45]Ibid., 17, 24 December 1893; 18, 25 March, 8, 15, 22 April 1894.
[46]Ibid., 15 December 1895.
[47]Ibid., 17 February, 6 March, 14 April 1895, 3 January, 1 April 1896.
[48]Ibid., 14, 19, 21, 28 June 1896.
[49]Sanger, 47.
[50]Session Minutes, 15, 22 November 1896.
[51]Ibid., 3 January 1897.
[52]Ibid., 21, 28 March 1897.
[53]Ibid., 2 May 1897.
[54]Ibid., 19, 26 September, 3 October, 7, 14, 21 November 1897.
[55]Ibid., 23 January, 6 February 1898.
[56]Ibid., 3 April 1898.
[57]Ibid., 3 July 1898, 16 April 1899.
[58]The Inflation Calculator, www.westegg.com/inflation/infl.cgi.
[59]Ibid., 5 January , 29 October 1899.
[60]Ibid., 29 January 1899.
[61]Ibid., 28 May 1899.
[62]Ibid., 22 September, 29 October 1899; 22 January, 18 February 1900.
[63]*Staunton Spectator,* 20, 27 April 1900.
[64]Ibid., 1 February 1901.
[65]Ibid., May 11, 1900.

Chapter Five
The Scott Era and a New House of Worship

A notice in the *Staunton Spectator* on April 5, 1901 reminded members of the congregational meeting the coming Sunday to hear its report of the Pastorate Committee and the recommendation of the man that Second Church should call to its pulpit. Colonel S. Brown Allen reported for the committee members that they had consi-dered forty-eight names before deciding unanimously on the Reverend William N. Scott, D.D. of Galveston, Texas. Thomas Colgate Morton, Benjamin Franklin Hughes, and Allan Moore Howison from the committee spoke strongly in favor of the call.[1]

Dr. Scott paid an extended visit to Staunton while considering the call. The *Spectator* reported on April 19 that he had arrived in town and was the guest of Captain Charles A. Holt and his son Frank T. Holt, who were prominent members of the congregation. He preached twice on Sunday at Second Church and administered communion. He also attended the meeting of Lexington Presbytery at Waynesboro and preached before that body, then visited in Richmond.[2] He returned to preach again at Second Church "to the largest congregation that has assembled in that church for many years, every conceivable space being occupied by worshipers, sitting or standing."[3] He moderated Session meetings on April 21 and 28, so that the elders would have a sense of his leadership style and the ways that they might work together. Scott promised that soon after his return to Texas he would telegraph his decision about accepting the congregation's call.

Fortunately for Second Church, on May 6, Dr. Scott wired T.C. Morton, secretary of the calling committee, of his acceptance of the call, saying that he planned to be on the job on June 1. The church officers met at the Y.M.C.A. the next morning to hear the news, and to respond to Dr. Scott's letter of suggestions for the work of the church.[4] On June 2, 1901, Session received the formal resolutions from First Church, Galveston, and from Brazos Presbytery congratulating the church on its good fortune in gaining his services.[5] In William Scott, Second Church acquired an exceptional minister, and one who proved to be just the right man at the right time for the needs of the church.

When Scott arrived in Staunton, he was a man with considerable successful experience who was at the height of his powers at the age of fifty-two. He had been born in Halifax County and educated at Washington College right after the Civil War, when Robert E. Lee was president of the college. He then went to Union Theological Seminary, and served at Third Church in Richmond before his call to Galveston in 1882. The Staunton paper described him to be "of striking appearance and an eloquent speaker," qualities that are a great help in attracting a following, winning souls for Christ, and building up a congregation. The paper also pointed out that he had ties to three prominent old families in Augusta County, Sproul, Christian, and Morton, and that his daughters had previously visited in the Bethel congregation as well as Staunton, and had many friends in the area.[6]

Scott was a widower with grown children. His elder son was in business in Galveston and remained there. The daughters, Agnes Morton and Annie Brook, and the younger son, John A., a college student, all transferred their memberships to Second Church at the end of June. The *Spectator* was also bold enough to write, perhaps in subtle criticism of a rival area newspaper, "The impression has been made in some quarters through a newspaper report that Dr. Scott is wealthy. This is a mistake. He is not a rich man, but is not a man to make a salary the main thing when considering a call."[7] This is an important point, however, for the inability of Second Church to pay much more than a modest salary had been a prime reason that the congregation had five ministers in its first quarter century, and that most could not long remain at the low salary. Scott may not have been wealthy, but it is clear from his lifestyle and his travel while at Second Church, that he had independent sources of income to supplement his salary.

Scott was installed in an evening service that drew a very large crowd on the third Sunday in July. Dr. A.M. Fraser of First Church preached a sermon on Calvinism, "which fully satisfied all the Presbyterians present," according to the newspaper, suggesting that the numerous visitors from other congregations found that discourse a bit heavy. The early observation of the newspaper that Scott was an excellent speaker must have been accurate for he was much in demand to speak in the region. In September 1901, he preached the opening sermon at Lexington Presbytery and gave a lecture in the Presbyterian Church at Bridgewater

The Reverend William Nelson Scott, D.D., sixth pastor, who served from 1901 to 1919, was the first minister to stay more than a few years. He oversaw the building of the present church structure, and guided the congregation through large growth in membership numbers.

on the devastating 1900 Galveston flood. In November he was in Millboro for several days' services and preaching in connection with the dedication of the new Presbyterian church there. In March 1902, he preached at the chapel at the University of Virginia and in April was in Clifton Forge assisting the Reverend Dr. E.W. McCorkle with a series of services. In May he preached the baccalaureate sermon for Augusta Military Academy at Augusta Stone Church in Fort Defiance.[8]

The first important matter that Dr. Scott helped the officers and congregation resolve was the question of what to do about the charming little church building they had outgrown. Session had been considering a plan for its expansion. The Ladies Aid Society, as recently as April 26, had held a tea at the manse from five to seven, selling cakes, ices, coffee, homemade candy, and "the novel 'George Washington cake'" to raise funds for new pews in the church.[9] Although surviving records tell nothing about the options under consideration, there were likely some among elders, deacons, and members who wanted to remodel and enlarge the church building, and others who thought that an entirely new house of worship was needed. Scott was undoubtedly of the latter persuasion, and argued the case well, for the *Spectator* reported that the officers had met the evening of June 10 and unanimously decided to build a new church on the existing site. A subscription paper for the capital campaign was circulated with excellent immediate results. The paper predicted wildly that the new building would be ready by fall.[10]

In the midst of the successful start to the new ministry and the excitement over the new church, there was a setback in the resignation in July of the Reverend R.C. Gilmore of Third Church. That new congregation, which owed so much to the efforts of Second Church, concluded that it could not continue, saying that "after three years experience that it was not expedient for the best interest of Presbyterianism in Staunton to have a third church in the city at this time." In August, Session called a congregational meeting to decide what to do with the Sears Hill chapel building that had reverted to Second Church. The newspaper speculated that the trustees might sell the building and apply the proceeds to the new church. Many of the members who had left Second to help form the new church now came back to their old congregation.[11]

Financing the new church building would not be easy, as it was a much larger structure than the original. When the local Ministerial Relief Fund came to Session with a plea for assistance, Session had to tell them that the demands made on the congregation for the new church had made additional contributions impossible. However, Session did decide to hold a "Pound Party" for the poor of Second Church. In January 1902, Session concluded that it must call a congregational meeting to seek authority for the trustees to borrow funds to complete the church. The authority was granted, but the negotiations with the lenders were still taking place in June.[12]

The women's organizations carried on an active role in the fundraising for the new church. The Ladies Aid Society agreed to furnish the new church, carrying on their earlier intention of supplying pews for an enlarged old church. One of their events for this was a "Handkerchief Shower" held in the room next to Singer's Confectionery on a Friday evening in October 1901. By June 1902, the women had raised nearly $800 through events such as this. The Church Workers had taken on the project of supplying a new organ, and had raised $400 by June. The children's arm of this organization, the Junior Church Workers, held an ice cream supper in July 1902 which realized another thirty dollars for the organ fund.[13]

Meanwhile the congregation worshiped at the Y.M.C.A. building (now known as the Clock Tower) at the corner of Beverley (Main) and Central (Water) while the new church was under construction. The Building Committee let the contract for the construction to G.W. Fretwell for $8,000 in September 1901. The last services took place on Sunday September 22, 1901, and the last official business transacted there was the election of four new deacons: Newton Argenbright, the longtime Clerk of the Court of Hustings and City Council Clerk, W.A. Wilson, William Frank Dull, designer of the new church, and Thomas Addison Bell who was with Hamrick's Funeral Home. On Tuesday, Fretwell's workers began to tear down the little Gothic Revival church built with such pride by the struggling young congregation a quarter century earlier.[14]

The ceremony to lay the cornerstone for the new church took place on Saturday, January 18, 1902, after being postponed two days because of bad weather. The choir opened the brief program singing "Rock of Ages," then the Reverend A.M. Fraser of First Church offered prayer. Dr. Scott reminded that it was sad to pull down the walls of a building that held wonderful memories, but that the new church

While the new church was under construction in 1901 and 1902, the congregation worshipped in the Young Men's Christian Association building, known today as the Clock Tower. For years the Board of Deacons held its regular monthly meeting here.

symbolized progress. Colonel S. Brown Allen gave a brief history of the congregation and its growth. Next, little Miss Ellen Howison, granddaughter of founding member, the late Major Jed Hotchkiss, placed the box containing symbols of the times in the cornerstone. The choir closed with "How Firm a Foundation," and the Reverend W.Q. Hullihen of Trinity Episcopal Church pronounced the benediction. The contents of the box were: rolls of pastors, elders, and deacons since the church's foundation; of current members; of superintendents, officers, teachers, and scholars of Sunday School; of Ladies Aid Society members; and of Church Workers Society; old coins from the former cornerstone; new coins placed by various members; a testament given to the Hotckisses at their marriage and carried by Major Hotchkiss during the Civil War; copies of Staunton and religious newspapers; and a certificate of Mrs. Mary S. Allen for reciting the shorter catechism perfectly.[15]

The architect for the new building was Frank Dull, who also served on the building committee along with Arthur Wilson, William Anderson Crawford, Colonel S. Brown Allen, and Dr. Scott. Dull was the manager for the George W. Fretwell Construction Company and lived at North Madison Street in Staunton. Although it is not clear that he had formal architectural training, Dull gained favor as a building designer. He also designed the old King's Daughters' Hospital building which stood on the campus of Mary Baldwin College and was demolished in 2001.[16]

As the building progressed, the congregation began to use parts of it. In July 1902 the basement area was sufficiently completed that worship services could be held there, and a large crowd turned out for that first occasion. The Session began meeting in the ladies parlor when it was ready, then in the basement, and finally on October 19 in the new Session room, which the Ladies Aid Society had furnished. The new pipe organ, for which the women's organization had worked so faithfully, was purchased from

W.W. Putnam & Co., and arrived in Staunton in late August, ready for installation. That work had been completed by early October, with only the finishing touches such as carpet installation to be done before the dedication on the third Sunday in October.[17]

Dr. Scott and the Session had been making plans for the dedication since August, and had invited the Reverend G.B. Strickler, D.D., of Union Theological Seminary and formerly pastor at Tinkling Spring to preach for the occasion. The elders had also invited all the former pastors of the congregation to be present, as, amazingly, all five of them were still living and still active. Unfortunately, none could attend.[18] The first pastor, MacDuff Simpson, sent a lovely letter from the manse in Edrom, Berwickshire, Scotland, to Capt. T.C. Morton in response to his invitation, in which he wrote:

> It is now 25 years since I lived amongst you, but the ties of affection that still bind me to you are as strong as in the olden days when we laboured together in founding the church which now enters upon a new era of prosperity.... A picture of the old brick building hangs in my Scotch study, and daily reminds me of the old place and the old friends who become dearer still as the years go by.[19]

The building was nearly filled to capacity for both dedication services. Many from Tinkling Spring attended in the morning to hear their former pastor, and in the evening, the service was a joint venture for both First and Second Churches. The offerings taken at the services brought an additional $1,400 toward the construction. The paper had reported that the total costs for building and furnishing the church would approach $14,000 (equal to $286,000 in 2001), but specific accounts do not survive to give actual figures.[20]

Dr. Scott's first eighteen months at Second Church had been a resounding success. Not only had the magnificent

The pale brick of the new church gave it an entirely different appearance from any other church in Staunton at that time.

new church become a reality, but also the size of the congregation had increased significantly. Of the 460 members on the rolls in the fall of 1902, 112 had been added since Dr. Scott's arrival.

The new church facilities offered much better opportunities for programs and events. Session worked on a policy for its use and named a standing committee for that purpose. Soon after, the Church Worker Society sponsored an entertainment in the church basement on Friday evening, November 21, 1902, from 4 to 10 p.m. to benefit the organ

"Whosoever Thou Art That Enterest This Church Leave it not without one Prayer to God For Thyself, For Him who Ministers and For Those who Worship Here"

Second Presbyterian Church,

Staunton, Virginia.

W. N. SCOTT, D. D. Pastor

Manse next door to Church. Telephone No. 373

Sunday Services

Divine Worship 11 a. m. and 7.30 p. m.
Sabbath School 9.30 a. m.
Y. P. S. C. E. 6.30 p. m.
Midweek Prayer Service Lecture Room
Wednesday 7.30 p. m.
Visitors Welcome   Seats Free to all

Welcome by the Pastor will be gladly extended to visitors and Strangers at the close of the Service.

An early service leaflet after the new church was occupied.

fund. Salads, coffee, ice cream, cake, and homemade candy were the featured foods offered to the public and church members. In October, the Ladies Aid Society sponsored a supper in the Lecture Room, featuring oyster patties, chicken salad, coffee, cake, ice cream, fancy hot sauces, homemade candies, and a variety of fancy work articles for sale. In February 1902 the Church Workers sponsored a free lecture program by Dr. Robert Kerr. A lively program of visiting preachers and special events, all well publicized in the local newspaper, also kept attention focused on Second Church as an exciting congregation. Dr. Dubose, a missionary to China, preached in December 1902, accompanied by former pastor, J.E. Booker.[21]

A special feature in January 1903 was the celebration of General Robert E. Lee's ninety-sixth birthday by the Stonewall Jackson Camp of Confederate Veterans. The group met at its hall at 10:30 in uniform. The members had invited the city's two military companies, the West Augusta Guards and the Staunton Rifles, to join them, in uniform, of course. The Stonewall Brigade Band, handsomely attired in marching uniforms, led the parade to the church for the 11 a.m. morning service. Seats had been reserved not only for the parade, but for the families of veterans as well. Dr. Scott, who was chaplain to the camp, preached what the newspaper described as "a capital discourse" to "an immense congregation." This began a tradition at Second Church, and for the next two years the congregation observed the Lee birthday in similar fashion.[22]

Dr. Scott continued to be a speaker much in demand. He exchanged pulpits with Dr. Thornton Whaling of Lexington in March, then in April, Lexington Presbytery sent him to Bridgewater to hold a week's services there, then at the end of that month, he was invited to address the Railroad Y.M.C.A. at Crewe, Virginia. He had the opportunity to visit with his brother, the Reverend Littleton E. Scott, minister there, who had also been a guest preacher at Second Church. In May, Dr. Scott traveled to Statesville, North Carolina, with his daughter Nannie, to deliver the commencement sermon at the college there. Another brother, the Reverend John A. Scott, Jr., was president of the college.[23] The Session and the congregation were so pleased with Dr. Scott's work, with the excellent spirit in the congregation, with the addition of seventy-six members by profession of faith in the past year alone, and with their two mission Sunday Schools at Englewood and Folly Mills, as they reported to Presbytery in the spring of 1903, that they voted to raise Dr. Scott's salary from $1,200 to $1,500.[24]

In April 1904, after making out another report of fiscal, numerical, and spiritual growth to presbytery, Session voted Dr. Scott a two-month leave of absence for a trip to Europe. On Wednesday evening, May 25 he conducted his final mid-week prayer meeting, then departed the next day with daughters Nannie and Agnes for Philadelphia, where they sailed on the American steamship *Westernland*. Dr. Scott was no stranger to Europe, and planned to show his daughters places that he had already visited in England, Scotland, and the Continent.[25] In his absence, the pulpit was filled by the Rev. Dr. W.C. Campbell of Roanoke, the Rev. C.W. Maxwell, superintendent of the Orphan's Home at Lynchburg, and by the Rev. Dr. H.W. Burwell of Augusta, Georgia.[26]

When Staunton's First Presbyterian Church celebrated its centennial in the fall of 1904, members and officers of Second Church also took part in the services and events. As part of the celebration, several ministers were invited to deliver talks detailing the history of Presbyterianism in Augusta County. Dr. Scott was one of those invited, talking of the growth of Second Church as a daughter of First Church. His own Session was so pleased with his historical sketch of the congregation, that it authorized the talk to be printed as a pamphlet and distributed to each family in the congregation at the expense of the church.[27]

At a time when the only married women who engaged

in paid employment were those from poor families, the married women of middle class status or higher depended on church organizations as one of the principal outlets for their intellectual and creative energies. So it was that the women's organizations of Second Church played an important role in the lives of their members. Each organization had its own program of study and spiritual enrichment, and each also undertook various fundraising projects. The funds raised could be applied to needs of Second Church, or sent to domestic and foreign mission fields or to institutions such as the orphanage that the Presbyterian Church sponsored in Lynchburg. The Ladies Aid Society, largest of the women's organizations at Second Church, had Mrs. Heiskell Argenbright as its stalwart leader from 1908 to 1920.[28]

The women applied considerable creative effort to their fundraising events, trying to offer something that would attract a wide range of the general public as well as church members. Notices of these events placed in the Staunton newspaper give a good idea of popular social activities as well as popular and new foods in the years before the First World War. The Church Workers held a "Colonial Tea" in the fall of 1904, offering "a substantial and tempting menu." In February 1907, the Church Workers held an "Orange Social" in the Lecture Room to raise funds, but the newspaper offered no explanation of what an "Orange Social" was. In the spring of 1905, the Ladies Aid Society held a "White Goods Sale" at which they featured handmade white items such as shirtwaists (blouses), along with a chicken salad supper. The following spring when the Ladies Aid held its white sale, the menu featured a hot supper of chicken, terrapin, French peas, hot biscuits, and cake and ices for dessert. The proceeds from these events were invested in repairs and improvements in the Lecture Room of the church.[29]

In March, 1906, the Ladies Aid Society gathered at the residence of Dr. and Mrs. Joseph Spencer DeJarnette on East Frederick Street. Mrs. DeJarnette, who was also a doctor, had been a member of the society for a number of years, and had recently married Dr. DeJarnette, the superintendent of Western State Hospital. The occasion for the meeting was a surprise shower for the couple, as each society member brought something useful for housekeeping or for the pantry.[30]

Another woman's organization that had been active at Second Church for some years was the Maria Pratt Missionary Society. In 1904, Mrs. H.M. Harman was president

Articles such as this one advertising a "White Sale And Supper" in the local newspapers encouraged a good attendance from the wider community for the fundraising events that the women's organizations sponsored.

WHITE SALE AND SUPPER

Ladies of Second Presbyterian Church Are Quite Successful.

The Ladies' Aid Society of the Second Presbyterian church held their annual white sale yesterday afternoon and night and had a most successful time. There were a large number of exquisite hand-made garments that found ready sale and the supper served was delicious. Mrs. Heiskell Argenbright is the efficient president of the society and she acted as cashier. Mesdames C. M. Zirkle, J. S. DeJarnette, J. S. Benson, J. T. Parr, W. A. Crawford, John Davidson J. H. Garlick, I. H. Trimble and R. A. Fulwiler had charge of the white garments and fancy work.

Misses Bessie Dunsmore and Maud Trimble did a flourishing business at the candy table. The supper was in charge of Mesdames W. A. Willson, Geo. E. Schmucker, Stickley, J. A. Noon, F. T. Woodruff, S. D. Gochenour, Nannie Fishburne and Kate Fauver, while the waitresses were Mesdames J. G. Dunsmore, J. B. Burwell, Minnie Diggs, A. G. Fifer, Hawkins and Misses Mamie Brown Allen and Annie Byers.

of the group, Mrs. A.M. Howison, Jed Hotchkiss's daughter, was secretary, and Mrs. T.C. Morton was treasurer. The group accepted the invitation of the Lexington Society to meet in that town to consider the formation of a Missionary Union for Lexington Presbytery in February 1905.[31]

A question that is always of some interest in regard to church practices involves the celebration and observance of Christmas. The Presbyterian Church, in its formative years in Scotland in the sixteenth and seventeenth centuries had taken a very negative attitude toward Christmas, not recognizing it as a valid liturgical occasion. This attitude prevailed among Presbyterians in colonial America and in the new republic in the early nineteenth century. Beginning in the mid-nineteenth century, however, Christmas became a popular home and family celebration among nearly all Americans. Christmas trees to decorate, a visit from St. Nick to fill stockings, and gift exchanges had become commonplace. The fact that the Episcopal, Lutheran, and Catholic churches provided Christmas worship services and Sunday School programs brought pressure on the Presbyterian churches to include some Christmas observance. Most had begun to do so in the final quarter of the nineteenth century. Second Church was typical of this new attitude, as its Sunday School had observed some Christmas exercises for a number of years. In 1904 the Session decided to change its previous policy of holding those exercises in the Lecture Room, and to move them instead to the church auditorium.[32]

Another activity to which the Sunday School children looked forward all year was the annual summer outing. In July 1905 that was held at Mt. Elliott Springs. Church leaders had made arrangements for additional cars to be added to the local westbound train leaving Staunton at 6:58 a.m. on Thursday, July 27, returning at 7:45 p.m., at very favorable ticket prices. With several hundred children in the Sunday School, this event was a large and well-coordinated celebration that involved the teachers, officers, and many parents as well. The next month the Sunday School held its annual picnic in the grove at Tinkling Spring. The newspaper reported that "the children and their friends were loaded into spring wagons, carriages, etc., and made a fine procession as [they] drove out of town at an early hour in the morning."[33]

Each December the Sunday School elected officers for the coming year, according to a plan that the General Assembly of the Presbyterian Church urged upon congregations. Elder Harry M. Lewis was chosen superintendent for many years, with William A. Crawford as his assistant. C. Wallace Wiseman was often the secretary, and sometimes the treasurer, and W.C.H. Hyde was librarian for a number of years. There were usually about two dozen teachers as well. Session liked to keep a careful eye on the operation of the Sunday School, and in 1906 when it received reports of "erratic teaching in one of the classes" it appointed two elders and the pastor to investigate and correct the problem if the report was valid.[34]

The Session continued its careful monitoring of the congregation, and when it learned that the Misses Laura, Leta, and Jesse Driver had gone into the United Brethren Church without notice, they were stricken from the roll of Second Church. Likewise, when another member, J. Luther Kelly, had been found guilty of forgery and sentenced to prison, the elders suspended him from "the sealing ordinances of the church until such time as he may give satisfactory evidence of true and sincere repentance of his sin." Fourteen months later, Kelly provided that evidence, was restored to membership at his request, and given a certificate of dismissal to a church in Richmond, where he and his wife hoped to start a new life. In the summer of 1907, a committee of three elders was to meet with three men in the congregation about their irregular attendance at church, and with another "to explain reports derogatory to his Christian character." The latter case was reported to Session as having been judged insane and committed to Western State.[35]

Pastor Scott was on the road again in 1906. The Session granted him a three-week leave in January so that he could visit his former congregation in Galveston.[36] At the end of June, Dr. Scott departed with his daughter, Agnes, and another of his clergy brothers, the Reverend Charles C. Scott of Sherman, Texas, for Boston, where they would sail on the *Parisian* of the Allan Line for Edinburgh. They planned to be in Scotland for six weeks. A letter to a member of the Session dated July 20 reported on trips out from Edinburgh to visit Linlithgow Castle and Dunfermline Abbey, and then plans to spend their remaining time in the Highlands.[37] His travels in 1907 were less dramatic, possibly because he was moderator of the Synod of the Virginias that year and attended the annual meeting in the fall in Charleston, West Virginia. He did take a rest of about ten days at Bolar Springs in Bath County, accompanied by his daughter.

Dr. Scott's most ambitious trip occurred in 1909. He and his daughter Agnes, Jed Hotchkiss's daughter, Mrs. A.M. Howison, and her daughter Ellen Moore Howison, who had laid the cornerstone in the new church eight years earlier when she was a child, took a three-month trip abroad that included a visit to the Holy Land. The party sailed from New York in February. Dr. Scott and his daughter returned in late April, but Mrs. Howison and her daughter remained an additional month. The Reverend J.R. Homerton filled the pulpit of Second Church on Sundays in Dr. Scott's absence. The Wednesday evening prayer meetings were placed under the Missionary Laymen's Committee of twelve men chaired by W.A. Crawford.[38]

Second Church continued its pattern of growth. In 1906 the congregational report to the presbytery showed the addition of fifty-six members, twenty-seven on profession of faith and twenty-nine by certificate from other churches, for a total membership of 582. The total amount of contributions to the church for all purposes was $4,270. It was also a matter of relief that the Sears Hill Chapel, closed for several years, had finally been sold that year for $215, with the concurrence of the congregation at a meeting. By the spring of 1909 the membership numbers had reached 634.[39]

F.T. Glasgow presented a resolution to Session to adjust Pastor Scott's salary upward, owing to the increased cost of living. Session had conferred with Scott, and hoped to raise the salary to $1,800, but found that the finances and debt of the church simply did not make that possible at the time. When Scott made a report to the congregation in 1907 at the close of his sixth anniversary, he noted that 400 members had been added to the church in that time.[40] Although the church had not been able to raise Dr. Scott's salary, the Ladies Aid Society made life more comfortable for him and for his daughter Agnes with extensive improvements carried out on the Italianate style manse. A columned Colonial Revival style porch, then much in vogue in Staunton, was added to the front of the house, wrapping around to the east side, and another large porch was added

The new church was featured on a Staunton post card along with the post office about 1908.

in the rear. An ornamental granolithic wall was added to the yard and a concrete walk, and extensive painting and re-papering brightened the interior. The construction work was designed and supervised by congregational member W. Frank Dull, manager for Fretwell & Co., contractors, and architect for the new church building.[41]

A great loss in the lay leadership of the congregation occurred in the summer of 1907 with the death of Colonel Thomas Colgate Morton. A native of Botetourt County and a lifelong Presbyterian, Morton served in the Confederate Army as a young man. He came to Staunton in 1875, the year after Second Church was founded, as a partner in the insurance business with William A. McCue and later James Ker. He later became a joint owner and editor of the *Vindicator* along with H.C. Tinsley, and became a prominent Valley journalist. He had joined Second Church at the request of his father when he moved to Staunton, and took an active role from the beginning. He was ordained and installed as a ruling elder on February 6, 1881, and was tireless in his work for the building up of the congregation. Ever an ardent Confederate, he was buried in his uniform, his casket draped with the Confederate flag, and borne to the cemetery by Confederate veterans. Session wrote a moving memorial to his life and service that was read to the congregation and published in the *Central Presbyterian*.[42]

Life settled into a fairly predictable routine for the pastor, officers, and members of Second Presbyterian Church in the second decade of the twentieth century. The Session continued its role as a moral monitor for the congregation, although cases seem to have been handled less frequently than in the late nineteenth century. In 1912, two cases came before the Session, both involving alcohol. One was a married or widowed woman who had been investigated the previous year, and who had been before Police Court several times and convicted for drunkenness. The other was a man who had confessed his drunkenness and promised amendment, but did not change his behavior. In that time when little was understood about alcoholism, punishments were severe. The Session suspended both persons indefinitely from the sacraments.[43]

Dr. Scott continued to be in demand as a speaker for special services such as the revival held at Second church in March 1910, the annual Week of Prayer in January 1911, and the baccalaureate service at Lewisburg Seminary in West Virginia in June 1910.[44]

The first book of deacon's minutes that survives for Second Church begins in 1910, even though a board of deacons had been active from the formation of the congregation. That group met regularly the first Monday of every month at the Y.M.C.A., and then had a quarterly meeting with the elders, also at the Y. The deacons oversaw the preparation of the annual budget for the congregation. In 1900 that amounted to $2,600, of which $1,500 was for Dr. Scott's salary. The organist and sexton were the only two other employees of the congregation, and each received $150. Lighting cost $100, coal for heating was only $40, insurance $50, music for the choir $15, pulpit supply during Dr. Scott's vacation was $75, repairs to the buildings $200, and incidentals $170. The Deacons had four standing committees: Executive, with S.P. Silling as chairman; Finance, chaired by Frank Holt, owner of a bookshop and stationery business in the Crowle Building on Beverley Street, who was also Treasurer; Poor Committee chaired by T.A. Bell; and Ushers, whose chairman was Richard Henry Bell, Jr.[45]

Charles Frazier was the sexton of Second Church at this time. In 1911, after having to take up a special offering to assist him with living expenses the year before, the deacons decided to raise his salary from $12.50 a month to $18.[46]

After a decade of use, the congregation found the Sunday School space at the new church inadequate, so the deacons began to explore ways of adding space. W.D. Dull, Harry Miles Lewis, and Richard H. Bell were the committee appointed. The deacons hoped to gain assistance from the Ladies Aid Society, but that group had already committed its funds for the year, so the issue of expanded Sunday School space was put on hold. Instead, over the next two years, the deacons discussed many ways to squeeze more space, such as cleaning out a storage room for an additional classroom, and changing rooms between an adult class and the infant's class. Another space accommodation in 1912 was the placement of stationary chairs in the gallery of the church as seating for the cadets at Staunton Military Academy.[47]

Around 1910 a great many modern devices were becoming available in America to make homes, schools, and churches more comfortable. These included central heating to replace the individual coal fireplaces in houses, electric wiring for lighting, and natural gas for cooking. The church heating plant installed at the time of construction had become inadequate, so lengthy discussion of replacing that occupied the deacons for much of 1911 and 1912. In July 1912, a contract was let for a new heating plant that Augusta Plumbing & Heating would install for $800. The old furnace and fixtures were given to Bethel Church. G.W. Fretwell, who had built the church in 1901-1902, presented a proposal to panel and paint the ceiling of the sanctuary, which had been judged unsafe. While they were considering these measures, the deacons also decided to wire the church for forty dollars. The manse received a new heating plant as well. When the Church Workers wanted to buy a new coal stove and cooking range for the church kitchen, the deacons refused this plan, but approved the group's purchase of a gas range.[48]

In the fall of 1915, in the midst of the World War that was raging in Europe, the deacons turned their attention once more to the expansion of the Sunday School space. They met jointly with the Session to prepare plans for financing an addition, and to approve plans for the building. In October 1915, the two groups met with the architect, agreed on plans, and solicited bids. J.M. Lee proposed to build the addition for $3,316; Mr. Hemp for $3,463, and Mr. Fretwell for $3,660. The deacons and elders agreed not to exceed $3,500 in building costs. Morton, one of the elders, proposed that the church undertake a capital campaign for $5,000 in the five-day period from October 29 to November 4, 1915, with pledges to be spread over two years in six payments.[49]

The General Assembly of the Presbyterian Church in the United States approved a sweeping change in the organization and administration of Sunday Schools in the southern Presbyterian church. For decades these religious educational arms of the local congregations had their own administration, and managed their own financial affairs separately from the budget of the congregation. In May 1913, the Session considered the request of the General Assembly and Presbytery that Sessions take responsibility for Sunday School finances, so that contributions of the children could go directly to benevolent causes. Session found at that time that it could not do so, but went on record as intending to do so as soon as possible. In 1916 the elders found their way clear to making the change, and from that time forward, the collections of the Sunday School would not go to a Sunday School treasurer to administer, but to the Treasurer of Benevolent Causes for the Session. The congregation as a whole would undertake the purchase of Sunday School literature and other operating expenses of the school.[50]

The summer Sunday School work that Second Church had undertaken at Folly Mills and Edgewood early in Dr. Scott's time as pastor seemed to have dwindled and been given up by 1910, as these schools cease to be mentioned in the annual reports to presbytery. In place of mentioning these schools, the answer to the question about evangelism efforts became, "no special efforts at this time." However, when First Church approached the Session of Second Church in August 1913 about organizing a chapel on Sears Hill, the

Session assured First Church that it approved of the plan and was willing to provide assistance in the project.⁵¹

In place of an emphasis on evangelism, Dr. Scott and the congregation seemed to focus on the possibility of recruiting several young men from the congregation to enter the gospel ministry. Reports to presbytery in the years from 1911 to 1916 indicate that Dr. Scott spoke forcefully on the subject, and that several young men were considering a call to the ministry. One of these was Christian Brand, whom the Session certified in June 1915 to be "of sufficient character to study for the ministry and commended him to presbytery for whatever assistance might be available to him to study for his calling.⁵²

Dr. Scott's health was declining in the World War I years. In February 1915 the Session granted him a sick leave, and passed a resolution assuring him that the congregation wanted him to extend his leave in order to get the full benefit, and not return to work prematurely. In May 1917, at a joint meeting of the elders and deacons while Dr. Scott was ill and unable to attend, the group voted to raise his salary to $1,800. The appreciative pastor sent the officers a letter of thanks for the kind way in which they did this without his knowledge. In November 1917, Dr. Scott's physician prescribed a three-month break for him to rest and seek restoration of his health. Dr. DeJarnette moved that they pay the pastor's full salary in his absence. The officers secured the assistance of Dr. Eggleston as pulpit supply while Scott was on leave.⁵³

The first sign of an impact that World War I had on the congregation was the vote of the deacons in November 1917 to make a monthly donation not to exceed ten dollars to the Armenian relief Committee. The plight of the Armenian Christian people who lived in the Muslim dominated Ottoman Empire that was allied with the Central Powers (the Austrian Empire and Germany) caught the attention of Americans, and became one of the principal international relief efforts of the decade.[54] In January 1918, the Session agreed to join with other Staunton churches to hold Wednesday evening prayer meetings at the Y.M.C.A. in response to a request from the Fuel Administration in order to conserve coal for war purposes.[55]

By March 1918, Allen Moore Howison, son-in-law of Jed Hotchkiss, a deacon from 1886-1907, an elder since 1907, and a close friend of Dr. Scott was reported seriously ill. Early in April he died, and was memorialized by the Session, who noted Howison's conscientious attention to his religious duties, regular attendance at church, devotion to Presbyterianism, and long service to the church and his God.[56]

The break from late 1917 into early 1918 did little to restore Dr. Scott's health. He realized that he could no longer continue his work with the church, and resigned his pastorate in a letter to the Session on March 16, 1919. A congregational meeting held the next Sunday considered the letter and accepted it with regret. In the late spring of 1919, just at the time Staunton's native son, President Woodrow Wilson, was in Paris negotiating a treaty to end the war, Dr. Scott sought treatment and rest in Tampa, Florida. It was there that he died on Tuesday, June 3, 1919. As soon as the news was received, a meeting of the congregation of Second Church was called, and five men were chosen to represent the congregation at the funeral in Richmond and burial at Hollywood cemetery there. They were B.F. Hughes, Dr. J.S. DeJarnette, Richard Bell, A.S. Morton, and Colonel S. Brown Allen.[57]

Dr. Scott had been an excellent leader for the congregation in an important stage in its development. His death brought to an end an era of nearly two decades in which the church experienced unprecedented growth and strength, and in which it attracted a wide range of membership from all walks of life, including many among the social, economic, and professional leadership of the community.

Chapter Five Notes

[1] *Staunton Spectator*, 5, 12 April 1901.
[2] Ibid., 19, 26 April 1901.
[3] Ibid., 3 May 1901.
[4] Ibid., 10 May 1901.
[5] Session Minutes, 2 June 1901.
[6] *Staunton Spectator*, 26 April 1901.
[7] Ibid., 12 April 1901.
[8] Ibid., 2, 20 September, 1 November 1901; 14 March, 11 April, 30 May 1902.
[9] Ibid., 26 April 1901.
[10] Ibid., 14 June 1901.
[11] Ibid., 15 July, 9 August, 23 August 1901; Session minutes, 11 August 1901.
[12] Session minutes, 22, 29 December 1901; 26 January, 1 June 1902.
[13] *Staunton Spectator*, 30 May, 25 July 1902.
[14] *Staunton Spectator*, 27 September 1901.
[15] Ibid., 24 January 1902.
[16] *Subscribers Directory*, Staunton Mutual Telephone Company, Staunton, Va. 1914.
[17] *Staunton Spectator*, 11 July, 29 August 1902; Session minutes 31 August, 19, 26 October 1902.
[18] *Staunton Spectator*, 29 August, 19 September, 3 October 1902; Session minutes, 10 August 1902.
[19] MacDuff Simpson to Capt. T.C. Morton, 22 September 1902. Printed in full in the *Staunton Spectator*, 24 October 1902.
[20] Ibid and the Inflation Calculator, www.westegg.com/inflation/infl.cgi.
[21] Session minutes, 1 November 1902, 22 February 1903; *Staunton Spectator*, 21 November, 12 December 1902, 23 October 1903.
[22] *Staunton Spectator*, 16, 23 January 1903; 8 January 1904; 13 January 1905.
[23] Ibid., 13 March, 17 April, 24 April, 15 May 1903.
[24] Session minutes, 1 17 May, 21 June 1903.
[25] *Staunton Spectator*, 27 May 1904.
[26] Ibid., 3, 17 June, 1 July, 12 August 1904.
[27] Ibid., 4 November 1904; Session minutes, 30 October 1904.
[28] Sanger, *A History of Second Presbyterian Church*, 60.
[29] Ibid., 14 April 1905, 30 March, 8 June 1906.
[30] Ibid., 9 March 1906.
[31] Ibid., 24 February 1905.
[32] Session minutes, 25 December 1904.
[33] *Staunton Spectator*, 21 July, 25 August 1905.
[34] Session minutes, 14 December 1902, 18 December 1904, 24 December 1905, 17 June 1906, January 1907, 17 January 1909, 10 April 1910.
[35] Session minutes, 15 April, 1 July 1906, 5 May, 14, 28 July, 4 August 1907.
[36] Session minutes, 14 January 1906; *Staunton Spectator*, 19 January 1906.
[37] *Staunton Spectator*, 29 June, 3, 17 August 1906.
[38] *Staunton Spectator*, 19 July, 1 November 1907; 15, 29 January, 5 February, 30 April 1909; Session minutes, 27 September 1908, 17 January 1909.
[39] *Staunton Spectator*, 11 June 1909.
[40] Session minutes, 4 March, 8 April, 16, 23 December 1906; *Staunton Spectator*,

30 March, 13 April 1906.
[41]*Staunton Spectator*, 13 December 1907.
[42]Session minutes, 11 August 1907.
[43]Ibid., 8 January, 23 April 1911, 17 March, 14 July 1912.
[44]*Staunton Spectator*, 18 March, 3 June 1910, 6 January 1911.
[45] Deacon's minutes, 1910-1911; 3 January, 5 December 1910.
[46]Ibid., 12 September, 7 November 1910; 10 April 1911.
[47]Ibid., 2 September 1912, 4 November, 6 December 1913, 5 January, 2 February 1914.
[48]Ibid., 1 July, 6 October, 4 November 1912.
[49]Deacon's Minutes, 1915-1921; 6, 13, September, 11, 18 October, 8 November 1915.
[50]Ibid., 25 May 1913, 3 April 1916.
[51]Session Minutes, 1911, 1913, and 1914 reports to presbytery.
[52]Ibid., 13 June 1915.
[53]Session Minutes, 28 February 1915; Deacon's Minutes, 7 May, 18 November 1917.
[54]Deacon's Minutes., 5 November 1917.
[55]Session Minutes, 4 January 1918.
[56]Ibid., 14 April 1918; Sanger, *History of Second Presbyterian Church,* 52, 54.
[57]*The Staunton Daily News,* 4 June 1919.

Chapter Six
Times of Transition

In the last quarter of the twentieth century, those who study the dynamics of Protestant congregations in America and their relationships with their ministers came to understand that the loss of a long-term minister brings about a type of grieving among the members of a congregation. They also understand that it is often difficult for that congregation to find a new pastor who will be as well received and who will be willing and able to stay for a long pastorate, as the former minister was.

These pastors and professors who have studied what happens to churches when it is time to get a new pastor now recognize that it is important for a congregation to have a temporary minister. This person is called an interim minister and has been trained in special interim ministry skills. The interim's job is to help a congregation tie off the relationship to the former pastor, examine carefully the strengths, weaknesses, needs, and goals of the congregation, and go through a careful selection process to find a new pastor who can help the congregation address its needs and goals positively. These studies of hundreds of congregations across the country have found that if a congregation fails to appoint an interim minister and moves directly to the selection of a new pastor, that new pastor is likely to have a very short pastorate. He or she will, in effect, fulfil the role of the interim minister that the congregation failed to engage.[1]

In 1919, when the aging and ailing Dr. Scott resigned, the notion that a change of pastors was a critical time in the life of a congregation was not clear. The concept of an interim ministry simply did not exist. The standard practice in the Presbyterian Church, and in nearly every Protestant denomination in America at that time, was to fill the pulpit as quickly as possible. Supply ministers, usually chosen among retired or part-time clergymen living in the region, filled in for two or three months until the new man could be chosen and brought to town.

The officers of Second Church did what was typical for their time. Dr. Scott's resignation was presented to the Session on March 16, 1919. By the next week, the Session had selected a supply minister, the Reverend Charles Andrew Lawrence, who moderated the Session meeting on March 23. A month later, on April 27, Session authorized a congregational meeting for Sunday, May 4 to elect a calling committee for a permanent pastor. Although the calling committee was often composed only of officers, Session recommended a six-person committee. Its members were elders S. Brown Allen and Harry M. Lewis, deacons Frank T. Holt, who was with White Star Mills, and Harold C. Gibson, manager of the Banner Store, and from the congregation, Charles R. McGuffin, a bookkeeper with Valley National Bank, and Rumsey S. Blakemore, who listed himself in the city directory as a clerk.[2]

No records survive to indicate how extensively this committee searched, or how many candidates were interviewed. Perhaps they considered a number of men. Perhaps not. Congregational minutes do not survive to tell when the selection took place, but the search was brief, for on June 15, 1919, Charles Andrew Lawrence, the supply minister, was installed by Lexington Presbytery as pastor of Second Presbyterian Church. Dr. A.M. Fraser, pastor of First Church, preached a powerful installation sermon, according to the

Charles Lawrence's pastorate, 1919-1921, was one of the shortest in the church's history, but he introduced important new movements in Presbyterianism.

newspaper, with Dr. D.K. Walthall of Waynesboro and the Rev. W.W. Sprouse of Third Church assisting in the service.[3]

The new pastor could hardly have been more different from Dr. Scott, the courtly, elderly Southern gentleman and admirer of the Confederacy, who, with his white goatee, might remind today's congregation of Colonel Saunders. Charles Lawrence was just over fifty when he arrived at Second Church, clean-shaven in the modern style, a widower with a son and a daughter in college in the north. Lawrence was himself a northerner, born in 1872 in Portville, New York. His background and education were not Presbyterian, but Methodist. He studied at Geneva Wesleyan Seminary, became a deacon and an elder in the Genessee Methodist Episcopal Conference, and served pastorates in the Methodist Episcopal Church from 1900 to 1913. He then became a Presbyterian and served pastorates in the Presbyterian Church U.S.A. (northern) from 1913 to 1919, and transferred into the Presbyterian Church, U.S. (southern) at the time he came to Second Church.[4]

Although Lawrence started his pastorate at the $1,800 salary to which Dr. Scott had only been raised in 1917, by May 1920, the elders and deacons were meeting jointly to consider three proposals for raising his salary: $2,100, $2,400, and $2,500. Each proposal received eight votes, so Colonel S. Brown Allen was called to the chair and cast the tie-breaking vote for $2,400. To some in the church this may have seemed an enormous increase — thirty-three percent. They may not have realized that Dr. Scott had a low salary, and that they were now being asked to offer a more normal, modern figure for a church of that size. The groups met again before the congregational meeting on the question, fearing the church budget could not take such an increase. They rescinded the motion and took the vote again. Although they reached same decision, three members refused to vote in favor of this raise — an early sign of dissension.[5]

Most new pastors in a congregation find some things that they would like to change and some new ideas and programs that they would like to introduce. Lawrence thought he would like to deliver the benediction from the back of the church, apparently an innovation that puzzled some at Second Church, and that required approval of the deacons to take place. Another innovation he brought to the congregation was a printed weekly bulletin. The deacons began to investigate the costs in May 1921, and by October were ready to begin issuing the bulletin.[6]

Pastor Lawrence took charge at a time of change, uncertainty, turmoil, and transition in the nation. Armistice had only been achieved in November 1918 in the Great War that we now call World War I. Staunton's native son President Woodrow Wilson, a child of the town's Presbyterian manse, was in Paris concluding the work of the Peace Conference and the Versailles Treaty draft. As Lawrence was being installed, Woodrow Wilson was preparing to sail home to try to convince the American people to support that treaty, and the United States Senate to ratify it.[7] As one means of helping with the transition to peacetime, in June 1919 the Session of Second Church appointed elders W.N. Clemmer, R.T. Moseley, and A.S. Morton to cooperate with the War Community League to welcome the church's returned soldiers home and help them secure employment.[8]

Transition to peacetime was more than finding jobs for veterans. The nation worried in 1919 about the Bolshevik Scare, as former ally Russia fell under communist control. The nation's Attorney General, A. Mitchell Palmer, was arresting without warrants hundreds of immigrants suspected of radicalism and deporting them without hearings. Half a million coal miners were threatening to strike. Influenza outbreaks were still a major fear. Race riots had broken out in many cities across the country, resulting in some of the worst racial violence in American history. Radical suffragettes had campaigned for votes for women, often supported by conservative southerners, who saw the votes of white women as a counter balance to votes for black men. Many Americans, especially conservative southern Protestants, campaigned for a prohibition of alcoholic beverages. The many tensions in the nation could easily have contributed to an atmosphere of doubting and testing of new programs and new ideas at Second Church.

One tension in the congregation appeared by the end of the summer of 1919 involving the Sunday School. It would appear that Pastor Lawrence and the Sunday School Superintendent, Harold C. Gibson, were in favor of an ambitious Sunday School program. An article in the Staunton paper called attention to an elaborate Children's Day program at Second Church on June 8, 1919, with songs, solos, recitations, an address by Lawrence, and a discussion of "The Seven Year Plan and the School's Participation." The article noted that "this wide-awake Sunday school has an enrollment of 456 members, with 222 in the Home Department and 38 on the Cradle Roll, making a total of 716 members." Lexington Presbytery carried on a contest among its churches to encourage Sunday School attendance. Of the five largest churches in the presbytery, Staunton's Second Church won the banner in 1919 for the highest average attendance, 350. Harrisonburg was second with 300, then Lexington and Staunton's First Church tied at 259, and Mt. Carmel was next at 216.[9] Some in the Session were unhappy with the aggressive vigor of the Sunday School program. One of the most strongly worded statements to appear anywhere in the Session minutes of Second Church noted:

> The Session is being seriously inconvenienced and the morning service of the Church hindered because the meetings of the Sunday school are extended beyond reasonable points and whereas; Persons often desiring to come from the Sunday School before the Session are prevented from doing so and Whereas; the morning service of the Church is often delayed because the Sunday School is held beyond the allotted time. Session insisted that the lessons terminate at 10:40 and instructed the superintendent to observe the rule.[10]

In December 1920, when the Sunday School superintendent asked permission of Session to use the church auditorium for the usual Christmas program, including a sacred concert, Bible readings, and a male quartet, the Session granted the request, but wanted it clearly understood that this was in no way to interfere with the regular Sunday evening service.[11]

One woman in the congregation caused considerable upset in the course of 1919, Mrs. Oliver.W. Robertson, a social worker with the Community Welfare League.[12] At the beginning of the year, she filed a complaint with church officers, accusing a Session member, Elder Hughes, a druggist, of selling "denatured alcohol to certain Drug Fiends" who were using it as a beverage. Elder Hughes appeared before the Session, made a full statement, which was acceptable to its members and to Mrs. Robertson. The incident was closed with the adoption of a resolution stating that:

> While mistakes may have been made all around we bow to the will of him who [knows] that it is 'human to err'& we here and now agree to reconsecrate ourselves to the work of uniting our church and members into a great Brotherhood where chief object shall be to promote good will and Christian fellowship between our members to the end that the Second Presbyterian Church of this city shall become a power for good in the future as it has always been in the past.[13]

Such a strong statement about unity and brotherhood would only be made when those very qualities had been seriously weakened in the congregation. Two days later, Mrs. Robertson was again the subject of a Session meeting when she requested to meet with the elders regarding statements that she and H.C. Gibson had made regarding church matters. The meeting ended with each promising "to cooperate with each other and with the Session in all things relating to the good of the Second Presbyterian Church," and both affirmed that they had never in any way questioned the consecrated leadership of the Session.[14] When a congregational meeting was held to elect elders in November 1919, Mrs. Robertson's husband, O.W. Robertson, was among those chosen.

The next month, Mrs. Robertson was once more the topic of a Session meeting. This time Captain Francis of the Salvation Army had brought charges against her. Session minutes give no detail about them. Session went on record stating their "unshaken faith in her Christian Character and high appreciation of the efficiency and importance of her work in the Welfare League and to express further belief that the rumors floating around the city — in which her methods are assailed and her motives questioned are not only with out foundation in fact but utterly false."[15]

Another issue that may have caused division in the church was the question of church music. In January 1920, the Session held a long discussion about the music at Second Church. Minutes give no details, but two elders, Harry Miles Lewis and Randolph Talcott Mosely, were appointed a committee in charge of music. Three days later, that appointment was rescinded and the entire matter of music placed in the hands of Session.[16] Such indecisiveness and contradiction can be a sign of a power struggle on the board, or of weak leadership and poor organization on that body.

An innovation in Lawrence's pastorate was the effort to emphasize family worship at home. For many years the Session's annual report to presbytery had indicated that this was a weak area and that little was done about it. In January 1920, Session formed a committee on family worship. The group adopted the Family Altar League program of the General Assembly of the Presbyterian Church, U.S. In May, the Reverend G.A. Wilson addressed the Session on the subject of "Family Religion and the Essential Feature of the Family Altar."[17]

Lawrence seemed also to have a strong interest in evangelistic work, both personal work on the part of members of the church, and outreach in the form of revival meetings. Session reported to presbytery in the spring of 1920 that "The Holy Spirit's power was plainly manifested in a Revival Service during the year and a goodly number were added to the church." In November 1920, Session had a lengthy discussion "of ways to promote more interest in personal evangelistic church work" and approved a tentative plan by the pastor, who, with the Clerk of Session, would map out details. Whether this placed pressure on the clerk, or whether he was simply tired and aging is hard to say, but two weeks later, he offered his resignation after twenty years service. In March 1921, the pastor and clerk were to prepare a letter on personal evangelism as a first step in preparation for the Evangelistic Campaign of Staunton Churches, beginning with cottage prayer meetings and occurring in all churches on Sunday, March 13. The revival must have had a strong impact, for some thirty new members joined the church on March 27. The deacons considered this protracted meeting successful, and voted additional payments of twenty-five dollars to Professor R.L. Middlekauf, the organist, ten dollars to Luther Howard, the sexton, and then took up a freewill offering that netted $107 for Pastor Lawrence for his work in the two weeks' revival.[18]

Missions were another important emphasis that Second Church displayed during Lawrence's pastorate. One aspect of this was the congregation's assistance to one of its young men, Louis C. Brand. In January 1920, the deacons gave him financial aid to attend the Student Volunteer Movement Convention in Des Moines, Iowa. Participation in this powerful and popular college Christian movement encouraged many young Presbyterians all over America to enter the mission field. Brand also received assistance from the Student Loan Fund at Second Church to attend college and medical school, and became a medical missionary in Korea. He married Alberta Dudley of Second Church, who accompanied him to Korea as a missionary.[19]

The congregation also undertook the full support of one of its own, Lelia G. Kirtland, who became a missionary to Japan. Miss Kirtland, who was called Missy, had transferred to Second Church in 1910 from First Presbyterian Church in Memphis. In 1920, that support amounted to assuming her entire annual salary of $1,350, as the Session notified the Foreign Missionary Committee at Nashville.[20] In addition to $650 more in foreign missions, the Benevolent Causes portion of the congregational budget in 1921 included $701 for General Assembly Home Missions, $425 for Presbytery Home Missions, and $542 for Congregational Home Missions.[21]

The Home Mission that excited a number of members of Second Church was the Irish Creek Mission near Cornwall in nearby Rockbridge County. Boxes of clothing had been sent there in previous years, but now the congregation had one of its own working there in the person of Alma McLaurin, whom Second Church helped to support.

Pastor Lawrence developed an unusual proposal, which Elder Harry M. Lewis presented to the Session in August 1921. Lawrence proposed that he share the manse with Professor Morrison M. Edgar of Seymour, Indiana, the new principal of Dunsmore Business College, and his family. With Lawrence's son, Alton,[22] and daughter away at college, there was plenty of room in the large Italianate house with its graceful porches, and the pastor felt the arrangement could be of benefit to both families. The Deacons approved. Edgar quickly became an active member of the congregation, and within a year was elected to Session.[23]

In spite of what appear to be innovative programs, healthy growth in numbers, and significant increase in the giving of the congregation, especially for benevolent causes,what is now called "outreach ministry" in churches, there were deep-seated divisions in the congregation that came to the surface in the fall of 1921. On November 6, the following minutes were entered in the Session book.

> A paper numerously signed by members of the Church and others in which the statement was made that the Church was in far better condition spiritually and financially than ever before was laid before the Session, with the request that it be made a part of the Session record. Elder Lewis moved that this paper be approved and recorded in the minutes of the Session. On a recorded vote the motion was lost. Elders Allen, Wiseman, Kester, Bell, Clemmer, and Moseley voting "no." With Elders Hughes, Robinson [sic Robertson], and Lewis voting for the motion.[24]

This unusual request and the sharply divided vote are indicative of turmoil in the congregation. This was borne out by the minutes of the next Session meeting a week later, in which Elder Moseley introduced a resolution that the Session instruct its commissioner, Elder Richard Bell, to present to Lexington Presbytery at its next scheduled meeting on March 15, 1921, during the Virginia Synod, a follow-up petition to the one Session had rejected the week before. This petition protested Session's action in refusing to place the paper signed by some 400 members of Second Church into the record. Session added, "and further that he [Bell] be instructed to state to Lexington Presbytery that serious trouble exists in our church and ask the Presbytery to appoint a committee to investigate and settle our trouble if possible." Kester, Wiseman, Allen, Clemmer, Bell, and Moseley voted for this. Lewis, Hughes, Silling, and Robertson voted against it.[25]

Lexington Presbytery took immediate action on the situation, not waiting for a spring meeting, and cited the congregation. Session called a congregational meeting for December 4 to answer the citation, and instructed its clerk to invite one of the nearby ministers, either C.D. Waller, Dr. D.K. Walthall, or Dr. Fraser to moderate the meeting, in that order. Unfortunately, minutes for that tense meeting do not survive to shed light on issues and personalities. It must have been long, difficult, and painful. Either before, during, or just after that meeting, Lawrence submitted his resignation as pastor.[26]

Lexington Presbytery held a special called meeting in Staunton the day after. Presbytery decided that it was in the best interest of all parties to accept the resignation. However, the Lexington Presbytery adopted a resolution about Lawrence and issued a public statement saying "Lexington Presbytery places on record an expression of appreciation of his work as a minister, of confidence in him as a man, of high regard for him as a presbyter and affection for him as a Christian brother; also our regret that circumstances have arisen which had led him to offer his resignation."[27]

Further, Presbytery required the resignation of all elders, deacons, and other male church officers, including the Sunday School Superintendent and assistant, the treasurers of current expenses and benevolent funds, the choir leader, chairman of ushers, and the congregational manager. No officers of any women's groups were asked to resign, as women were not considered to be in a governing role in the congregation. Presbytery appointed a commission to direct the affairs of the church until a new election could be held, and instructed the congregation not to elect officers until presbytery directed it to do so.[28]

The commission appointed to handle the affairs of the church was comprised of the Reverend John R. Rosebro of Hebron Church, chairman, the Reverend David B. Kirby Walthall, D.D., of Waynesboro, the Reverend Charles DeVries Waller, and Elders William H. East of Loch Willow, and S. Finley McClure of Mt. Carmel

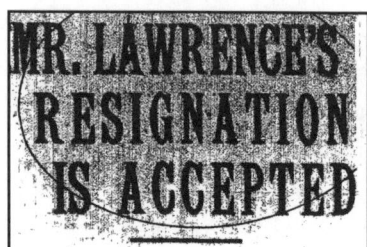

MR. LAWRENCE'S RESIGNATION IS ACCEPTED

Lexington Presbytery Decides to End His Pastoral Relation With Second Church and Asks for Resignation of All Church's Officers; Commission to Direct Church.

Lexington presbytery, in special session here all day yesterday and last evening, decided to accept the resignation of the Rev. Charles A. Lawrence as pastor of the Second church of this city, and to ask for the resignation of all of the officers of the church. Presbytery appointed a commission to conduct the affairs of the church until a new pastor can be called and new officers elected. The church remains in status quo until January 1.

In accepting the resignation of Mr. Lawrence, to take effect on January 1, presbytery adopted the following resolution:

"In accepting the resignation c the Rev. C. A. Lawrence as pastor of the Second church of Staunton Lexington presbytery places on record an expression of appreciation o, his work as a minister, of confidence in him as a man, of high regard for him as a presbyter and affection for him as a Christian brother; also our regret that circumstances have arisen which have led him to offer his resignation."

The commission of presbytery named to direct the affairs of the church until new officers are elected is as follows:

The Rev. Jno. R. Rosebro, the Rev. D. K. Walthall, D. D., the Rev. C. D. Waller, and Elders, W. H. East and S. Finley McClure.

Presbytery asked the elders and deacons to resign and instructed the congregation not to elect officers un til such time as the presbytery shall direct the same to be done. The commission appointed is to have charge of the affairs of the church until the new officers shall be elected and installed.

The pastor's resignation made front page headlines in the Staunton News-Leader on December 6, 1921.

Church.²⁹ It is not clear how often this group met or visited Second Church. By late February, they believed that the congregation was ready to undertake its own government once more. On March 1, 1922, the commission installed Harry M. Lewis, Benjamin Franklin Hughes, Stuart Preston Silling, and Oliver Walker Robertson, all of whom had been elders previously. These were called to meet as the Session and proceed with the ordination and installation of elders and deacons.³⁰

The new elders ordained and installed were H. Newton McCutchan, Charles Robert McGuffin, Morrison McClurkin Edgar, Frank Thomas Holt, and Dr. Isaac Henry Trimble. Holt had long been active as a deacon. McCutchan had joined Second in 1906. McGuffin, who was a bookkeeper with Valley National Bank, had transferred from First Presbyterian in 1916, and Dr. Trimble, who had joined some time around 1910, was chosen a deacon in 1913. Edgar, as the head of the Dunsmore Business College, had only recently arrived in town.

Eight new deacons were elected and installed: D.B. Wilson, who was in the grocery business; Delmar Ross Cox, a painter; Charles Gates Clinedinst, Frank Bartley Kennedy, a lawyer who was active with the Stonewall Brigade Band as secretary; William McClanahan Chittum, the ticket agent for the B&O Railroad; Dr. Joseph S. DeJarnette, superintendent of Western State; Arthur Sydnor Morton, the circulation manager of the *Staunton News-Leader*; and Emmett G. Robertson, a cabinetmaker with Forsythe Antiques. Some of these men were old members, some new. Morton had first been chosen deacon in 1900 and Dr. DeJarnette in 1907. Clinedinst and Chittum were longtime members. Kennedy and Robertson had joined Second in 1901. Cox had come from Stuarts Draft in 1917. Swiftly, seven new deacons were added to that list: Howard Craig Wilson, Raymond Charles Wymer, a life insurance agent; Robert Elmore Christian, vice president of Staunton Lime Products; James Stuart Lotts,

Lewis Valentine Harris, a plumbing and heating contractor; and Thomas Addison Bell, a manager at Hamrick's Funeral Home.[31]

The following week, Session met to elect the other officers of the church, and chose M.M. Edgar as Superintendent of the Sunday School. This was apparently a good choice, for he remained in the position for sixteen years, until 1938. S.P. Silling, long a city councilman, was treasurer of benevolences, C.R. McGuffin was Clerk of Session, and H.N. McCutchan was chairman of the Music Committee. Then they named a committee for Pulpit Supply. Its members were H.M. Lewis, chair, H.N. McCutchen, and C.R. McGuffin. Whether the committee was only concerned with temporary supply and was not also the committee on Pastoral Call is not clear.[32]

The statistics this new Session reported to presbytery showed the terrible toll that the divisions had extracted. Membership had dropped by one hundred persons, from 674 in 1921 to 573 in 1922, and the congregation had not been able to meet its benevolences budget.

The committee to select a pastor reported to the congregation on September 13, 1922, after a six-month search, undoubtedly lengthened by the widespread knowledge of the difficulties that the church had experienced. Their recommendation, accepted by the congregation, was the Reverend Watson Emmet Davis, D.D. Davis, a young man not yet thirty, was a lifelong Presbyterian, educated at the Presbyterian College of South Carolina and at Columbia Theological Seminary. His only pastorate had been at Fort Hill Presbyterian Church at Clemson College in South Carolina since 1917. His successful work there with young men made him especially attractive to Second Church, with its large and active Sunday School, and with several young members studying for the ministry or missionary work. Davis was not a stranger to the Staunton area. For the three summers that he was in seminary, 1915, 1916, and 1917, Davis was

Watson Emmet Davis, D.D., pastor from 1922-1926 was an engaging man who brought stability and vigor to the church.

the assistant pastor to the Reverend William C. White, D.D., at Loch Willow and Union Churches in the Churchville area.[33]

Lexington Presbytery received Davis at its meeting at Second Church on October 23, 1922. Presbytery named Elder Harry Miles Lewis, a descendant of Staunton's founder, John Lewis, and a senior member of the Session and congregation, to plan the installation service along with the Reverend E.W. McCorkle, D.D. The service took place on November 19, 1922, with Davis's former mentor, Pastor White, preaching.[34]

Davis's energy and enthusiasm may have helped to make up for his lack of experience. He appears to have worked closely with the Session elders, seeking their advice. Together they developed a quarterly spiritual canvass of the congregation, besides the usual canvass for financial contributions. Session and the pastor made a special effort to be aware of sick members, so that they could receive a pastoral call. Although Session budgeted a reduced contribution for benevolences of $5,250 for 1923, as conditions in the congregation improved, they were able to raise this to the $6,500 that presbytery had requested. Gradually, the membership began to climb again, with 643 reported in 1923, 635 in 1924, and 658 in 1925.[35]

As the congregation recovered confidence and members, it also grew financially. By 1925, the budget included $6,700 for operating expenses and $7,000 for benevolences. That year, the deacons recommended a congregational meeting to amend the pastoral call to increase Dr. Davis's salary to $3,000. The congregation was so pleased with their minister, that when T.A. Bell offered an amendment to raise the salary to $3,600, it passed unanimously.[36]

A fire at the manse on Frederick Street in the fall of 1924 probably caused the church to take a careful look at housing for its minister. In the spring of 1925 a good opportunity came along. In April, when the Session called a meeting to consider the unanimous recommendation of a joint committee of elders and deacons to purchase the Yost property on North Lewis Street directly behind the church, the congregation voted unanimously to buy it for $18,000. Pledge slips distributed at the meeting resulted in pledges of $4,133 to be paid by June. Thus the church acquired the handsome colonial revival house that was the finest manse Second Church has had in its history.[37]

Various groups at Second Church began to make use of the facilities at Massanetta in nearby Rockingham County while Davis was pastor. The deacons took an active role in soliciting funds for sending church youth to camps there. Davis leased a tent and a cottage there for the full five week summer conference in 1924, the tent costing four dollars a week and the cottage seven dollars. Second Church also ran an active Daily Vacation Bible School, a program that caught on with Protestant churches all across America in the 1920s.[38]

Davis initiated a complete reorganization of women's work when he called all the women of the church together in the spring of 1923. The formal change took place on April

The Yost house made a handsome manse for Second Presbyterian Church for many decades.

23, 1923, when the Woman's Auxiliary was born. This new organization brought together all the women's groups that had functioned over the years, such as the Ladies Aid Society, the Church Workers, and the several Missionary Societies. Those groups ceased to exist, and the new Woman's Auxiliary included in its membership every woman who was a member of Second Church. A group that large could not meet efficiently, so was divided into several circles.[39]

The first president of the Woman's Auxiliary at Second Church was Mrs. A.M. Howison who, a decade earlier, had played an active role in organizing the Woman's Auxiliary for the entire Southern Presbyterian Church. This daughter of founding member, Jed Hotchkiss, was at that time a widow, living with her daughter Ellen and her son-in-law, Robert E. Christian, at Oakenwold. She had been the treasurer for that church-wide group, so brought strong leadership skills to her local role. All the other officers had extensive experience in women's work. Mrs. J.S. DeJarnette was vice president, Mrs. L.L. Putney, whose husband was a physician on Dr. DeJarnette's staff at Western State, was secretary, and Miss Ruth Brand was treasurer. The Woman's Auxiliary continued until 1948 when a new reorganization of women's work in the church brought into being the Women of the Church.[40]

Another innovation in Davis's tenure was the organization of the Men of the Church, a recommendation from the General Assembly of the Presbyterian Church in the U.S. This took place in December 1924. About seventy-five men were present at the organizational dinner that the Woman's Auxiliary served. Dr. Davis gave an address, and several men gave pep talks about the organization. The men decided to adopt such an organization and to meet monthly for programs and fellowship. The first officers they chose were Frank B. Kennedy, president, Omri C. Hemp, a bookkeeper as secretary, and Cecil Burton, manager of the Piggly Wiggly grocery, treasurer. This group continued active for a decade, when its work was taken over by the Men's Bible Class in 1935.[41]

Under Davis's leadership, Second Church also took part in a large evangelistic campaign in the spring of 1926. A principal service took place on a Sunday. Session authorized Davis to send a personal letter to everyone who planned to unite with the church and to all who reconsecrated their lives during that Sunday revival. Session also authorized services held throughout the following week, the last week of May, and met daily in the presence of the congregation at each evening service to examine and receive new members. This proved an effective tool for increasing congregational membership.[42]

In four years, Davis had worked wonders in bringing the congregation together, in leaving former divisions behind, in strengthening youth work, in developing summer programs, and in bringing new organization and new life to the work of the men and the women. Church budgets were the largest in the history of the congregation, and a handsome new manse was probably the finest ministerial accommodation in all of Staunton. In the wider community, Davis also played a role. He was president of the Staunton Ministerial Association for two years, and was a leader in the Staunton Kiwanis Club, serving as a trustee and member of the board of that recently founded civic organization.

It is little wonder that the congregation was distressed when Dr. Davis received a call to Central Presbyterian Church in Atlanta, Georgia. At a called meeting on October 3, 1926, the congregation adopted a resolution noting the wonderful progress the church had made under his leadership, and requesting earnestly that he decline the call from Atlanta. He gave the matter much careful and prayerful thought in the week after the meeting. On Sunday, he told the congregation that he had tried "to see it my duty to remain here" where, as he said, "the surroundings have been most congenial," but he believed that "the Lord had directed very plainly His desire for me to go."[43]

Central Presbyterian Church had a membership of 1,500, nearly triple that of Second Church, and an annual budget of $215,000, more than ten times as great as that of Second Church. It was a rare opportunity for a capable young man. When the congregation of Second Church held its next meeting on October 17, the members had come to understand that their minister was firm in his resignation, and agreed to join with him in asking presbytery to dissolve the pastoral relationship. His resignation was effective on October 31, 1926. The congregation bid him and his family farewell with the warmest of wishes, and turned its thoughts to the future. Davis's successful, short tenure of four years would prove to ease the transition to the next pastor.

Chapter Six Notes

[1] The Alban Institute in Washington, D.C., is an interdenominational, non-profit, membership-based organization dedicated to research, study, consultation, training, and publication in topics that encourage strong, healthy congregational life and ministry. Among the pioneering studies that the organization has published, and that address the findings about the importance of changing pastorates and using interim ministers are: Loren B. Mead, *Critical Moment of Ministry: A Change of Pastors*; Martin F. Saarinen, *The Life Cycle of a Congregation*; Ralph Macy, *The Interim Pastor*; and Roger S. Nicholson, editor, *Temporary Shepherds: A Congregational Handbook for Interim Ministry*.

[2] Session Minutes, 16, 23 March, 27 April 1919.

[3] Ibid., 15 June 1921; *Staunton Leader*, 17 June 1919.

[4] Sanger, *A History of the Second Presbyterian Church, Staunton, Virginia, 1875-1975*, 48.

[5] Deacons minutes, 19, 24 May 1920.

[6] Ibid., 6 October 1919; 3 May, 7 June 1920; 3, 5 October 1921.

[7] Gene Smith, *When the Cheering Stopped* (New York: William Morrow and Company, 1964), 44-59.

[8] Session minutes, 1 June 1919.

[9] *Staunton Leader*, 8, 15 June 1919.

[10] Session Minutes, 21 September 1919.

[11] Ibid., 5 December 1920.

[12] The Robertsons had transferred to Second Church with a certificate from Old Providence Associate Reformed Presbyterian Church in Spottswood (Augusta County) in 1912. Robertson was a farmer, and his wife a social worker. The large Robertson family, with probably mother-in-law who was superintendent of the Welfare League Home and widowed sister-in-law who was housekeeper at the Welfare League Home, lived together at 310 Kalorama Street. *Staunton City Directory, 1919-1920*. Later, in the 1920s, Mrs. Robertson was the city probation officer. They lived with their daughter, Miss Reta Robertson, at the Kalorama Streethouse according to the 1924 *Staunton City Directory*.

[13] Ibid., 1 January 1919.

[14] Ibid., 3 January 1919.

[15] Ibid., 30 November, 7 December, 21 December 1919.

[16] Ibid., 30 January, 10 February 1920.

[17] Ibid., 31 March, 9 May 1920.

[18] Ibid., 7 November 1920, 6 March, 27 March 1921; Deacons Minutes, 4 April 2 May 1921.

[19] Session Minutes, Sanger, 28.

[20] Deacons Minutes, 17 December 1919; Session Minutes, 27 March 1921; and Sanger, 28. See also the Register of Second Church, in volume of Session Minutes 1910-1920.

[21] Session Minutes, 22 September 1920; Sanger, 29.

[22] Alton A. Lawrence, son of Charles A. Lawrence, is listed on the Register of Baptisms at Second Church, probably in 1919, although the entry is not dated. Register is part of the Session Minutes volume 1910-1920.

[23] Ibid., 2 August 1921.

[24] Ibid., 6 November 1921.

[25] Ibid., 13 November 1921.

[26] Ibid., 20, 27 November 1921.
[27] *Staunton News-Leader,* Tuesday 6 December 1921.
[28] Ibid., Session Minutes, 25 December 1921.
[29] *Staunton News-Leader,* 6 December 1921. For identification of church affiliations of pastors and elders, see Howard McKnight Wilson, *Lexington Presbytery Heritage.*
[30] Session Minutes. Insertion following meeting of 25 December 1921.
[31] Registers with Session Minutes of 1898-1910 and 1910-1920.
[32] Session Minutes, 8 March 1922.
[33] Sanger, 48; *Staunton News-Leader,* 10, 24 October 1922.
[34] *Staunton News-Leader,* 24 October 1922.
[35] Session Minutes, 22, 23 October, 3 December 1922; 4 February, 11 March, 8 April 1923, 4 April 1925.
[36] Deacons Minutes, 5 January 1925; Congregational Minutes, 19 April 1925.
[37] Session Minutes, 3 May 1925; Congregational Minutes, 10 May 1925; and Deacons Minutes, 1 June, 6 July 1925. The Deacons worked out a five-year plan to eliminate the manse debt. Minutes 2 November, 7 December 1925.
[38] Deacons Minutes, 2 June, 4 August 1925.
[39] Sanger, 31.
[40] Ibid.
[41] *Staunton News-Leader,* 5 December 1924; Sanger 34.
[42] Session Minutes, 17, 25, 26, 27, 28 May 1926.
[43] *Staunton News-Leader,* 14 October 1926.

Chapter Seven
Second Church in Depression and War

As the congregation faced the replacement of its popular and successful young minister, it elected a calling committee to which it added Miss Ruth Brand, the first time a woman had been permitted to participate in the selection of a pastor for the congregation. That committee worked exactly two months, and on December 19, 1926, its chairman, M.M. Edgar of the Dunsmore Business School, reported its recommendation of the Reverend Ray Lawrence St. Clair of Portland Avenue Presbyterian Church in Louisville, Kentucky.[1] The congregation elected him unanimously, and as events unfolded, accepted him without a difficult grieving period, and stood behind him with almost unanimous voice for nearly four decades.

Neither the members of Second Church nor their new young minister could have imagined in the lively and upbeat days of 1927 that the ministry he exercised in that congregation would be focused on the nation's most severe economic crisis and on a second World War. However, the fact that the deacons had to solicit contributions among themselves and others in the congregation to defray the St. Clairs' moving expenses from Louisville to Staunton should have been a hint that this church often had to operate on a slim margin. Fortunately, a kind member of the congregation, Gus Dull, who had a trucking company, volunteered to move the St. Clair family at no expense to the church.[2]

Ray Lawrence St. Clair, a graduate of Louisville Theological Seminary, began his pastorate in 1927. He is shown here with his family in the 1930s on a visit to his former church.

St. Clair was an earnest, down-to-earth young man. A native of Louisville, he had received his education at Berea College, so knew well the struggle that so many of the Appalachian students at that college experienced to gain an education. After his graduation from Berea, he prepared for the ministry at Louisville Theological Seminary, and served a church there for six years before his call to Staunton.

The new pastor titled his first sermon, preached masterfully to a full congregation on Sunday, January 16, 1927, "In the Land of Beginning Again." His scripture text from the fifth chapter of Second Corinthians, "If any man be in Christ, he is a new creature: old things are passed away; behold, all things are become new," was carefully chosen. To a congregation that had been through considerable dissension, loss, and pain in recent years, he said, "I wish there were some mysterious place — The Land of Beginning Again — where all our mistakes, heartaches, and griefs might be dropped off like a coat, never to be put on again." To a congregation longing for a fresh and successful relationship, he assured them that the avenues of humiliation, repentance, confession, and faith would indeed bring a new beginning. The newspaper reported that St. Clair was of Scotch descent, and opined that there was "something of the Scotchman in his smile, pleasing personality, and voice."[3]

In 1920 St. Clair had married Helen Bundy.[3] She and their two boys, David and Harvey, arrived on the C&O a few days after this successful beginning to his ministry. Over the years, the home they made together at the manse behind the church on Lewis Street became a second home to everyone in the congregation. In reminiscing about this much-loved couple, older members of the congregation who gathered in 2001 recalled that "Mrs. Saint" often invited the elders and deacons to enjoy the hospitality of the manse. The door was never locked. She often welcomed children in for games and gave them milk and cookies after school. Among the adults she was famous for her cheese straws, which were a standby at Family Night suppers and many other occasions.

"Mr. Saint" had a talent for reading palms, a rather un-Presbyterian behavior, but one that delighted the young folk on many occasions, including Halloween. The St. Clairs were famous for their Halloween parties in the manse attic. One member of the congregation, Betty Van Fossen, had vivid recollections of being blindfolded and handed what she was told were eyeballs. Next she had to plunge her hands into a dish full of "brains." Only later did she learn that the "eyeballs" were grapes and the "brains" a bowl of spaghetti!

A relatively new organization, the Men of the Church, was already into its second year of activity when St. Clair arrived. At their first 1927 meeting, Group 1, headed by J.K. Sheets, served a dinner to sixty men from the entire organization. Roy Halderman, leader of Group 3, received a silver loving cup on behalf of his group, which achieved the greatest number of goals of any of the groups. Several members of the Billy Sunday Evangelistic Club attended as guests.[5]

Youth Work in many forms was an important emphasis of the 1920s and 1930s at Second Church. In 1927 the

Session appointed a committee with J.L. Scrogham, M.M. Edgar, Dr. Cox, and C.K. Morrison to see about organizing a Boy Scout troop in the congregation. The church received a charter as a sponsor that year. William F. Beltz agreed to be the first Scoutmaster for Troop 7. Beltz, a member of the congregation, had donated a baptismal basin to Second Church that year. Donald V. Whitbeck, who had come from Fredericksburg a few years before, succeeded him in 1931 and ran a successful program for four years and assisted for a number of other years. During this time, the deacons granted the troop members permission to fix up a room in the basement of the church home for their use at their own expense and to erect a flagpole in the yard of the church house to display flags for special occasions. In 1933 the troop had been in existence long enough to be eligible for an excellence award that President Herbert Hoover had established for scouting. The troop re-organized in January 1935 with John F. Brown as Scoutmaster and Whitbeck and Ronald Woodrum as his assistants. In 1936 there were fourteen boys in the troop. Session had a Boy Scout committee that kept the elders apprised monthly of the troop's progress and needs. By 1938 Randolph Gardner was Scoutmaster, with Walter Hanger, L.B. Bosserman, and former Scoutmasters John Brown and Whitbeck as his assistants.[6]

The Junior and Senior Christian Endeavor groups, which had been the principal youth organizations since the late 1890s, had ceased to exist at Second by 1930. Session transferred the small balance in their bank account to the church's debt fund.[7] The organizations may have ceased, but youth work was quite active in the 1920s when Mabel Speck was employed to work part time with youth and as parish secretary. The Session had added the salary of a full time youth worker at $1,100 to the annual congregational budget in the late Twenties when Marguerite Edgar was employed as Young People's Worker. The next two young women to hold the post, Manira Hoon from 1928 to 1930

A July 4 parade was part of the fun and fellowship for Second Church youth at Massanetta in 1929.

and Elizabeth Lynn from 1930 to 1931, both left to marry young ministers.[8] Margaret Bowen of Bluefield, West Virginia, held that position successfully from September 1931 until she was called in the summer of 1937 to a church in Charleston, West Virginia. Session sent her a letter of "appreciation of her splendid services as Young People's Worker of this church, and to wish her much success in her new field."[9] Her successor, Susan Hill Goodwin of First Church, Williamson, West Virginia, was chosen over twelve other applicants in those times when jobs were at a premium. She remained through the summer of 1941, when she left for Bristol, Tennessee. A recently married member of the congregation, Elizabeth Morrison Grim, filled in as secretary.[10]

In those years when the mainline Protestant viewpoint dominated public life in America, and before issues of the separation of church and state were routinely raised, Bible instruction took place often in the public schools. In Staunton, the Session of Second Church cooperated with the Ministerial Association and other Protestant churches in sharing the costs of the salary of Miss Agnes Stokes, employed to teach Bible at Robert E. Lee High School. In 1927, Second Church's share was $180, which the deacons raised to $198 in October 1929, shortly before the stock market crash. The church continued its support of this program into the 1940s. Miss Stokes reported in 1934 that she had 110 students, thirty-seven Presbyterian, thirty-four Methodist, twenty-one United Brethren, seventeen Baptist, eight Lutheran, one Catholic, and one Pilgrim Holiness.[11]

For younger children, the church continued its earlier work with Daily Vacation Bible School every summer. In the summer of 1928, for example, Second Church had something over ninety children enrolled in the program, which was "better than we expected," according to St. Clair. This was a better show than the DVBS that First Church and Central Methodist joined to sponsor that year, which had a smaller enrollment than anticipated, according to the newspaper. In 1929 the committee on Young People's Work was allowed to take a special collection in Sunday School to help with expenses of Daily Vacation Bible School.[12] Older members of the congregation recollected in 2001 that they had learned their books of the Bible as well as many Bible verses and hymns in the Daily Vacation Bible School of the 1920s and 1930s. The program ran two weeks in the mornings, from nine until noon, and included crafts and a snack as well as lots of learning. Some years they cooperated with Central Methodist and traded classes.

St. Clair was a strong believer in evangelistic services, and in preparation for special seasons of the church. At Easter time, for example, he convinced the Session to have pre-Easter services beginning the Sunday before (Palm Sunday) and continuing each evening through Friday (Good Friday). He instituted a change in the traditional preparation for communion. From colonial times in the Valley of Virginia, the Saturday before a Communion Sunday had been the time for the preparatory service. St. Clair changed that to combine it with the Wednesday evening prayer ser-

The Massanetta Cottage that belonged to Second Church was an important focus of camps and conferences for all ages for many years.

vice, apparently with no negative repercussions. St. Clair was interested in church attendance, and told his congregation at the outset that his preaching was far stronger to a large congregation than a small one. He reported to Session near the end of his first year that average morning attendance was 264 and average Sunday evening attendance was 204, in addition to the eighty cadets from SMA who attended. Over the years of his pastorate, those numbers grew considerably.[13]

Second Church had two special evangelistic weeks annually in spring and fall. St. Clair continued the tradition. In November 1927, for example, the guest leader for the services was Dr. C.C. Carson of Bristol, the General Assembly's Evangelist. I.M. Ellis of Roanoke was engaged to provide the special music for these services, at a salary of $125 plus room and board at the manse. For the spring evangelistic services in 1935, in addition to the special prayer services on Wednesday evening beforehand, Session agreed to arrange prayer services in six homes scattered over the congregation one evening. A goal at the fall evangelistic services in 1936, in the Depression, was simply to raise a collection of $100 to pay the visiting evangelist. A special feature of the 1938 spring revival was that Professor Nelson

Huffman of Bridgewater College would lead song services. His payment was $50, an indication of the effects of the Depression, for it was less than half what was paid for the same professional service in 1927.[14]

In the early years of St. Clair's pastorate, four beloved older church leaders died, B.F. Hughes, Thomas Addison Bell, Dr. I.H. Trimble, and William Atwell Haines. Hughes, born in Charles Town [West] Virginia in 1854, had come to Staunton as a young man and worked in a hotel, but soon started his own retail drug store. He joined Second Church in 1879, and filled many leadership positions. When he died at age seventy-four, he was the oldest druggist in Staunton, and one of the oldest in the state. Elder Bell, an Augusta County native, had worked for Hamrick Funeral Home his entire life, and had served Second Church in many leadership roles. Dr. Trimble, also an elder, was born in Monterey in 1849, educated at the University of Virginia and at Bellevue Hospital Medical College in New York City. He practiced at Monterey until 1919, and then in Staunton until his death. He was an active Mason and devoted member of the Session at Second. Elder Haines was a quieter member of Session than the others. Born in Winchester in 1867, he came to Staunton as a child, was educated at Dunsmore Business College, and spent his career in banking as cashier at Farmers & Merchants and then at Planter's.[15]

An interesting episode in the relationship between First Church and Second Church occurred in 1930. Although the two congregations and their pastors were generally friendly and worked cooperatively, there is also no doubt that a certain sense of rivalry existed between them, and that there were areas of work that each guarded jealously. The entire issue of "turf" was raised over a desire to open new mission work in Staunton. The four Presbyterian ministers in town, Fraser at First, St. Clair at Second, J.E. Wayland Assistant at First, and W.W. Sprouse at Third, met in January 1930 with the Reverend W.E. Hudson, D.D., superintendent of

Home Missions of Lexington Presbytery, to explore possibilities. They agreed that new work should begin in the Selma area north of Gypsy Hill Park, and that Second Church should take the lead in the work, assisted by First Church. The ministers also reached some agreement about how to approach new Presbyterian residents in Staunton so that they would not be competing with each other.[16]

Two weeks later, the Session of Second Church received a letter from the Session of First Church regarding the resolutions of those five ministers in their meeting. First Church endorsed the leadership of Second Church in starting a mission in the Selma area, but informed them that they could not be much help, as they were still committed financially to helping Third Church. On the question of geographic boundaries for enrolling new members, the Session of First Church noted that they had always favored and usually practiced this. They suggested that all of the city north of the C&O railroad tracks and east of the center of Central Avenue should be for First Church, all west of the Central Avenue midpoint should be for Second Church, and everything south of the C&O tracks would be the territory of Third Church.

Fraser and St. Clair had meanwhile met and St. Clair had negotiated successfully on behalf of Second Church for the line to be moved eastward to the middle of Augusta Street. While this division probably reflected to a large extent the actual areas of the city from which each congregation already drew its members, by adopting the clearly-drawn geographic boundaries, the churches committed themselves to a sharper socio-economic division in their membership. The members of Second Church could not know it at the time, but over the next fifty years, the neighborhood assigned to them would undergo dramatic change. It experienced significant out-migration of the middle class, encroachment of business and urban renewal, and an in-migration of poorer, unchurched populations that were not readily attracted to a mainline church.

It would be difficult to over emphasize the effects the Great Depression had on many aspects of congregational life at Second Church. One of the most significant of these was most clearly the budget. The budget figures adopted in February 1929 for the coming year were $8,500 for current operating expenses for the church and $5,680 for benevolences. In February 1930, before the severity of the Depression set in, the deacons again proposed a budget of some $8,700 current expenses and $5,700 benevolences. It would be many years before the congregation would see another budget exceeding $14,000.[17]

When the church's financial year closed in April 1930, the effects of the Depression were already noticeable. Receipts for church expenses had been only $8,053, which was $500 less than budgeted. Pledges for the coming year for church operating expenses had fallen below $8,000. Frequently throughout the Depression years, the treasurer was authorized to go to the bank for a loan of several hundred dollars to pay outstanding bills. The deacons had the unpleasant duty of visiting families whose pledges had fallen in arrears "in an effort to stimulate the church income which is at a very low ebb at present," noted their minutes in February 1931.

The pastor, elders, and deacons worked hard to make ends meet throughout the Depression. In a measure that meant sacrifice for his family, the pastor chose to share the hard times of his people. In January 1933, at his own request, the Session reduced St. Clair's salary to $3,000. In the next two years' budget meetings, he announced to the Session that he would expect a salary of $600 less than that stated in their call to him. This was a sixteen percent reduction in pay. The $10,000 budget for the year allotted $7,000 for church operation and $3,000 for benevolences. This was a twenty percent reduction in the local church budget and a fifty percent reduction in the benevolences, or outreach budget, from the good years of the late Twenties. Even the amount contributed toward the salary of the Bible teacher in the high school was cut by forty percent. Session and the Board of Deacons watched every possible way to save money, ending the contract for regular organ maintenance, and going with the least expensive person who could do spot repairs when needed, for example.[18]

One measure of help that the congregation could offer to some of its young people in those hard times of dashed dreams came from the Student Loan Fund. Remembering an earlier scholarship fund in memory of Dr. Scott, Session created this fund in April 1928 from volunteer offerings by members of the congregation. Session initially named five women to administer the fund, Mrs. I.H. Trimble, Mrs. D.B. Wilson, Mrs. F.W. Brand, Mrs. M.M. Edgar, and Mrs. L.V. Harris. From 1929 the committee consisted of three women and two men. A young man in the congregation, Palmer Stover, was recipient of the first loan. At a time when many families could not contemplate paying tuition costs for education past high school, yet when that education was so important as job opportunities shrank, this fund could make the difference in young lives. It offered low-interest loans to students of high Christian character and good academic promise who were planning to enter a Christian college or graduate school. One portion of the monies, the Martha Cline Trimble Memorial Fund, was restricted to $500 loans to those who were preparing for a church career as a missionary, minister, or director of religious education. In the Depression years, $500 covered a substantial portion of the annual tuition at many Virginia private colleges.[19]

While the size of pledges, contributions, and budget was shrinking, the size of the congregation and the Sunday School was not. Those numbers showed a steady growth, year by year. In 1927, when St. Clair arrived at Second Church, the membership roll showed 720 persons. By 1944, that number had reached 833, representing a steady net growth of seven or eight persons per year. The Sunday

School classes, both children and adult, had grown considerably, indicating a stronger interest in participation among members of all ages. In 1929, the Sunday School enrollment, including adults, was 669. The facilities in the church basement and in the church home had become seriously crowded by 1934.

The depth of the Depression was not a good time to undertake a major capital improvement program. The Session developed a modest plan to excavate the basement of the church home to gain a nine-foot ceiling, and presumably pour a concrete floor, then to re-arrange rooms on the second and third floors of the former manse in order to gain more classrooms. The congregation adopted the plan, using $2,300 that was in the Building Fund, soliciting the members for what they could pledge, and borrowing the rest. The total for this work and some copper guttering and repairs to the church auditorium came to about $6,000 (about $79,000 in the year 2001). The deacons raised the insurance on the old manse by $5,000 in light of the improvements.[20]

In a few years, these improvements were inadequate to handle the continued growth of the church's classes. The Religious Education Committee reported to Session in December 1938 that on a typical Sunday with no special emphasis to swell the numbers, attendance was 400. The Cradle Roll class was caring for twenty-six infants and toddlers in a room that should not have held thirteen. The Primary Department needed four additional classrooms, the Senior and Young Peoples classes had to be combined for lack of space, but really needed to be separated, and the Pioneer Department needed two classrooms so that it would not have to meet in the pastor's study. The adult classes were operating under equally poor conditions: the men's groups in the basement, where the Sunday school children trooped noisily through, one group was in the kitchen, and two of the women's classes, the Sunshine and the Gleaners, had to meet in the church auditorium with its fixed pews.[21]

Sunday School classes that were taxing the space available in the former manse called Church Home included these four groups taken in the early 1940s.

The committee that Session appointed to recommend solutions reported in January 1939 its recommendation for a three-story building fronting Frederick Street that would join the church house and the church building, provide new church offices, and add the classrooms needed for all but the adults. A re-arrangement of the church basement would solve the adult class needs. The price tag for the work was estimated at $15,000. By May, a joint meeting of the elders and deacons developed a financial plan for the work that called upon each of the 800 members of the congregation to give five dollars. The less expensive basement alterations would begin as soon as the funds were in hand, and the connecting building would begin as soon as $4,000 had been subscribed. The remainder would be financed with long-term bonds. The basement alterations were completed by February 1940 at a cost of nearly $2,100, plus contributed labor by members valued at $800. In addition, the Woman's Auxiliary had bought a new kitchen stove for $135.[22]

A most unexpected form of damage occurred to the church in 1935. A Works Progress Administration project for Staunton as part of President Franklin Roosevelt's New Deal to provide jobs in the Depression was a new post office. The old Romanesque style post office at the northeast corner of Frederick and Lewis Streets had been built around the turn of the twentieth century, not so long before the present church was built. In Jed Hotchkiss's time, when the first church was built, the Staunton Iron Works Foundry stood on that corner. The old post office came down, and foundations were dug for the building that still stands on that spot. The workers soon encountered rock, and blasted to break it up. The blast broke some stained glass windows in the church auditorium directly across Lewis Street in September of 1935. The Session instructed the church attorney to write Mr. Black, the contractor, about the damage. In December, the deacons appointed a committee to see about repairing the windows and replacing the stained glass. The work, done by R.D. Morris of Lynchburg, was completed by May 1936 for $101.[23]

Another sign of the times in the troubled Thirties was the appearance of poliomyelitis as a serious health threat for young people. In August 1935, Sunday School for the beginners, Primary, Junior, and Intermediate Departments—all the pre-school and public school age children—had been cancelled due to the polio epidemic.[24]

The music program at Second Church went through some turbulent times in the early Thirties before it reached a point of excellence. A. Douglass Cullum was choir director as the decade opened, and also was supposed to give voice instruction to some choir members, for which the church paid him additionally. The post of organist was a separate position on a month-to-month basis, but Cullum was on contract. The Music Committee of Session, the deacons, and the other elders disagreed over Cullum's services, and after they learned he had not given the contracted music lessons for which he had been paid, there was pressure to terminate his position. The Music Committee chair resigned and Session voted to abolish the committee, naming C.K. Morrison the liaison with the choir. Cullum's contract was terminated, but only after he negotiated a paid vacation and leave.[25]

When the organist, Mrs. W.J. Bodie, resigned, a new Music Committee was able to combine the organist and choir director positions, and employ Mrs. R.P. Wall at forty-five dollars per month. She was the right person at the right time for a difficult job. She immediately began a rigorous choir training program, and prepared the choir for a Christmas Cantata that was a great success. This became a holiday tradition at the church. The Music Committee reported to Session early in 1935 that the Christmas Cantata had been excellent, and that new choir robes had arrived and been put into use. Committee members stated further that the choir at that time was the best in the history of the church. Mrs. Wall was well liked and doing a good job, so the Session was pleased to be able to raise her annual salary from $540 to $630 in 1935. It was the beginning of a long and happy relationship between congregation, Session, and organist-choir director.[26] Another musical high point of the era was the formation of a quartet. This suggestion was first put forth by the Music Committee in 1928. Session instructed them to look into the matter.

By the late Thirties, the economic situation had eased some in the nation and at Second Church. The deacons had been able to retire some of the church debt. The pastor's salary had been raised from $3,000 to $3,300, still below what he had been promised in his call in 1927. The contribution toward the Bible teacher in the high school had returned to its pre-Depression level, and the overall congregational budget had crept up to $11,000.[27]

The Woman's Auxiliary played its usual important role in the life of the congregation. The great majority of the women in the church were homemakers, many with children and teenagers at home. Their participation in one of the circles was an important activity in their social calendar as well as in their spiritual life. Some of the members worked, and for them two circle groups met outside business hours — the Business Women and for the younger ones, the Business Girls. The auxiliary was also an outlet for good works through the collection of clothing for the Irish Creek Mission or for missionaries, and in the fund raising projects that the auxiliary carried out. Throughout the Thirties and wartime years, the Woman's Auxiliary typically raised and contributed around $2,500 annually to church and benevolent projects. One of the women's projects in 1945 was to contribute $300 toward a special room for the church's Boy Scout Troop 7.[28]

Women who took a leadership role serving as officers of the organization in the Depression and war years included presidents: Mrs. T.C. Craig, Mrs. C.K. Morrison, Mrs. Glenn Yount, Mrs. W.E. Lucas, Mrs. B.S. Sadler, Mrs. W.A.

Betty Wall shown here later in life, began her long career as organist and choir director in 1934 with a successful Christmas cantata, the first of many.

Brand, Miss Lucille Lohr, and Mrs. Virginia Marcus. Among the vice presidents were Mrs. R.S. Smiley, Mrs. R.C. Keller, and Mrs. D.C. Sensabaugh. Secretaries included Mrs. O.C. Hemp, Miss Eliza Fauver, Mrs. Cecil Prestwood, Mrs. Ronald Woodrum, and Mrs. O.P. Bowman, while treasurers included Mrs. J.W. Tomes, Mrs. Turner Marcus, Mrs. Dell Harris, Mrs. Hugh Scrogham, and Mrs. J.W. Fix. For a number of years Mrs. C.K. Morrison was the historian, faithfully keeping the scrapbooks and writing reports of each year's activities. The considerable rotation in office indicates that leadership among the women was democratic, and not limited to a small elite group, nor limited to wives of elders and deacons.

In addition to the women who served as general officers of the organization, each of the nine circle groups had its own leader every year, and the organization as a whole had a "cause officer" for each of the causes or areas in which the auxiliary had an active interest at local, presbyterial, or southern church level. Those causes were Spiritual Life, Foreign Missions, Assembly Home Missions, Synod and Presbytery Home Missions, Christian Education and Ministerial Relief, Social Service, Pastor's Aid, Social Activities, and Religious Education. When the chairmanship of each of these circles and programs is considered, it means that in the course of a decade there were opportunities for 200 women to exercise some group leadership in their congregation.

Missionary work was a strong interest at Second Church, which had borne significant parts of the salaries of several missionaries. In addition to Lelia Kirtland and Dr. Louis Brand, in the late 1920s, Second Church undertook a $500 salary contribution to Dr. and Mrs. Z.E. Lewis in Cuernavaca, Mexico, which terminated in 1928 at his retirement. He visited Second Church on his return. The congregation also assisted with work among Italian immigrants in a settlement at Ensley, Alabama. In 1928 that work was transferred to another Italian community mission in Kansas City, Missouri, under the Reverend J.B. Bisceglia. The Reverend Mr. Bisceglia spent the month of November 1931 at Second Church.[29] In 1933 the congregation was distressed

The women who worked so hard in behalf of the congregation and benevolent projects throughout the year enjoyed a week together in the summer at the congregation's cottage at Massanetta in Rockingham County.

to learn of the destruction of Dr. Louis Brand's hospital in Korea. In January 1934, Session set aside a special Sunday offering to be taken toward the rebuilding of the hospital.

During this period, Second church lost three members who long had played an important part in the life of the congregation. In March 1938, Session recorded its memorial resolution on the death of Dr. Brand, "our beloved missionary to Korea." As a member of a family that was long active and prominent in the work of Second Church, Dr. Brand had been an early recipient of financial assistance with the good offices of the Session, to enable him to study to become a medical missionary. For years the congregation had contributed $500 annually toward his salary as a missionary, and followed the reports of his work, sent boxes to his family, and welcomed him back on furlough. In April 1940, the congregation's last Confederate Veteran, Francis Marion Trimble, died at the age of ninety-three. That fall, Stuart P. Silling, first a deacon then an elder, and teacher of the Men's Bible Class for years, died at the age of seventy-three. He had been in the retail meat business, then operated an orchard on the edge of town, and served on Staunton City Council at the time it pioneered the city manager form of government.

In August 1941, Morrison M. Edgar died at the age of sixty. For twenty years, since the death of its founder, J.G. Dunsmore, he had been president of Dunsmore Business College, where hundreds of young men and women in western Virginia had been educated for useful careers in business. He had served as a trustee of Mary Baldwin College, was an elder at Second Church from 1922, had been its Sunday School Superintendent for a decade, and represented Lexington Presbytery at General Assembly for the entire southern church.[30]

From the time Second Church initiated the first efforts for an outpost Sunday School on Sears Hill in the 1890s, the congregation had been interested in outpost work, and in

The congregation followed eagerly the work and worries of its own missionaries abroad, Dr. Louis Brand in Korea, Lelia Kirtland in Japan, and Virginia Brand shown here in Africa.

getting as many unchurched children into Sunday School instruction as possible. One example of this is the effort that C.K. Morrison spearheaded in 1935 to bus children from outlying areas to the church. In 1935 he reported at a congregational meeting that two busses, supported completely by individual private donations, were operating to bring children from the Parkersburg Pike, Springhill, and Churchville Roads to church and Sunday School. The elders discussed purchasing buses, and looked into the costs of used and new ones, but concluded that they must continue to rent them. This project was discontinued in the spring of 1938.[31]

The next project for Christian educational outreach came during World War II when the pastor reported to Session in April 1943 that there was a need for an outpost Sunday School in the Greenville Road area. Session asked the Religious Education Committee to investigate this. The opportunity in October 1943 to have the vacant Dennison store building for this was appealing, but it was rented by January 1944 before details could be worked out with deacons and Session. An alternate space was found, and the little

Sunday School began operation, taking in just enough in donations from the children each week to cover the cost of the religious literature distributed to them in their classes.[32]

Another change in the administrative structure of the church was the elimination of the position of young people's worker combined with part-time parish secretary. In 1943, in the midst of the war, the position expanded and changed focus to the entire religious education program. The new title became Director of Religious Education. Many of the larger Presbyterian churches in southern cities were adding this professional post to the staff. The young women employed in the position were usually graduates of the School of Christian Education (known then as the Church Training School) affiliated with Union Theological Seminary in Richmond. Hortense Pruitt, from Central Presbyterian in Anderson, South Carolina, came to the position in June 1943 and remained for a year and a half. Her successor for the remainder of 1945 was Virginia Steagall, daughter of missionaries to Africa, who resigned to marry a young minister in Texas.[33]

Pearl Harbor was attacked on December 7, 1941, the day that would "live in infamy" according to President Franklin D. Roosevelt, who was then serving an unprecedented third term in the White House. This plunged the United States into the war that had already engulfed Europe and Asia in 1939. One of the first signs of its effects on civilian life in the form of shortages, and eventually rationing, came in March 1942. Session authorized the pastor to notify the Moderator of Lexington Presbytery that, "due to tire shortage, we extend an invitation to Presbytery to meet in our church April 20th instead of at Franklin, W. Va. as scheduled." The elders apparently thought that travel to Staunton, in the heart of the presbytery, and accessible to many by train, would cause less wear on tires than reaching remote Franklin.[34]

In February 1943, Session gave permission for the Red

Cross to use the lecture room one day in April to receive blood donations for the Blood Bank. Another way that Second Church helped with the war effort was to take up special offerings, such as one for the Defense Service Council. In 1945 that group received $191 in special offerings.[35]

As many of the church's regular activities as possible continued during the war. In the summer, Second Church joined with other downtown churches, mainly Central Methodist, St. Paul's United Brethren, and Christ Lutheran, in sponsoring Wednesday evening services in Gypsy Hill Park. The usual evangelistic services that had been a tradition at Second Church in spring and fall continued during the war as well.

In February 1945, the congregation lost one of its most faithful and active longtime leaders, Frank Bartley Kennedy. "Pop" Kennedy had been born near Stuarts Draft in 1867, educated at Augusta Military Academy, and graduated from Washington and Lee College. He came to Staunton to practice law in 1891. A decade later he joined Second, and was elected a deacon in 1919 and elder in 1926. For years he was the inspiring teacher of the D.F.O. (Do For Others) older couples' Bible class. In his will he left the church $1,000, to be used as the elders and deacons thought best. They placed it in the building fund. His widow, Isa Bishop Kennedy, had always been active, and his daughter, Mrs. Virginia Marcus, was then a leader of the Woman's Auxiliary. They gave an additional $1,000 for a suitable memorial to him, and this also went to the Building Fund.[36]

Young men from Second Church began joining the armed forces immediately after the declaration of war. In 1942, Session agreed to list the names of members of the armed forces at the back of the Session record at the end of the church year. In May 1943, the Woman's Auxiliary purchased a service banner on which a blue star was placed for every member of the congregation serving in the armed forces and a gold star for anyone who gave his or her life in service. Initially Session thought the banner should hang in the adult Sunday School assembly room, but changed its mind and conferred with the auxiliary leaders on another location. The place chosen was the church sanctuary. By May 1944, that flag had eighty-five stars and by April 1945 there were ninety-eight stars. Fourteen more names were added before the war ended in Europe in May 1945 and in Japan in August 1945, bringing the total to 112.

The sound religious training their church had provided and the support it offered from afar while they were in the service undoubtedly meant much to these young men and women whose lives were on the line in the service of their country. During the war, the Session received a notice from a chaplain at a United States Naval Training Center that one seaman stationed there had made a profession of faith and wished to be united with Second Church, an unusual method of being put on the roll.[37]

The congregation was fortunate that the loss of lives among its service personnel was low, but every life is precious, and the sad news of those lost was met with heavy hearts. On January 30, 1944, one of the young men, Owen Gilliam "Buddy" Jones, was reported missing in action and on April 19, 1945, he was declared presumed dead. Howard Walton died in service in 1944, and John Dennison was killed on Mindanao in the Philippines on May 7, 1945.[38]

It was with grateful hearts that the people of Second Church greeted the news of the end of the war, and could turn their attention to welcoming their servicemen home, rebuilding families that had been separated by the wartime circumstances, and look to a future of growth.

The service flag of the Women of the Church hung in the sanctuary throughout the war, as a reminder to the congregation to pray for the safe return of its men and women in the services.

Chapter Seven Notes

[1] Congregational Minutes, 17 October, 19 December 1926.
[2] Deacon's Minutes, 3 January, 7 March 1927.
[3] *Staunton News-Leader*, 18 January 1927.
[4] Sanger, *A History of the Second Presbyterian Church, Staunton, Virginia, 1875-1975*, 49.
[5] *Staunton News-Leader*, 8 January 1927.
[6] Session Minutes, 18 September 1934, 15 January 1935, 3 May 1938; Deacons Minutes, 2 November 1931; Sanger, 38.
[7] Ibid., 17 March 1934.
[8] Ibid., 26 February 1928; Sanger, 35.
[9] Ibid., 4 August 1937.
[10] Session Minutes, 7 September 1941
[11] Session Minutes, 18 April 1934.

[12]*Staunton News-Leader,* 19 June 1928; Session Minutes, 18 June 1929.
[13]Session Minutes, 27 February, 28 June, 1 November 1927.
[14]Ibid., 20 November 1927; 9 April 1935; 6 October 1936, 4, 25 January 1928.
[15]Ibid., 8 April 1928, 3 February 1929, 22 November 1930, 6 July 1932.
[16]Ibid., 12 January 1930.
[17]Deacons Minutes, 2 April 1928, 4 February 1929, 3 February 1930.
[18]Session Minutes, 21 March, 1933; 17 February 1935; Deacons Minutes, 3 February 1930, 2 February 1931.
[19]Session Minutes, 10 April 1928, 5 April 1929; Deacons Minutes, 23 October 1934. The minutes of this meeting list the rules for the administration of the funds. The fund usually lent around $1,500 a year, divided among three or four students.
[20]Session Minutes, 4 June, 22 July, 1 October 1934; Congregational Meeting Minutes, 17 June 1934; Deacons Minutes, 3 August 1934.
[21]Session Minutes, 6 December 1938.
[22]Session Minutes, 17 January, 2 May 1939, 15 February 1940; Congregational Meeting Minutes, 14 May 1939.
[23]Session Minutes, 27 September 1935; Deacons Minutes 2 December 1935, 2 June 1936.
[24]Ibid., 13 August 1935.
25Session Minutes, 13 November 1930, 19 May, 20 October 1931; 19 January, 16 February, 6 July 1932.
[26]Ibid., 15 March, 21 June, 18 October 1932; 15 January, 17 February, 9 April 1935.
[27]Ibid., 5 January 1937, 15 March 1938, 3 February 1939.
[28]Annual Congregational reports, Session Minutes, passim; Joint elders and deacons meeting 25 March 1945.
[29]Session Minutes, 22 April, 5 May, 3 June 1928; 20 October 1931.
[30]Ibid., 20 March 1938, 26 November 1939. The Misses Alice and Martha Brand who transferred into Second Church from the church in Kangfu, Korea, were probably his daughters. Ibid., 14 April 1940. Silling Memorial Resolution, 13 October 1940; Edgar Memorial Resolution. Session Minutes, 7 September 1941.
[31]Congregational Meeting Minutes, 27 March 1935; Session Minutes, 20 June, 2 September 1935; 3 May 1938.
[32]Session Minutes, 21 April, 16 September 1943; 5 January 1944.
[33]Ibid., 21 February, 1 August 1943; January 1945; Sanger, 36.
[34]Session Minutes, 18 March 1942.
[35]Ibid., 16 September 1942; 21 February, 21 April, 26 May 1943; 18 April 1945.
[36]Ibid., 21 March, 18 April 1945.
[37]Ibid., 27 May 1945.
[38]Ibid., 18 April 1945, 17 April 1946.

Chapter Eight
The Boom Years

Peace ushered in an era of growth and prosperity unprecedented in the history of Second Church, and unmatched since. With the surrender of the Axis Powers in the spring and summer of 1945, the young men and women of the congregation set about building new lives, new careers, and new families, with their church as one of the focal points. By November 1946, the congregation had put the wartime experience far enough behind that Session ordered the service flag taken down from the sanctuary wall and returned to the Woman's Auxiliary.

Sadly, the booming postwar era started on a discordant note in the church. The idea of sponsoring an outpost Sunday School in the Betsy Bell area, begun with enthusiasm early in 1944, was taken up again by the Joint Committee from First and Second Church. St. Clair reported that the Joint Committee had secured a store building on Greenville Road for the purpose, and desired for Second Church to take on the work. Session authorized this undertaking and Donnie Dyer contributed a piano for the outpost. Within a month, a delicate diplomatic problem had arisen, for Third Presbyterian Church, to which all territory south of the railroad had been assigned earlier, had taken offense at being left out of this project, and at Second Church's invasion of its area. Elder R.C. Keller, Sunday School Superintendent and chairman of the Religious Education Committee, reported to Session in late August that he had requested Lexington Presbytery's Committee on Home Missions to meet, review problems raised by the new outpost, and give advice. The committee did so in early September, and renewed its request that Second Church operate the outpost.[1]

Meanwhile, Elder A.M. "Mack" Woodside represented the Session at the fall meeting of Lexington Presbytery and reported on September 30 that a special report had been adopted at that meeting about the Greenville Road outpost. The Presbytery's Home Missions Committee stated that the welfare of the Kingdom was more important than the momentary divisions, and suggested ways to address the issue. The committee members acknowledged that the Home Missions committee had made an initial error in judgement in failing to include Third Church in planning the venture, but that they had understood from an early approach to that congregation, that it was not interested. The committee took Third Church to task for not considering its limited resources and the health of its pastor as impediments to its ability to carry out the work, and deplored the fact that Third Church aired the outpost issue in the local press before bringing it to presbytery.[2]

The Home Missions Committee recommended that the Greenville Avenue outpost be operated by Second Church, in consultation with two elders of Third Church, but with the ultimate view of turning it over to Third Church when presbytery saw fit. Meanwhile, Second Church should make the outpost building available to Third Church for prayer meetings and similar activities.[3] Second Church went ahead with the work. Woodside was superintendent at the outpost, and Mrs. Marvin Miller and Evelyn Collins were teachers. Unfortunately, the project ended after two years in July 1947, when the owners of the building sold it. Second Church was by then so involved with its own pressing physical plant problems that it could only run a bus to that neighborhood to bring children in to Sunday School classes at the church.[4]

The steady growth in the size of the congregation and the Sunday School had led to cramped quarters. This was obvious even in the middle of the war, so in 1943, Session had given the Building Committee authority to renovate the auditorium and church basement when funds became available and to borrow if necessary. The participatory fundraising plan was the "penny-a-meal bank." Each family in the congregation had a small bank that it was to place on its table, and deposit there a penny for each meal. Every two months, they were to bring their banks to church for the treasurer to open and collect the funds. In addition, a Building Fund had been set aside for the long-discussed expansion of the Sunday School. By October 1945 the work on the auditorium and basement was finished, and $5,500 had been collected in the Building Fund. That Building Committee received the thanks of the elders and deacons and was disbanded. It was time to appoint a new Building Committee for the new Sunday School construction, with three elders, three deacons, and three from the Woman's Auxiliary.[5]

The new Building Committee worked in 1946 to prepare a plan that included expansion of the church auditorium along with a new Sunday School building. They could never have dreamed the manner in which their plans would be realized!

Sometime around 10:40 p.m. on Monday, December 2, 1946, a person passing by the church on Frederick Street saw smoke "rolling from under the doors of the edifice's front entrance and immediately turned in the alarm."[6] Staunton's volunteer firemen, fortunately housed in the old firehouse on Baldwin Street at the corner of Central Avenue, rushed to the scene. Among them were the late L.B. Bosserman, Jr., Juanita Mullins's brother, and Wade Mitchell, a member of the church then and in 2000 as well. The fire broke out in the southwest corner of the building, the area

Smoke and water poured out of the church as firemen fought the fire near midnight on December 2, 1946.

to which flames were confined. The fire generated a huge amount of smoke, which spread all over the business district and adjacent residential districts.[7]

Word of the fire spread swiftly among members. Some of those who arrived immediately took the communion service and other valuable items from the church to the manse. Some older members reminisced at an oral history gathering in 2000 that they left home immediately and arrived at the scene about 11 p.m. to see "water flowing out the church doors and down the street."[8] The firefighters had attached hoses to every nearby hydrant and poured water into the building from both the Frederick and Lewis Street sides. Hundreds of spectators gathered to watch. It was Staunton's coldest night of the year. The firemen's suits froze, and the water in the streets froze. Mrs. Gilpin Willson, Jr., who lived in the lovely Gothic Revival house that stood opposite the church where the city parking lot now is, brought hot coffee to the firefighters. Several of the firefighters sustained cuts, but fortunately there were no serious injuries. By 12:15 they had determined that the fire was definitely under control. As it turned out, another blaze flared up in the Session room area about 2:30 a.m, and the firemen had to return to the site.⁹

The elders, deacons, and pastor were busy all day December 3 talking with the insurance agent, inspecting the damage, receiving offers of space and other assistance, talking with the press, and reviewing informally with the Building Committee the options facing them. The flames had broken through the floor of the basement storage room in which the fire apparently originated, destroying woodwork in the Session room area. Flames also broke through and damaged the balcony and scorched the underside and fronting of the balcony. Two basement rooms were gutted, a piano destroyed, large amounts of plaster had fallen or was ruined, hymnals destroyed, carpeting ruined, two stained glass windows broken, and the pipe organ damaged beyond repair. In addition, there was smoke and water damage throughout the building, inside and out.¹⁰

The elders and deacons met that evening to make significant decisions about issues that the emergency had raised.

L.B. Bosserman, Jr., pictured here in his uniform as a member of the Staunton Fire Department, was one of those who fought the fire on December 2. Another congregation member in that role was Wade Mitchell.

They instructed the clerk to write a letter of thanks to Fire Chief Eugene H. Dabney for the efficient work of his department in bringing the fire under control. The deacons had followed the prudent practice of reviewing the fire insurance annually and increasing it to reflect improvements and inflation, so the property was well covered. The elders and deacons were familiar with the plans that the Building Committee had already prepared for enlarging the auditorium to accommodate a new organ and to enclose the vestibule. They probably recognized what an older member expressed in retrospect in 2000, that the fire had been "a blessing in disguise." Those leaders voted unanimously that evening to follow an extensive remodeling plan in their rebuilding, "rather than to restore the building as it was before the fire." They gave the Building Committee blanket instruction to proceed with that plan, using fire insurance proceeds, and to raise additional funds as needed.[11]

The Building Committee that carried out this charge was chaired by Randolph C. Keller, with Glenn E. Yount as assistant chair, Mrs. Frank W. Dice (Irene) as secretary, and John F. Brown as treasurer. The other members of the committee were Mrs. W.E. Lucas, Mrs. Virginia Marcus, W.A. Brand, and J. Luther Kelley. Although many persons believe that Pastor St. Clair designed the reconstructed building, he was not, of course, an architect. For that purpose, the committee engaged the outstanding Staunton firm of T.J. Collins and Son. It is likely, however, that many of the ideas for the new interior arrangement came from St. Clair.

First Church, several other churches, Mary Baldwin College, the Strand Theater, and the Visulite Theater all made generous offers of space for the congregation to worship in while the extensive renovations were under way. The elders and deacons considered them all and voted unanimously that the offer of John Herndon, manager of the Visulite Theater, would meet the congregation's needs best. The theater was only two blocks from the church and the undamaged Sunday School rooms could be used for both the congregation's regular 11 a.m. Sunday worship hour and 7:30 Sunday evening service. However, St. Clair told the newspaper that other churches would be used for weddings and funerals.[12]

The plans that the Building Committee had prepared called for enclosing the vestibule and moving the south wall out to obtain additional balcony space. The north wall would be extended twelve feet and its choir balcony removed in order to gain space for a new pipe organ, and to add a new Session room and other meeting space. The expansion of the north wall was possible because on January 6, 1947, the trustees purchased from the trustees of First Baptist Church and the King's Daughters' Hospital Corporation an alley four-and-one-half-feet wide that separated the church lot from the manse lot.

In their characteristic fashion, the members of Second Church took the emergency in stride and figured ways to make their worship meaningful and successful in the strange setting. With the deacons supervising, a schedule was worked out each month for the men who were to do the work of transforming the movie theater into sacred space. Herman Adkinson remembers well going to the theater after the last show each Saturday night to pick up popcorn and vacuum the floor. A railing was put on the stage and a red curtain put on that. Chairs from the Third Presbyterian building were set up on the stage for the choir, elders, and pastor. A piano had been moved in for Mrs. Wall to play. After the Sunday evening service, all this had to be taken down and trucked back to storage, only to have the process repeated week after week for a year. Joining Adkinson in that work were Francis Ramsey, Guy Deaver, W.H. Stump, Harry Dice, Ronald Woodrum, and Tracy Wenger.[13]

The ordinary routine of the church continued throughout the fourteen months that the congregation worshipped at the Visulite. The 1946 Christmas pageant, under the direction of Helen Rowan, had the theater stage for its venue.[14] A special social occasion lightened spirits in January 1947. The occasion was St. Clair's twentieth anniversary as pastor. On Sunday, January 19, he preached the same sermon he had given at his arrival in Staunton, "In the land of beginning again." What could have been more appropriate after the devastating fire? On Thursday evening, January 23, the congregation gathered at the manse for a reception to show appreciation of his two decades of faithful leadership through depression, war, and fire.[15]

At that first worship service at the Visulite, on December 8, 1946, members recall that $10,000 was pledged to the rebuilding effort. In January 1947, the Building Committee recommended accepting the $31,293 that the insurance company offered for the fire damage. On January 29, construction work began on the church, with J. Luther Kelley, a contractor and member of the board of deacons, as the supervisor. By September 28, 1947, the Building Committee reported to the congregation that the building was under roof, that the auditorium plastering under the supervision of W.A. Brand was "beautiful," and that the boxing and refinishing of the ceiling trusses is "considered by many who have seen it as a masterpiece of beautiful architecture." Howard Baylor handled electrical work and J. Carson Gardner the plumbing and heating.

Many interior details remained to be done, including the laying and finishing of the auditorium floor, setting and finishing of the pews, building and placing of the choir and pulpit furniture, finishing the wood trim, and hanging doors. A contract had been signed with Möller of Hagerstown, Maryland, for a new organ, but this would not be available until September 1948.

An acute shortage of building materials and labor in the postwar building boom had made it difficult for the contractor to keep on schedule. There was also an acute shortage of funds to pay for the work. The committee estimated that it needed between $30,000 and $40,000 more and sought congregational approval to borrow the funds.[16]

As the work neared completion, the cornerstone was laid on February 8, 1948. The first day of worship in the new church was February 29, 1948. First Church, Third Church, Olivet, and Hebron all sent letters of congratulations on the occasion. That from Hebron was especially meaningful, as its members noted that their congregation had gone through a similar fire experience forty-eight years earlier. Elders and members of these three churches joined with the congregation of Second Church in the evening worship, with the Reverend Freeman Parker, pastor of Olivet, as guest preacher.[17]

Laying the new cornerstone for the church took place on February 8, 1948. The local paper listed the contents of the cornerstone. The church, Sunday School, Church Workers, and Ladies Aid society rolls from 1902 and newspaper article from January 16, 1902 were all returned to the cornerstone. Items added were the church roll and Woman's Auxiliary roll for 1948, description of changes made to the building, and service bulletins of December 8, 1946, January 26, 1947, and January 15, 1948.

St. Clair, in his sermon, "What Came Out of the Fire," spoke of the extensive changes brought about in the reconstruction. Of special significance was the new arrangement of the chancel area. Presbyterian churches traditionally have the pulpit, from which the Scriptures are read and the Word expounded in the sermon, as the focal point of worship. This pulpit is traditionally on a raised platform, with the communion table beneath it on the floor of the sanctuary auditorium. The new arrangement at Second Church was a dramatic departure from that traditional American Presbyterian practice. The new arrangement returned to the earlier practice all over Europe and Britain of having the altar or communion table as the focal point, and dividing the reading and the preaching of the Word between a lectern on one side and a pulpit on the other. As Pastor St. Clair explained, by placing the communion table in the center, "this reminder of the atonement of our Lord is given its rightful place as the center of attention and worship."[18] In addition, the new arrangement provided a sedilia with thirteen stalls, to allow all elders and the minister to be seated on the platform for a communion service. Traditional Presbyterian practice had provided three chairs on the platform, for two elders and the minister.

Isa B. Kennedy had commissioned six completely new stained glass lancet windows as a memorial to her husband, Frank Kennedy, a longtime elder. The three for the chancel worship center behind the choir in the north wall of the church depict Christ the King in the central window, with an angel on each side adoring Him; the triangle, a symbol of the Trinity with a hand for God the Father; and the Dove, a symbol of the Holy Spirit, and the Alpha and Omega Greek letters as a symbol for Jesus. The birth of Jesus and the atonement are pictorially represented in these three windows as well as symbols for the four evangelists, Matthew, Mark, Luke, and John. Once more, Second Church was breaking new ground for Presbyterian church design. Traditionally,

Presbyterian churches had rejected stained glass windows with representation of human figures in favor of simple symbolism.

The three lancet windows over the Frederick Street entrance to the church where the wall had been extended over the vestibule were designed to be viewed by the congregation as it leaves worship to go out into the world. The theme is the Great Commission with symbols of the teaching, preaching, healing, and charitable work of the church. The handsome new lighting fixtures were a memorial to M.M. Edgar, elder and longtime superintendent of the Sunday School, as a gift of his widow.[19]

With the advice of Professor Carl Broman of Mary Baldwin College, the congregation had previously decided to purchase a pipe organ produced by M.P. Möller, Inc., of Hagerstown, Maryland. Although an organ concert had been planned for October 1948 with a world famous organist, Marcel DuPré of Paris, this was postponed when it was learned that installation would still be under way in October. By November, the new three-manual organ was in place. Its first use for a worship service took place on November 7, 1948, when Mrs. Wall played Handel's Largo for the prelude. The next week the first public concert took place when Broman presented an organ recital on Sunday afternoon, November 14.

When all the figures were tallied for the church, the bill had come to $117,962, equal to about $900,000 in 2001. This included the $21,874 for the new pipe organ. The insurance payments were $32,587. The old building fund had $12,435 to place toward the work, and new contributions had amounted to $31,140 by 1950. That left the congregation with a debt of $41,800. A year later the debt had been reduced to $32,300. Bequests of $2,500 from the Byers estate and $4,142 from the David Silling estate reduced it to $9,000 by October 1953.[20]

The long-awaited organ concert took place on January 17, 1949, when DuPré performed before a full house at an

The new chancel arrangement in the renovated and enlarged sanctuary was a departure from Presbyterian tradition, both in making the communion table the focal point rather than the pulpit, and in the stained glass windows with pictorial, rather than purely symbolic, representation.

admission fee of $1.20. This was the last American appearance for the famous organist of St. Suplice Church, Paris, and Professor of Organ at Paris National Conservatory. The program included works by Bach, Liszt, Cesar Franck, Olivier Messiaen, and two works of the organist's own composition. For many years following that concert, Mrs. Wall would not change the registration that DuPré had set up on the organ.[21]

Occupying the wonderful new church building came at a time of great growth and vigor in the congregation. The building itself surely contributed to this spirit, but it was also a sign of the times. The new families being formed after the war were coming to church. Membership was fairly stable, growing from 845 reported to Presbytery in 1945 to 888 in 1950. The number of marriages and births in the congregation was high in this period. Between April 1946 and March 1947 there were fifteen marriages and twenty-nine births. The next year saw twenty-two marriages and nineteen births, and the following year seventeen marriages and twenty-seven births. The 1950 report to presbytery noted fifteen marriages and twenty-nine births. Nearly all of those babies were brought to church for baptism in the year following their birth. The 1951 report noted that the church membership had reached 900, its all-time high. The marriages were thirteen and the births nineteen.[22]

One result of the new emphasis on young families was the introduction of Family Night programs at Second Church. These began in the fall of 1948, shortly after the remodeled facilities became available. Session assigned a different elder and a different adult Sunday School class to be responsible for the program each month. When Session reviewed Family Nights in October 1949, it considered them such a success that the program was extended for another year and a tradition was under way.[23] That year, a different elder and church organization were responsible for the program each month. Older church members who gathered to reminisce in 2000 remembered the Family Nights as wonderful occasions of fellowship, food, and fun. A typical program was that for June 3, 1950, when the Crusaders Class, with Mrs. Harry Dice as program chair, presented "A Beautiful Garden." Class members had decorated the stage to look like a garden, and presented a pantomime that included the primary children all dressed in yellow. Joseph Wine of Bridgewater sang "In the Garden," and "The Beautiful Garden of Prayer."[24]

Another form of family activity that the church sponsored was an Athletics Committee. Session voted in 1949 to sponsor a team in the Church Softball League for the summer. Elder John Brown represented the Session on the league board and as a player, and St. Clair served on the board. Games took place at Olivet field. Highlights of the 1950 sea-

One of the most active adult Sunday School classes in the postwar years was the Crusader's Class. This group of young men and women sponsored wonderful Family Night programs and the Tom Thumb Wedding. They are pictured here on the steps of the church, probably in the fall of 1946, before the fire.

son included Second Church's victories over Fishersville Methodist and Central Methodist. This was so successful that the congregation next participated in the Church Basketball League.[25]

An important occasion was the forty-sixth annual meeting of the Women of the Church of Lexington Presbytery at Second Church in April 1950. Mrs. John Irvine, President of the National Council of Presbyterian Women and delegate to the First Assembly of the World Council of Churches and Dr. Frank Bell Lewis, President of Washington and Lee University, addressed the 400 women attending. Mrs. W.A. Brand, and Mrs. C.K. Morrison, president of the local chapter, presided.[26]

With the awareness that the church's seventy-fifth anniversary would take place in 1950, Session appointed a committee to steer the celebration, consisting of A.M.

A highlight of 1950 that illustrates the rich social and community life of the congregation was the Tom Thumb Wedding that the Crusader's Class sponsored as a public fundraiser at the Beverley Manor School Auditorium in August. Ray Houser provided the special music for the show.

Woodside, Mrs. Frank W. (Irene) Dice and Mrs. C.K. (Rose) Morrison. Those energetic workers organized quickly and developed subcommittees to prepare a commemorative plate with the church picture, a history booklet, a roll of former members, a major reception with elaborate invitations, decorations, and publicity. The celebration took place on Sunday, November 12, with the popular former pastor, W. Emmet Davis, as preacher for the morning service, and the pageant as focus for the evening service. It was just a year later that the news that both their former ministers, Lawrence and Davis, died on the same day, December 26, 1951, saddened the congregation.[27]

For Pastor St. Clair, 1952 and 1953 were years of reflection and consolidation of a ministry of unusual length and strength. Virginia Synod honored St. Clair by electing him moderator in 1952. Special emphasis in his tenure in that position was placed on recruiting young people as missionaries, and expanding the collection of clothing and blankets for world relief. In his capacity as moderator, he had the honor of reading Scripture at the cornerstone ceremony for the new Westminster Presbyterian Church in Alexandria. There he shared the platform with President Harry S Truman, who laid the cornerstone as a favor to his military aide, General Harry Vaughan, a member of that congregation. St. Clair served on many synod and presbytery boards and committees, including Home Mission, Stewardship, Challenge Fund, Minister's Annuity Fund, Sunnyside, Orphan's Home, and Judicial Committee. He was the person responsible for establishing the paid position of executive secretary of presbytery, and was chosen several times as a delegate to General Assembly.[28]

John Knox Press in Richmond published St. Clair's book, *We Met Jesus*, in 1953. This was based on a series of popular sermons he had preached at Second Church about New Testament personalities. St. Clair admitted that his own favorites were Zacchaeus the Publican and Judas the Traitor. The congregation showed its deep appreciation of his devotion in a surprise Family Night program in January 1952 that honored the St. Clairs. A.M. Woodside, his longtime right arm on the Session, was toastmaster for the occasion. The congregation presented the St. Clairs with a silver tray and pair of silver candlesticks as a token of its affection.[29]

The large numbers of "baby boomers" born in the congregation in the postwar years were enrolled in the Sunday School and by 1953 were testing its space limits. Session authorized a committee to explore with adjacent property owners the possibility of acquiring an additional building. One of the finest residences in the neighborhood, the Todd House at the corner of Frederick and Fillmore, came on the market. The Session authorized acquiring it at auction, and the trustees did so in September 1953, at a good price of $13,500, which they borrowed. After refurbishing the house and naming it the Primary Building, it was opened to the public at an open house in May 1954, and became the new home of the young children's classes.

More space was needed. The doctors in the nearest house on Frederick Street did not plan to move until an office complex was built near the new King's Daughters' Hospital. Session even pondered tearing down the manse in order to build a Sunday School, but considered the house too lovely. Constructing a building where the old manse then stood seemed the best solution. Session authorized engaging an architect to draw tentative plans and investigated a professionally run fundraiser for the necessary capital campaign. The congregation met in January 1954, to hear the plan and to vote on it. The recommendations to proceed with the plan were defeated by one vote.[30]

Pressures on downtown property were considerable in the 1950s and 1960s as old residential areas of the town saw families moving to suburban housing developments and large older buildings were turned into offices or cut up into apartments. The sharp increase in automobile ownership in the years since World War II had crowded Staunton's narrow streets and created a demand for parking space. In June 1955, Session learned that the heirs to the Augusta N. Dull property across Lewis Street from the manse wanted its residential restrictions lifted, but had to gain permission of Session by terms of their deed. There was strong sentiment on Session to acquire the property for church parking, but on recommendation of the Board of Deacons, the Session opposed lifting the residential restriction. In negotiations with representatives of the church, Second Church offered to agree to lift the residential restriction for a payment of $5,000 from the estate. The heirs rejected this offer and were prepared to sue Second Church to force the Session to lift the restriction. In August 1957, attorney Wayt Timberlake wrote the Session offering a compromise of $1,500 if the church would agree to remove the restriction. Failing that, the suit would proceed and the case would go to court. Session recommended that the congregation accept the compromise offer, and on September 8, 1957, the congregation voted to do so.[31] Unfortunately, this cleared the way for another downtown structure to be destroyed, but failure to accept the compromise offer could have left the church facing costly legal fees, a questionable stewardship situation. Session voted to place the $1,500 received from the Dull heirs, less $250 in legal fees, in the Building Fund.

In a rare stand on a public issue, the Session of Second Church recorded a unanimous vote in April 1954 in opposition to the opening of motion picture theaters in Staunton on Sunday as "unwarranted commercialization of the Lord's Day" depriving the citizens of the restful day they have enjoyed for two centuries, and making the task of raising children more difficult.[32]

A development that Second Church supported heartily was the Sunnyside Home. Session agreed in April 1955 that the church would participate in Lexington Presbytery's major capital campaign for it. The Mother's Day offering of $850 was for Sunnyside that year. The Session, Board of

The stately Todd house served for several years as the Primary Sunday School building until the new building was constructed. In the 1960s when Victorian architecture was considered ugly, and when federal urban renewal programs were tearing down acres of downtown property across the nation, the congregation concluded that the land on which the house stood was more valuable as a parking lot. The house was demolished and the lot paved. Top photo, c. 1900; bottom photo c. 1950.

Deacons, and Women of the Church each named members to serve with St. Clair on the campaign committee.[33]

In August 1956, Session authorized the Music Committee, working with several women choir members, to plan a reception and suitable gifts for Betty Wall in recognition of her twenty-five years of service as organist and choir director. The event was a great success, for Mrs. Wall was much loved by the entire congregation.

The Boy Scout program begun in 1927 continued strong at Second Church throughout the 1950s. The highpoint of the decade was the dedication of the Johnny Reb Scout Troop Hut in August 1959. This realization of a long-held dream was made possible largely through the generosity of two members of the congregation, John F. Brown and Charles Sensabaugh. In May 1958 Session voted to accept Brown's gift of a lot at Third and Orchard Streets on which the hut could be constructed. Construction of the 28 x 60-foot cinderblock building was done by Scouts, their parents, and members of the congregation. The building contained two patrol rooms, two rest rooms, a kitchen, and an assembly room with fireplace. More than 200 members of the congregation and others were on hand on a sunny Sunday afternoon for the dedication ceremony. Brown and St. Clair unveiled the marker for the building, then St. Clair gave the dedication key to Scoutmaster Fred Miller, and reminded everyone attending that scouting is one of the best ways to build character in youth.[34]

The post-war years were truly boom years at Second Presbyterian Church. The membership and the Sunday School enrollment reached their all-time high numbers in those years. Young families flocked to the church and helped to make it one of the largest and most active in Staunton as well as one of the largest churches in Lexington Presbytery. The beloved pastor marked his Silver Anniversary with them in this period, and demonstrated the maturity of his ministry in his numerous significant committee appointments in presbytery and synod, in his selection for foreign exchange and service, and in his publication of a book of his sermons.

And yet, at this very high point of the life of this worshipping community, forces were at work in the local community, in the presbytery, and in American society that would place great pressure on the vigor, growth, and success that the congregation and its pastor had achieved.

Chapter Eight Notes

[1] Session Minutes, 1 July, 8 July, 26 August, 13 September 1945.
[2] Ibid., 30 September 1945.
[3] Ibid.
[4] Ibid., 16 April 1947, 17 September 1947.
[5] Ibid., 23 June, 13 October 1943; 5, 14 October 1945.
[6] *Staunton News-Leader,* 4 December 1946.
[7] Ibid., 3 December 1946.
[8] Oral history recollections of members, taken at a dinner in 2000.
[9] *Staunton News-Leader,* 3 December 1946.
[10] Ibid., 4 December 1946.
[11] Session Minutes, 3 December 1946.
[12] Ibid.; *Staunton News-Leader,* 4 December, 5 December 1946.
[13] Deacons Minutes, December 1946, January 1947; Recollections of Herman Adkinson at Oral History gathering in 2000.
[14] *Staunton News-Leader,* 5 December 1946.
[15] Woman's Auxiliary Scrapbook, 1941-1956.
[16] Building Committee Report, Congregational Meeting Minutes, 28 September 1947.
[17] Session Minutes, 17 March 1948.
[18] Service Bulletin leaflet, Second Presbyterian Church, 28 February 1948.
[19] Service Bulletin leaflet, 28 February 1948.
[20] Congregational Meeting Minutes, 29 January 1950, filed with Session Minutes; Session Minutes 11 April 1951; Board of Deacons Minutes, 8 July, 12, August 14, October 1953.
[21] The author is grateful to William J. Haessly, who compiled much of the information about the organ.
[22] Session Minutes, 18 April 1945, 17 April 1946, 16 April 1947, 15 April 1948, 14 April 1949, 5 April 1950, 11 April 1951.
[23] Session Minutes, 29 September 1948, 19 October 1949.
[24] Family Night Program, 3 June 1950, Woman's Auxiliary Scrapbook.
[25] Session Minutes, 16 March, 20 November 1949; 15 March 1950.
[26] Woman's Auxiliary Scrapbook, 1945-1955.
[27] Session Minutes, 14 April, 20 July 1949; 18 October, 15 November 1950.
[28] *Staunton News-Leader,* 20 January, 17 September 1952.
[29] Ibid., 17 December 1953.
[30] Session Minutes, 24 November 1953; 14 January 1954. Congregation Meeting Minutes, 24, 31 January 1954.

[31]Session Minutes, 24 August 1955, 20 June 1956., 21, 29 August 1957, 8 September 1957.
[32]Session Minutes, 25 April 1954.
[33]Minutes of Joint Meeting of Elders and Deacons, 13 April 1955.
[34]*Staunton News-Leader*, 24 August 1959. The persons who took part in the actual construction were Herman G. Adkinson, Baxter Barger, R.W. Bridges, Frank Brown, Jim Cash, Dick Cason, Walter Cason, Earl Chittum, A.L. Clemmer, Willis Clemmer, Ronnie Coiner, John Howard Craig, Richard Culpin, Ricky Culpin, Walter Hodge, Larry Jenkins, John Jones, Dallas Keyser, Phillip Knopp, Bob Landes, Byron Lessley, John Lessley, Winfred Link, Joe Mader, Lewis Mader, Elwood Masincupp, David Miller, Fred Miller, Robert Morris, Calvin Parrish, Walter Ralston, Russell Ramsey, Marshall Reid, Floyd Reid, Donnie Reid, Lloyd Sanger, Sammy Sanger, Butch Seaton, Charles Sensabaugh, D.C. Sensabaugh, Dickie Sensabaugh, Kenneth Sensabaugh, Lewis Sensabaugh, Forrest Sheffer, Larry Sheffer, Gerald Shiflett, Harry Simmons, Harry Swarzel, Jim Thomas, Carlyle Wilkerson, Calvin Wood, Eddie Wood, and David Wood.

Chapter Nine
The Decision

The 1950s was an era of growth and optimism in the United States, especially once the Korean War was over in 1953 and the economy entered an upward cycle. The expansion of automobile ownership in the post-war years continued, with amazing machines in a palette of pastels, large tail fins, and chrome galore by the mid-fifties. Car ownership transformed the face of America in ways that would have a striking impact on Second Church. This congregation was born at a time that Staunton was a community of 12,000 persons who lived in a compact "walking city" that stretched east-west from the Virginia School for the Deaf and Blind to Thornrose Cemetery, and north-south from Staunton Military Academy to Sears Hill.

By the mid-1950s, the city had expanded its physical space dramatically by annexation. The young households that had been formed in the congregation at the rate of fifteen to twenty marriages annually in the decade after the war set about being fruitful and multiplying with three or four children each within a decade. The parents of these "baby boomers" tended to reject the lifestyle of their parents who lived in the Italianate houses of Victorian Staunton or the foursquare houses of the 1910s and 1920s. With their accumulated savings and the help of a generous federal home loan program for veterans, the young families preferred to own modern three-bedroom ranch houses in one of many new subdivisions that were being developed in the expanded city limits or on the fringes of Staunton. Increased automobile ownership made this all possible. This changing residential pattern tended to blur the clearly drawn district lines for membership in the city's three Presbyterian churches plus Olivet on the outskirts.

Many American Protestant denominations in the 1950s formed new churches in the suburbs where the lively young families were moving. Popular taste viewed schools, train stations, post offices, schools, and churches in Victorian Gothic and Romanesque styles as ugly and outdated. Modern architecture excited many, causing A-line churches to sprout like mushrooms across the land. More traditional tastes revived colonial and classical houses of worship, dotting the face of America with churches plucked from New England village greens or Christopher Wren's London.

Fortunately for Second Church, the massive renovation of the old church after the fire had created a remarkable positive spirit in the congregation and had provided an exciting new worship space with a form that varied sharply from traditional Presbyterian Victorian architecture. This forestalled the possibility of members looking upon their church building as dreary and old-fashioned.

But that alone could not protect the congregation from the effects of the winds of change. The southern Presbyterian church, from theological seminaries to General Assembly, Synod, and Presbytery, was alert to the need to expand, grow, and meet the needs of changing patterns of living and working especially in larger cities and towns across the South. The General Assembly had a Board of Church Extension that was especially active in the 1950s. This board had an Urban Church Department. From that department came Hal Hyde in the spring of 1955 to carry out a survey regarding church expansion possibilities on behalf of presbytery.[1]

Much, if not most, nineteenth-century church expansion in Lexington Presbytery had occurred as "unplanned growth" when a group in one of the churches wanted to form a separate congregation, either for their greater worship convenience or from disagreement with the minister or current policy in the church. Second Church itself was born in that way. Presbytery in the mid-twentieth century took a different and proactive stance on new church formation. Church leaders perceived the formation of new congregations as desirable occurrences that should be carried out on a planned basis in concert with presbytery. One example of such planned development was the formation of Westminster Presbyterian Church in Waynesboro with the assistance of the Home Mission Committee of Lexington Presbytery and First Presbyterian Church there, beginning in 1953. This congregation began with a colonization program from First Church and organized formally with 240 members in October 1955.[2]

The longtime interest of Staunton's Presbyterian churches could be seen in the attempt to form an outpost in the Selma area in the late 1920s and in the Greenville Road outpost right after the war. As 1956 opened, that interest took formal expression with strong encouragement from Lexington Presbytery. In June 1955, in concert with the desires of presbytery, Session adopted a resolution to elect two representatives to serve on a council formed by the Presbyterian churches of Staunton to study the possibilities of expansion and to make recommendations to the Sessions of their churches.[3]

The result was the formation of the Staunton Presbyterian Church Extension Council at a meeting at First Church on November 20, 1955. The new group's constitution was inserted in the Session minutes of Second Church on January 22, 1956. The council consisted of the pastors of the existing churches, two additional representatives of each church whom Sessions would appoint annually, the Executive Secretary of Lexington Presbytery, and one other member appointed annually by the Committee on Church Extension of Lexington Presbytery. A majority of the Council could vote to add other members. The original officers were the Reverend Richard Potter, pastor of First Church, as chairman, Gilbert Bowman of Second Church as vice chairman, the Reverend Freeman B. Parker, pastor of Olivet, as secretary, and Mrs. Clyde A. Wade of Third Church as treasurer.[4]

The purpose of the group was to explore jointly the "need for additional Presbyterian churches in Staunton" and take steps to meet those needs. The group was empowered to select suitable sites for new churches and acquire options on them, to work out a procedure to purchase the land, and to organize a new church. In May 1957, Session learned that the council was in the process of acquiring land near Westside Elementary School (now A.S. Ware School).[5] A letter in July 1957 from Potter informed Session that the council planned to purchase sites for future expansion work. He asked financial support from each of the four churches. Session of Second Church agreed to contribute $200 from the benevolence fund toward that effort. By October 1957, Potter reported to Session that the council had secured a minister to start work in one of the three locations, and to ask a ten percent increase in the benevolent contribution of each church to that purpose. The council acquired three sites for a total of $49,500 with funds from the four participating churches, from the Church Extension Committee of presbytery, and from the same committee at the synod level. One site was on the growing West Side of town at 5th and G streets, near the new Hillcrest housing subdivision. Another was in the Skymont-Selma area near Springhill Road and Lambert Street, where the Springhill Village Apartments were later built. The third site was at Triangle where North Augusta Street and the recently extended North Coalter Street met, near the new Baldwin Acres housing subdivision and the little Triangle Tea Room. This is where Covenant Church now stands.[6]

While the council deliberated ways to extend presbyterianism in Staunton, the elders, deacons, and congregation of Second Church moved ahead with their own extension plans. The failure of the congregation to adopt the Sunday School building plan and capital campaign by only one vote in 1954 encouraged Session and the Board of Deacons by 1957 to place the idea before the congregation again. In June, a joint Session of elders and deacons recommended the plan at a congregational meeting, which approved it in July 1957. A new educational building would be constructed west of the church, replacing the old church home and annex. A committee of three elders, three deacons, and three women chosen by the board of the Women of the Church would plan this project. By October 1957, Fleming Hurt of Waynesboro had been selected as architect and promised preliminary plans in thirty to sixty days.[7]

The planning committee reported in April 1958 to Session, and the next month to the congregation. The Session recommended 1) that the preliminary plans be adopted, 2) that a Building Committee be appointed, and 3) that the new committee be authorized to conduct a fundraising campaign, secure blueprints and specifications, and recommend a contract to the congregation if sufficient pledges were on hand and a borrowing plan in place. The members named to the Building Committee were Robert Wetzel, chair; Glenn E. Yount, Francis M. Ramsey, Tracy Wenger, D.W. Sensabaugh, Robert S. Landes, Mrs. L.J. Kiger, Mrs. Lloyd A. Sanger, Mrs. W.C. Link, and the pastor.[8]

When presbytery held its spring meeting at Hebron Church on May 20-21, 1958, it concluded that downtown Staunton could no longer support two Presbyterian churches, and that one of them should move out of the city center. Presbytery authorized its Committee on Church Extension, in cooperation with the Staunton Presbyterian Church Extension Council, to negotiate with First Church and Second Church for one of them to move to one of the three locations described above. As an inducement to moving, presbytery's committee was empowered to offer the church that agreed to move $5,000 a year for ten years to help defray the costs of relocation and new construction.[9]

The Reverend James Sprunt, minister of Bethel Church, was chairman of the Lexington Presbytery Committee on Church Extension. The other members included the Reverend Frank L. Goodman, minister of Union Church near Churchville, vice chairman, and W.I. Grove. The Staunton Presbyterian Church Extension Council had concluded that Second Church would be made the offer. The presbytery committee presented it to Session on June 25, 1958, and asked that Second Church take some action in a reasonable amount of time. Sprunt also read to the Session a petition by seventy-six Presbyterians who lived in the Triangle area expressing a desire that a new church be organized and located in that area, and indicating that they would join and support a church there.[10]

This meeting occurred after the St. Clairs had sailed to Scotland on May 29 for a summer abroad. That trip was a pulpit exchange, long in the works, that Session had approved on March 2, 1958, before the action of the presbytery committee had been taken. It was a wonderful opportunity for St. Clair to preach, study, travel, and participate in congregational life in Edinburgh, the home of the Presbyterian Church. The Reverend Ronald H.G. Budge of the Murrayfield Presbyterian Church in Edinburgh filled the pulpit at Second Church in Staunton that summer. But, the exchange meant that St. Clair was not in Staunton to be with his congregation and his elders and deacons at a time that a crucial decision was looming.[11]

On July 2 another meeting took place with the Session, the Board of Deacons, the Board of the Women of the Church, teachers and officers of the Sunday School, and officers of the Senior Fellowship. The Reverend Howard M. Wilson of Mossy Creek presided and the Reverend Frank L.

Goodman presented the presbytery's offer to the entire elected leadership of the congregation. Goodman also presented the petition of the seventy-six persons who wanted a church at Triangle. A lengthy discussion of the issues followed.[12]

All those church leaders present understood that their beloved Second Church was at a crossroads. Whatever decision was made on the offer, the future of the congregation would change dramatically. Nonetheless, it is not likely that many of them could have guessed just how great the stresses would be in the coming decade as their faithful leader left them, as downtown Staunton underwent serious decline and change, as social protest and an unpopular war occupied the minds of Americans, and as a new church in the Triangle location became the center of exciting growth in local Presbyterianism.

At a joint meeting on July 16, the elders and deacons decided to hold a canvass of church members after presenting the offer to the congregation.[13] Session announced the formal offer to the congregation on August 3, 1958, noting that Second was the church that presbytery and the extension council deemed "most likely to benefit" from the offer. Session had arranged for cards to be placed in the pews on August 3 and August 10 through a committee with Walter Donald as chairman, and Elwood Masincupp, Earl Chittum, Robert Landes, Mrs. John F. Brown, and Mrs. Winfred Link as members. Members were to indicate on the card whether they favored or opposed accepting the presbytery offer to move to a new location, along with $5,000 a year for a decade, and if they favored moving, which of the three locations they preferred.

The pew cards were a survey to help guide the committee and Session in their deliberations. It was not a vote. The congregation's vote on this decisive matter would come later. When the results of the poll were tallied, of the 567 replies, 293 voted not to move, 213 voted to move, 36 were undecided and 25 had no opinion. Of those wanting to move, 109 chose the Triangle location, 81 chose Skymont-Selma, and only 23 preferred Westside.[14]

Once the pastor returned from his Scottish exchange, informal meetings were set for September 30 and October 1 to give every member of the congregation an opportunity to hear a discussion, ask questions, and express opinions. These meetings coincided with the fall presbytery meeting at Timber Ridge, where it was reported that Second Church had the proposal under consideration. Presbytery was occupied with a resolution against racial discrimination and the massive resistance to integration policy of the state government that had led to the closing of public schools in some parts of Virginia.[15]

The congregational meeting to vote on presbytery's offer was set for two months off, on December 7, 1958. Whether the choice of Pearl Harbor Day for the vote was a coincidence or an unintended statement by the officers cannot be said. By that time, the elders and deacons planned to make a recommendation to the congregation on whether to accept or decline.

The deacons and elders reached their decision at a joint meeting on November 12. There is no record of individual opinions, but simply the note that, based on the congregational survey, they had decided to recommend a vote against moving. They named John F. Brown, Clerk of Session, to present their recommendation against accepting the offer. The vote itself was probably the single most decisive event in the life of the congregation.[16] Although the congregation voted with the recommendation of their officers to decline presbytery's offer, the poll makes clear that a substantial minority of the congregation was disappointed in the outcome. In their tradition of closing ranks and accepting the outcome of an election there was no indication of acrimony. Still, when two new churches were formed in the next two years, a number of communicants from Second Church became their charter members.

The progress with the plans for a new Sunday School

building was undoubtedly what led many members to vote against the move. In February 1958, the Sunday School teachers had an opportunity to review the preliminary plans and give suggestions that would meet their needs. With the vote about moving behind them, the building committee could proceed. By February 22, 1959, the congregation learned that the capital campaign would begin March 25. To aid in that, Session obtained the services of Paul Sheahan, an elder at Second Presbyterian Church in Roanoke, who was a professional fundraiser. It also engaged Mrs. W.A. Simantel as secretary to the capital campaign, with its slogan "In His Name We Build." By Easter (March 29) the campaign staff was at work in their office in the education building.[17]

A Loyalty Dinner took place in the Bessie Weller School Cafeteria on April 15, 1959, to develop enthusiasm for the new building. The choice of the name for the dinner may indicate something of the tension in the air about the future of the congregation. The event was free to all members of the congregation, and they were assured that no pledges would be sought that night, only a time of fun and fellowship and learning about the exciting new plans for the future expansion of the church's education program.[18]

On Sunday, April 19 the capital campaign began. In traditional professional fund-raising techniques, the donors with the best potential to make a large gift are lined up first, so that the campaign can begin on a strong, positive note, preferably with at least half of the funding already pledged before a public campaign begins. To an extent this practice held true for Second Church's campaign. By April 26, after just one week, the committee could announce to the congregation that pledges for $41,622 were already in hand. This was forty-two percent of the goal. There were 210 cards not yet turned in. The news in the Sunday *Bulletin* on May 3 was that $60,026 had been pledged, sixty percent of the goal. By this time, only eighteen pledge cards had not been turned in.[19] This meant that the 192 cards turned in since

Fleming Hurt designed a modern education building attached to the church and flush with the street. Detailing in the brickwork at the cornice tied the new with the traditional church.

April 26 had produced an average of ninety-five dollars per household toward the campaign goal. If the remaining eighteen cards were turned in at that same rate, the campaign for $100,000 would end with less than $65,000 raised. It would be necessary for the congregation to undertake a large debt.

Second Church had often been in debt in the past, and its officers knew that the congregation had always managed to pull through and pay off its obligations. By early June the planning and fund-raising committees and the officers felt confident enough to set March of 1960 as the beginning of construction. In reality, the building plans were not completed in March, so that it was May when the congregation met to authorize the beginning of construction. The firm of J.B. Wine and Son was the contractor on a fixed fee basis. The anticipated cost for the building and the furnishings was $140,000. The cash, investments, and outstanding pledges amounted to $70,000, just half of the total cost. The congregation authorized the trustees to borrow the remainder.[20]

Construction continued through the winter of 1960-1961. The building of cement, steel, and concrete block with a brick veneer was the first purpose-designed and built education facility in the nearly ninety-year history of the congregation. Its sturdy, modern, functional interior included a spacious church office for the secretary, a Sunday School office, a pastor's study, a chapel, modern restrooms, and twenty spacious, cheerful, well-lighted classrooms. The construction work also included a remodeling of the annex and its four classrooms, and some work in the church basement to secure a fellowship hall out of the old assembly room, and improvements in the kitchen.[21]

The congregation gathered with pride and a deep sense of satisfaction on Sunday morning, April 16, 1961, for the dedication of the Education Building. At the dedication service, Kenneth Sensabaugh sang "How Great Thou Art" and St. Clair preached his sermon on "The Place of Teaching in the Program of the Church." He noted the social revolution taking place in America, and stressed the importance of teaching the Christian principle of brotherhood and social justice for all people.

The public ribbon cutting ceremony took place that afternoon at 2:30, when J.B. Wine, representing the contract-

Cutting the ribbon on the new Education Building, April 16, 1961.

ing firm, presented the keys of the building. The architect, Fleming Hurt, was also on hand for the occasion. Each teacher was in his or her classroom to welcome the general public touring the new building, and the Women of the Church served refreshments to all who visited.[22]

In the meanwhile, after Second Church's vote to decline presbytery's offer and the decision to proceed with its own new, modern Sunday School building, the proponents of church extension in Staunton had continued their work. From the three sites selected as possible future homes of churches, one was dropped, the Selma-Skymont location. Plans continued at the other two, and by 1960, there were two new Presbyterian congregations in Staunton, added to the four existing ones. Covenant Church was formed with a base of seventy-five households in the growing north end of town that attracted middle class and upper income residents. Fifty-nine of its charter members came from Second Church. Bethany was destined to serve the growing west side of Staunton, a mixed blue collar and middle class area with twenty-four from Second Church among its charter members. Would the growth pattern of the 1950s continue in the 1960s, with large families, conservative values, and a strong undercurrent of evangelical growth in the Presbyterian Church? That was a question that no one could answer in April 1961 as the members of Second Church gathered to dedicate their fine new education building.

Chapter Nine Notes

[1] Report of History and Work of Presbyterian Church Extension Council of Staunton. Filed with Session Minutes, 23 July 1961.
[2] Howard McKnight Wilson, *The Lexington Presbytery Heritage* (Verona: The McClure Press, 1971), 268-269. The membership of that new church had reached 520 by 1970.
[3] Session minutes, 15 June 1955.
[4] Report of History and Work of Presbyterian Church Extension Council.
[5] Statement of Organization of Staunton Presbyterian Church Extension Council, Session minutes, 22 January 1956; Session minutes 15 May 1957.
[6] Session minutes, 17 July, 16 October 1957.
[7] Session minutes., 26 June, 14 July 1957. The persons named to the planning committee were William F. McCormick, W. Tracy Wenger, Robert Wetzel, Meredith Silling, W.C. Link, D.W. Sensabaugh, Mrs. Carl Harlowe, Mrs. Joe M. Greene, and Mrs. John Brown.
[8] Session minutes, 25 April 1958; Congregational meeting minutes, 4 May 1958, filed with Session minutes.
[9] Sanger, *History*, 43.
[10] Session Minutes 25 June 1958; Bulletin, 3 August 1958.
[11] Bulletins, 2 March 1958, 22 June 1958.
[12] Session Minutes, 2 July 1958.
[13] Sanger, *History* , 44.
[14] Session Minutes, 17 September 1958.
[15] Lexington Presbytery Minutes, quoted in Sanger, *History*, 44; "Presbytery Assails State's Massive Resistance Policy" in *Staunton Leader*, 1 October 1958.
[16] Bulletins, 3, 10 August, 21 September, 7 December 1958; Session Minutes 12 November, 7 December 1958; Sanger, *History*, 44-45.
[17] Bulletins, 22 February, 22 March 1959.
[18] Session Minutes, 18 February 1959; Bulletin, 22 March 1959.
[19] Bulletins, 19, 26 April, 3 May 1959.
[20] Congregational meeting Minutes, 1 May 1960, filed with Session Minutes.
[21] *Staunton Leader*, 15 April 1961.
[22] Ibid.

Chapter Ten
Challenge, Change, and Centennial

With another goal behind him in the successful completion of the new education building, St. Clair felt free to consider an interesting mission assignment from the Presbyterian Church in the U.S.A in July and August 1962 in British Guiana, on the north coast of South America. He was to assist the Canadian and Scottish branches of Presbyterianism there to federate into an autonomous church drafting a constitution for the new Presbyterian Church in British Guiana. Session granted the leave and was pleased to receive a letter commending St. Clair for his work.[1]

Second Church faced the sixties with the largest debt in its history, $92,000. The construction cost of the new building, including architect's fees, was $140,075 and pledges had covered less than half of that. Church officers were eager to reduce the debt; so with the new building happily occupied, they determined to launch another capital campaign. Elder Robert Landes introduced the Session to the Reverend B.B. Breitenhirt, campaign director. His committee included John F. Brown, chairman, Mr. and Mrs. Glenn Yount, the pastor, Mrs. W.C. Link from the Women of the Church, W.T. Lynn, and A.M. Woodside.[2]

In spite of shouldering this large debt, there must have been a suggestion at presbytery that Second Church members were not giving enough financially. In October 1962, the Reverend William H. Ramkey, executive secretary of Lexington Presbytery, met with the Session to review presbytery's stewardship program. He reviewed Second Church's gifts of the three past years, comparing them with those of other churches to see if Second was doing as well as it should.[3]

The membership of Second Church had declined from the all-time record of 915 in 1955, in part by losses to Bethany and Covenant when those congregations were formed. By 1962 there were 799 members on the books, and a year later only 759. That left a smaller base for fund raising. Sunday School enrollment had also declined, from 589 in 1955 to 478 in 1963. The average attendance was lower, having reached its peak in 1957 at 367.

A dramatic change in the Sunday School occurred in 1963 and 1964 when the Presbyterian Church nationally introduced a new education program for all levels from primary through adult, called the Covenant Life Curriculum. Elder Richard T. Beard was Sunday School Superintendent as its staff confronted the new materials. In February 1963, the Christian Education Committee recommended meetings for the Session and school staff to discuss the new curriculum with Ramkey, executive secretary of presbytery. A leadership training school on the new curriculum took place at Waynesboro's First Church from April 28 through May 2. On May 15, 1963, on recommendation of the Christian Education Committee, Session voted to adopt the Covenant Life Curriculum.[4]

With the new curriculum came a restructuring of the Sunday School, including the adult classes. A point of great strength at Second Church for half a century had been the adult classes such as D.F.O. (Do For Others), Sunshine, Fellowship, and Crusaders. Each had its own membership composition, whether men, women, older couples, or young couples. Several classes had the same teachers for a long stretch of years and had developed a special *espirit de corps*. The Crusaders, for example, had such strength in numbers, youth, and enthusiasm that they often provided wonderful Family Night programs and fun events such as the Tom Thumb Wedding for the entire congregation and even for the community. It was not easy to give up this familiar structure for a new experiment. Change can be helpful, but change often comes at a cost.

The new curriculum clearly caused some uneasiness and concern at Second Church as reactions to it developed over the summer of 1963. Session spent much time discussing the reactions, but took no immediate action. Elder Beard reported difficulty in recruiting teachers for the senior department. Several teachers in the Junior and Pioneer Departments had indicated a few weeks into the new curriculum in the fall that they wished to give up their classes when the new year rolled around in January. Beard urged Session members to visit classes and observe the difficulties, expressing his concern that attendance overall was too low.[5]

For several years, ever since being turned down by two young women to whom the position of Director of Christian Education had been offered in 1960, Second Church had not filled that staff position.[6] The burden of the education program thus fell on the shoulders of the Session member who Chaired the Christian Education Committee. That person was also expected to be the Sunday School Superintendent. It was the equivalent of a full-time job expected of a volunteer who had to serve as a church officer and hold a full-time job of his own in the secular community. The issue was presented to Session, with the result that the two positions were separated.

Another of the great changes the congregation had to face in the 1960s was the loss of its much-loved pastor. The members were aware that he planned to retire, but until he presented his request to Session on June 28, 1964, for dissolution of the pastoral tie, the situation had not been faced directly. The retirement would be effective at the end of August. The Sunday *Bulletin* on July 5 brought the word to

A.M. Woodside presented the silver service to the St. Clairs on behalf of the congregation.

the congregation, and announced that the St. Clairs would be moving to a house they had purchased at 914 Grove Lane.[7]

The congregational meeting on July 12 voted to accept the dissolution and agreed that a committee of three members each from the Session, the Board of Deacons, and the Women of the Church be named to the nominating committee. It had been thirty-seven years since any member of Second Church had experience in conducting a search for a pastor.[8]

The St. Clairs held an Open House for the congregation on July 23. For his final sermon on Sunday, August 16, St. Clair preached the same sermon he had delivered on his first Sunday as pastor in 1927 then again in 1947 when the congregation re-occupied the remodeled church after the fire, "In the Land of Beginning Again."[9]

It was indeed a new beginning for everyone at Second Church. For the St. Clairs, a new ministry as pulpit supply lay ahead. For the congregation, nearly all of whom had grown up under his pastoral care or had been attracted to join Second Church because of St. Clair and the leadership qualities he brought out in the congregation, the loss was profound and the future uncertain. At the farewell reception for the St. Clairs, Ronald Woodrum recalled for the crowd that in his thirty-seven years at Second Church, St. Clair had received 1,956 members into the congregation, baptized 346 adults and 556 children, and married 634 couples. On behalf of the grateful congregation, A.M. Woodside presented a generous purse and a handsome five-piece silver coffee serviceto the St. Clairs.[10]

The Session committee of Elders Francis M. Ramsey and Eugene Mullins reported on August 11 that Dr. J.J. Murray of Lexington had agreed to preach each Sunday and come once a week to visit the sick for a period of three months at $300 a month. Thus, for the same amount that the congregation had paid the summer student assistant seminarians, Second Church had the services of a distinguished minister. Murray, a graduate of Davidson College and Union Theological Seminary, had long been pastor of Lexington Presbyterian Church, then until his retirement, was professor at Louisville Theological Seminary. He was a former moderator of the Synod of Virginia, chairman of the board at Union Theological Seminary, and was the author of several books.[11]

The manse now stood empty, but the congregation probably assumed that a new pastor would soon occupy it. When the Palmer property adjacent to the Manse on Lewis Street became available in September 1964, the elders and deacons in joint meeting considered but rejected its acquisition.[12]

By late October, it was clear that the committee to nominate a pastor would not have a name to present the congregation, so the pulpit supply committee asked Dr. Murray if he could stay longer. He agreed if arrangements could be made to replace the annuity payments he must forgo.[13]

In December 1964, Session adopted a budget for 1965 of $37,500, including a total of $8,500 for benevolences,

$7,000 for the new pastor, the usual $2,100 for the organist, and $4,000 for a Director of Christian Education, a position that had not been filled for some time. When the parish statistics for 1964 were compiled the following month, the membership was 767. There had been only two marriages, eight births, and five infant baptisms in the congregation that year, about one-third the number in the boom years of the late forties and the fifties.[14]

Session Minutes in this period convey a sense of discouragement and confusion. Without a Director of Christian Education to manage the complex Covenant Life Curriculum that had been in place only a year, the chairman of the Christian Education Committee, D.C. Sensabaugh, and the Superintendent of Sunday school, Richard Beard, requested that a temporary part-time Christian education worker be employed. Session approved this, and in January 1965 authorized Sensabaugh to offer the position to Mrs. J.G.M. Ramsey. Soon after, Deacon Lynn reported to Session on behalf of the Board of Deacons that the church finances were in bad shape. Meanwhile, the church secretary resigned. Fortunately, Martha Wilkerson stepped up to fill that position.[15] Uncertain whether the nominating committee would have a pastor by March, A.M. Woodside, who then chaired the pulpit supply committee, arranged with Dr. Herbert S. Turner, former pastor at Bethel and professor of religion at Mary Baldwin College, to come as interim when Dr. Murray had to leave.[16]

At the end of February, the nominating committee informed Session that they had a candidate, so the Session called a congregational meeting for March 14. Elder J. Walter Hodge, Jr., chairman, presented the name of the Reverend Ralph Malcolm Piland, pastor of Second Presbyterian Church, Waynesboro. The congregation elected him unanimously with 215 votes. The members must have felt relieved and encouraged that the half year of uncertainty about the direction and leadership was about to end.[17] The relief was premature. Piland decided to remain in Waynesboro and the nominating committee returned to its work. Realizing that the search for a pastor might extend beyond the three months that Dr. Turner could give the church, Woodside reported that the pulpit supply committee had engaged the Reverend W. Chalmers Jamison as supply beginning June 1 for $225 per month plus $25 monthly for an auto. Jamison, an alumnus of Davidson and Union Seminary, had been pastor of Union Church in Augusta County before becoming executive secretary of Lexington Presbytery. He served the presbytery for twenty years before retiring in 1961.[18]

In the midst of those negotiations, Elsie Ramsey, the new Director of Christian Education, indicated that health problems were causing her to resign from that position.[19] No attempt was made to replace her. The Christian Education Committee was determined to maintain a quality program in spite of setbacks such as this and some resistance to the new curriculum. It recommended a teacher training program and a visitation evangelism program that would stress the importance of better Sunday School attendance for both adults and children. The committee also promoted a party for college students and other young singles and an Easter breakfast for Young People.[20]

The youth of the church had a successful organization at this time and a program that combined fun social occasions, outreach service, spiritual development, and fundraising. Their activities for the calendar year in 1964 included a banquet for parents, a bottle drive to raise funds for their activities, attendance at a conference on world missions, a rally at a Charlottesville church, a retreat at Massanetta, swimming parties at Shenandoah Acres and Seawright Springs, a hike up Humpback Mountain, a hayride to a drive-in movie, bowling, and miniature golf. At Thanksgiving the youth provided a basket for a needy family, and in December they sponsored the traditional Christmas pageant.[21]

As the nominating committee continued its work to select a pastor for the congregation to consider, it realized that the manse was a problem. The old Yost property, purchased in 1925, had served the St. Clair family well for nearly four decades. However, among younger Presbyterian ministers across America as well as those of many other Protestant denominations, the traditional manses, parsonages, and rectories had fallen out of favor. Often these were rambling Victorian houses in older sections of towns and cities. A new generation of younger ministers wanted to raise their families in the ranch houses of suburban developments, along with other middle class professionals. Second Church's manse, one of the finest Colonial Revival houses in Staunton, was located in a neighborhood that was undergoing radical transformation, and not for the better. Downtown properties were being destroyed to make way for parking lots and commercial structures. Urban renewal was a catchword of the times as well as a major program of the federal government that encouraged the wholesale destruction of older neighborhoods in the hopes that new, modern construction would replace aging nineteenth-century buildings.

Elder Hodge, speaking for the nominating committee, presented this problem to the Session. The elders recommended that a manse allowance be provided for the new minister, and named a committee chaired by D.W. Sensabaugh to report on this. His committee suggested a manse allowance of $125 a month, which Session raised to $150. Armed with this more attractive offer, the nominating committee presented the name of the Reverend Robert C. Bradford at a congregation meeting on May 9, 1965. The terms of the offer showed a salary increase of $250 over the previous one, plus the $1,800 manse allowance, $1,000 car allowance, and the health insurance and annuity payments. The generous offer could be made because the pulpit had been empty for nine months, and the supply ministers were paid less than half what a pastor would receive. The congregation accepted the nomination by a unanimous vote of the 179 members attending.[22] Unfortunately, this call was not carried through either. That news must have been discouraging to the nominating committee members who had worked hard to find men whom they considered good potential pastors. It must have been disheartening to the general membership as well.

The Sunday School picture continued to be discouraging. D.C. Sensabaugh reported for the Christian Education Committee that the visitation evangelism program had been completed and produced some helpful information. The Sunday School was dropping both in attendance and in contributions, so that less than thirty percent of the church membership and less than fifty percent of the enrollment in the Sunday School was actually attending classes. Nonetheless, the committee recommended adoption of the Covenant Life Curriculum at all levels for the entire Sunday School.[23]

In the interim while Chalmers Jamison served the congregation, a new practice of having the elders take communion to the homes of any shut-ins who requested it began. Also in his months with the congregation the suggestion of having some other regular means of communicating with the congregation besides the Sunday *Bulletin* came up. Those who did not attend church missed any announcements made. The summer seminarian, Jeffrey Wampler, was enlisted in the project to start a monthly newsletter to be mailed to all members.[24]

On July 25, 1965, Elder Hodge of the Nominating Committee indicated that the Reverend Julius S. Garbett was a serious candidate for pastor, and had asked two pointed questions that the Session would need to answer. One was whether the Session was ready to reorganize itself according to the structure recommended in the *Plan Book*. The other was whether the officers were willing to employ a Director of Christian Education. It seems clear that Garbett would not be interested in the pastorate unless both questions could be answered in the affirmative. It was clear that the Session was not familiar with the new organizational plan, but moved swiftly to learn it by setting a joint meeting with the deacons for the Reverend David R. Freeman to explain the new plan. The plan abolished traditional Session committees, and replaced them with new standing committees: Strengthening the Church, Witness, Service, Worship, and Commitment. Elders would be provided copies of the *Plan Book* ahead of time to prepare for the meeting. At the meeting with Freeman, the joint Session went on record favoring the reorganization and also favoring the employment of a Director of Christian Education, and for raising the pastor's salary to $7,500.[25]

Negotiations with Garbett continued most of August, so it was August 29 before the congregational meeting could be held. Garbett received a unanimous standing vote of the 170 members present. It must have been with the greatest relief that the Session received his letter on September 5 informing them of his acceptance of the call.[26] Garbett, his wife, and their three children moved into temporary housing until he purchased the house at 1113 Preston Drive. The Women of the Church hosted a reception on October 10 to welcome the Garbetts to Second Church. Among the many who turned out was the only elder emeritus, J.L. Kelley, and his wife.[27]

Garbett, a native of Richmond, was a graduate of the University of Richmond and Union Theological Seminary. He had served pastorates in Emporia and Rock Hill, South Carolina, before being called to Hilton Presbyterian Church in Newport News, Virginia, in 1958. In his seven years there, that church built a new education building, started Boy and Girl Scout troops, and began a day school for preschoolers. In addition to leading a lively congregation, Garbett was moderator of Norfolk Presbytery and was active in United

Julius Garbett came to Second Church after a successful pastorate in Newport News.

Fund, Traveler's Aid, and in Parent-Teacher Association work.[28] His installation service took place on Sunday evening, October 31, 1965.

With the new pastor settled in, the deacons brought to Session in October a suggestion that a joint committee be named to consider the future of the old manse and the former Todd property at the corner of Frederick and Fillmore. A committee reported to Session in November that they had received an offer of $100 rent a month for the old manse. The committee recommended asking a rent of $110, as real estate taxes on the property, now that it was not being used for church purposes, were $131.[29]

"A new broom sweeps clean" is a phrase often applied to the administration of a new executive in an organization. A fresh mind from the outside may see ways in which an agency or institution could be made more efficient and more effective. Garbett saw several things that could be made more efficient at Second Church. Even before taking the position, he had made clear that he wanted to work with a Session organized on the new model, and the Session set about doing so. The Board of Deacons was also reorganized, with only four committees: stewardship, property, finance, and ushers.

Another change in the operation of Session was Garbett's suggestion that it not meet every Sunday morning, as had been the practice from the founding of the church. He preferred instead a monthly business meeting on a week night. The Session decided to give it a two-month trial, and at the end of the time liked the arrangement and extended it indefinitely.

As the elders and deacons worked on the budget for 1966, it was apparent the church was in a financial bind. The current expense budget was $32,483, an increase of more than ten percent over 1965. At the request of Lexington Presbytery, the Session adopted an increase in benevolent giving to $9,613, for a total of $42,096, the largest budget in the history of the church. Pledges from members, however, only amounted to $28,452, leaving a deficit of $13,643.[30]

When the figures were compiled two weeks later for the annual statistical report, they were not good. The number of marriages increased sharply, births were the same, but membership, which was 773 at the beginning of 1965, had dropped ten percent to 701 at the beginning of 1966.[31] It had been thirty years or more since the membership at Second Church was that small.

Union Seminary had launched a major capital campaign early in 1966, and the chairman of the local effort spoke in February to the Session of Second Church, noting that this congregation was being asked to raise between $15,000 and $22,000 for the seminary over a three-year period. Within a month, it was clear that response from the congregation was quite weak.[32]

In its effort to deal with the other of the two issues Garbett had raised before accepting the call, the Session looked into employing a Director of Christian Education. Garbett had corresponded with the Presbyterian School of

Christian Education in Richmond, formerly called the Training School, and reported little chance of filling the post from there. The Session was pleased to learn of a well-qualified and interested person in Staunton, Mrs. T.R. Elliott, and voted to offer her the position at $4,200. She accepted and began work on July 1, 1966. Mrs. Elliott, who had been educated at the University of California at Berkeley, had been a consultant on children's work for Lexington Presbytery and a member of the Christian Education Committee of the Synod of Virginia. The congregation welcomed her and her family with a reception in Fellowship Hall.[33]

Mrs. Elliott took over the administration of the Christian Education program, steering the congregation into the third year of the Covenant Life Curriculum. Mrs. Elliott met with the Session and board of deacons in a joint Session to discuss her work and her relationship with the officers of the church and made a plea to the officers to help all people in the total life of the church.[34]

D.C. Sensabaugh, chairman of the Committee on the Strengthening of the Church, a key committee in the new organizational structure, reported to Session in September on improvements needed in the adult division of church school. The six recommendations included establishing a training program for leaders, developing neighborhood meetings for Bible study, prayer, and service, starting a special class for college students, instigating a rotation system for leaders and teachers, forming divisions of fifteen to twenty adults with mixed membership, and changing the group membership yearly or every second year.[35]

The laboratory school movement had become a popular, perhaps trendy, method in the Presbyterian Church of providing training for Christian education instruction and youth leadership. To introduce Second Church to the movement, a Family Night program in April 1967 brought the synod youth worker to show a film about such a school. The Committee on Strengthening the Church recommended that the church bear the costs of its teachers to attend the Children's Laboratory at Charlottesville. Unfortunately, response to attending was poor, but was better when Second Church was the site of a youth lab in August 1967.[36] The youth of the church were also involved in performing a youth mass, "Rejoice," another trendy means that both Protestant and Roman Catholic churches used in the sixties to interest young people in attending worship. The youth of Second Church joined with those of First Church for this production on May 28 and June 4, 1967.[37]

In the summer of 1966, A.M. Woodside chaired a committee to evaluate all facets of program work at Second Church. He presented the committee's report to Session in August. There were twenty-two areas in which the committee found the church weak, and in which steps should be taken to improve and strengthen work. In areas relating to Christian education, committee members found the library totally inadequate, leadership training weak, a need to improve the training of young people for church membership, and a need to form children's and youth choirs.

In areas of communication, the committee found that the church newsletter needed "systematic direction"; that the church needed to purchase a folding machine; that contact with non-resident members was weak; that the church needed to be enrolled in the every member plan for the church publication, *Presbyterian Survey*; that the evangelism program had difficulty getting names of contacts; and that the greeting program at services needed improvement because some considered Second a "cold church."

Financial matters came in for scrutiny in the survey as well. The evaluation revealed the need for greater effort to reduce the church debt, for a year-round stewardship program, and for better administration of the youth conference scholarship program. In terms of giving, the committee learned that per capita giving to current expenses in 1965 was only fifty-eight dollars, and that per capita giving to benevolences was below the average of presbytery, synod, and General Assembly. Evaluations suggested that a percentage of funds should be assigned to benevolences, that supplemental offerings should receive better promotion, and that all departments in the church should be allowed to present requests when the budget is being prepared. Another aspect of the evaluation report was the recommendation that an assistant pastor be employed.[38]

The suggestion of dramatic change was in the air with a new minister, a New director of Christian Education, an evaluation report that recommended widespread changes in the operation of the church, and another plan for change in the adult education program. A change of another sort came to Second Church in September 1966. The congregational meeting on September 18 heard the names that the nominating committee put before them for election to Session. Among the names were those of three women who had provided exemplary and long service to the congregation through the Women of the Church and the Sunday School. They were Eileen Brown, Elizabeth Kirkpatrick, and Mrs. C. Russell Ramsey. When the ballots were counted Mrs. Brown had been elected the first woman elder of Second Presbyterian Church.[39]

In the following year, two more women were elected as elders, Miss Kirkpatrick and Nancy Swisher. Although women were nominated for deacon in 1966, none was elected, but in 1967, Mrs. Frank A. Dull, Jr., was elected the first woman deacon.[40] In 1968, Nellie Reeves and Lucille Sanger joined the ranks of elders, and Betty Landes and Mrs. Charles Simpson were chosen deacons. From that time on, the women of the congregation have played an important role in its elected leadership. Another woman honored by the church was Ruth Brand, whom the Women of the Church selected in 1967 for Honorary Life Membership in "grateful recognition of the many years of faithful and loyal service in the Master's work at Second Church."[41]

There were certain indications of unhappiness among some church leaders. These appear mainly in the form of resignations from key positions, and have no explanations attached to them. Within a few months in 1967, John Brown and Guy Deaver resigned as elders, and Mrs. Wall resigned as organist and choir director. She reconsidered and asked Session to rescind her decision.[42] The resignations may be typical of shifts that occur in any organization when top leadership changes. These can only have been exacerbated at Second Church by the pressures of competition from two new churches in town, a long period without a pastor, a decline in membership, and major changes in the governing structure and in the education program.

Although there is no mention of it in the records of Second Church, the mid-1960s was a difficult time for the nation, with a civil rights movement, new social programs, a war in Vietnam that was unpopular with many, a growing drug use problem, a sexual revolution, and disaffection of many youth with mainstream culture. The General Assembly of the church, in close votes, took stands affirming the right to civil disobedience and on raising questions about the Vietnam War that most members of Second Church might not have agreed with.

The choir in 1966 numbered twenty-seven voices. Mrs. Wall, longtime director, is forth from the left in the front row.

In the midst of dealing with changes in society, the Presbyterian Church, through its participation in ecumenical endeavors, brought to its members in 1966 a proposal that would give more than lip service to the idea of church unity. The 106th General Assembly of the Presbyterian Church in the U.S. in 1966 had voted to participate in a plan called COCU—Consultation on Church Union. The ten denominations participating comprised twenty-five million members, and looked to form a single denomination in the future. Before union among many various Protestant churches, questions loomed about union with the Reformed Church and with the Presbyterian Church in the U.S.A. Closer to home, the General Assembly would call a conference on restructuring presbyteries and synods that could change familiar patterns among church leaders.[43]

When the statistical reports for 1966 were tallied for presbytery in February 1967, the elders must have been relieved to see that membership, which had dropped to 701 in 1965, increased slightly to 708 in 1966. Their pleasure was short-lived. The statistics for 1967 showed another decline in membership, down to 675. The total budget for the church was $55,704, with $33,719 going to current expenses, $11,530 to building fund, $7,778 to budgeted benevolences, and $2,667 to non-budgeted benevolences. The 1968 statistics were even less encouraging. Membership experienced a loss again, down to 656. Current expenses had risen to $39,431, and the pastor's salary had risen to $8,100.[44]

The elected leadership of the congregation faced some difficult decisions about the physical surroundings in the downtown neighborhood that had been their home for nearly a century. The former manse was rented to Dunsmore Business College.[45] The Todd house at the corner of Frederick and Fillmore was not providing adequate income. A committee of deacons studied the building and reported a bleak prospect for its profitability. They recommended that it be torn down for a parking lot whose spaces could be rented, and noted that they had a firm that would demolish it for $200. Session voted in favor of that recommendation, and called a congregational meeting for the purpose. Today, historic preservation zoning would make it nearly impossible to destroy a handsome historic residential structure, but no such zoning or sentiment existed in the sixties. The congregation voted unanimously on October 30, 1966, to raze the house.[46] In February 1968, Garbett reported to Session that representatives of the Retail Merchants Association had spoken with them. They requested the attitude of the Session to that group's long range plan calling for the purchase of every building except for Central Methodist Church in the block opposite the church on Frederick Street from Lewis to Washington and all along West Beverley Street opposite Trinity Church. The downtown merchants intended to tear down all those buildings, pave the entire block, and have a parking lot for 400 cars. The Session of Second Church adopted a motion expressing its support for the plan.[47]

The relationship with Mrs. Elliott as Director of Religious Education, which had started with such promise, did not work out. In June 1968 she sent a letter of resignation to the Session, effective September 30, 1968, when the new church school year began. She wrote that she felt the congregation had not supported the work of Christian education, and that she believed her work was not effective. The Session accepted the resignation with regret. They made some effort to find a successor, but by September had little progress to report.[48]

The social problems that had upset much of the nation for most of the decade of the sixties finally made their way into Session records near the end of the decade. In the summer of 1969, the Stated Clerk of the General Assembly sent several communications to the churches regarding issues that body struggled with. One was information about an organization called "Concerned Presbyterians." Another was a communication entitled "On Law, Order and Justice," which the Session referred to the Committee on Strengthening the Church. The third concerned the "Black Manifesto."[49] Problems within the denomination, some stemming from differences of views on such social issues, came to a head in 1972, and led to the formation of a group of moderate ministers called the Covenant Fellowship of Presbyterians. Their president, Dr. Andrew Jumper, wrote the Session of Second Church requesting an opportunity for a representative to visit Session to learn of Covenant Fellowship's effort to "heal the threatened disruption of our Denomination."[50]

The 1970s brought calmer times to Second Church. Session voted to be one of the six pilot churches in Lexington Presbytery in a study of the nature and mission of the church. One important event for the congregation in 1970 was the clearing of indebtedness on the Church School Building. The debt elimination ceremony was held September 13.

The long relationship between Second Church and Troop 126, Boy Scouts of America, ceased when the troop was re-chartered in 1970 under the sponsorship of the Johnny Reb Corporation. The land on which the Scout hut stood had been given to the church by Mr. and Mrs. John F. Brown, who requested that the Session take action to ensure that the hut would remain with the troop. Session called for a congregational meeting to make the decision on the property. The congregation voted to transfer the land to the troop.[51]

Membership at the end of 1970 was at 658, with 230 enrolled at some level in the church school, and an average attendance of 144.[52] The budget adopted for 1972 totaled $55,954. Garbett's salary had reached $9,660, thanks to the efforts of Lexington Presbytery in behalf of all its ministers to have salaries adjusted according to the cost-of-living increase in those days of inflation. The statistics continued to be discouraging regarding membership, which at the close of 1971 was down to 627.[53]

Session appointed a study committee to investigate the possibility of establishing a day school at the kindergarten level at the church. That committee reported in April 1971 and recommended that the church proceed with the plan in the church school building. Mrs. Ward Reubush was engaged as director of the kindergarten, at a salary of $250 a month. First Church lent a considerable amount of equipment and the church spent $480 on additional equipment, with a target opening date of September 13, 1971.[54]

Second Church continued its longstanding interest in evangelism crusades during this period. Billy Graham crusade movies were shown in the 1960s. A crusade by the evangelist Myron Augsberger took place in October 1971, and Second Church provided counselors for that event. Gordon Shipp of the Bill Bright Campus Crusade for Christ spoke at morning worship on October 31, 1971, to encourage interest in an Evangelistic Institute at Massanetta. In the spring of 1972 a film about underground evangelism in the Iron Curtain countries under Soviet dominance was shown. The pastor and Dr. Mardre Bell were especially strong advocates of an active evangelism program, using a General Assembly Key 73 program as the basis for presbytery and congregational evangelism. Another long-standing interest of the congregation continued in the 1960s and 1970s, the work of medical missionaries. Dr. Peter Olivero, a medical missionary to the Quichua Indians in Ecuador spoke to the congregation in September 1971.[55]

The cottage at Massanetta, which had served the congregation so well in the years since its construction in 1927, became a cause for concern by 1970. First, Tinkling Spring, which owned the cottage next door, planned a major expansion, in the course of which it was learned that their line was closer to Second's cottage. Deacon Stephen Anderson reported to Session of the serious need for major repairs at the cottage, and noted that it was scarcely used any more by the people of Second. The deacons had inquired into the

Interest in the congregation's cottage at Massanetta declined in the 1970s. It was turned over to the parent corporation, with rights to two weeks a year for the congregation's use.

possibility of selling the cottage, so Session named two members to join them in investigating the advisability of repair or sale as a path of action.

The property committee of the Diaconate brought to Session in April 1973 its recommendation that the cottage be sold. After much discussion, the motion to sell carried, although there were some dissenting votes. It would mark the end of a very special kind of fellowship that had served dozens, if not hundreds, of members of Second Church in deeply meaningful ways over the years, but it did not mean that the use of the cottage was totally lost. In negotiations, the congregation gave its lease to Massanetta Springs, Inc., with the understanding that Second Church would have free use of the cottage for two weeks during any of the conferences, except Music Camp and Bible Conference, for fifteen years. At the end of that time, the agreement was up for renewal.[56]

Deacon Anderson reported to Session that the Möller organ, installed in 1947, needed serious repairs, requiring an expenditure of $9,000 and necessitating a capital campaign. The initial appeal for funds garnered only $1,100, so

Session called a congregational meeting to authorize the trustees to borrow the needed funds.[57]

In these years in which American youth seemed very much at peril from the revolution in values, the relaxation of traditional sexual standards, and the availability of drugs, the congregation of Second Church placed special emphasis on youth programs. Dr. and Mrs. Mardre Bell led the youth group, and when Dr. Bell was elected to the Session, he undertook a strong campaign to provide evangelism for youth, bringing a lively series of films, and urging congregational involvement with the Campus Crusade for Christ.[58]

The congregation was looking forward to the celebration of the centennial of the church. A committee reported to Session that they thought E.E. Mullins should chair the event. When Mullins did not feel able to serve, Session agreed to invite John and Eileen Brown to co-chair the celebration. The Browns also declined to serve, so Betty Van Fossen was the next choice of Session for the leadership role. Mrs. Van Fossen graciously agreed to undertake this challenge and met with Session to inform them that Geneva Westhafer and Juanita Mullins would co-chair with her, and to discuss budget matters for the celebration and gain approval for having plates made with a picture of the church.[59]

By 1973, the budget had risen to $61,947, with $11,340 in presbytery, synod, and General Assembly benevolences, and an additional $7,350 in local outreach work in the church's kindergarten, the weekday religious education program, and the Valley Rescue Mission. The pastor's salary was $10,460. The number of communicants had risen slightly from 627 at the end of 1971 to 639 at the end of 1972, and 250 enrolled in the Sunday School, but at the end of 1973 the number was back down to 628. The next year brought more bad news about numbers, for the membership was down to 600 and the church school to 208. In spite of the warm feeling throughout the congregation in the centennial year, 1975, the numbers did not climb, and for the first time since 1920, they fell below 600. In spite of declining numbers, the budget continued to rise, with anticipated expenses in 1976 of $85,634. Some $7,000 was designated for debt retirement and $16,000 for benevolences. Current expenses of the church rose faster than any other figure, and the pastor's salary had reached $13,131.[60]

The reorganizations at synod and presbytery levels that had long been under discussion took place in 1973. Elder A.M. Woodside attended as representative of Second Church at the organizational meeting of the Synod of the Virginias on June 18-19, 1973. The merging of Lexington and Winchester Presbyteries was under consideration, and attendance was urged at a meeting at Loch Willow Church to discuss the proposed merger. The last actual meeting of Lexington Presbytery took place at Second Church on November 8, 1973. The History Committee planned a short service in the sanctuary to mark the historic occasion. Elder Sensabaugh attended the organizational meeting of Shenandoah Presbytery at Massanetta on January 5, 1974. St. Clair, in his time as minister, had convinced Lexington Presbytery to locate in Staunton, and it acquired a building adjacent to Second Church as its headquarters. With the merger of the two presbyteries, Harrisonburg was a more central location, so the new presbytery purchased a building there, and wished to sell its Staunton property. Second Church was given the opportunity to purchase this for $55,000. The word from St. Clair that another buyer had indicated willingness to pay $15,000 more for the building caused Session to call a congregational meeting. The congregation voted to purchase the building.

Another merger would affect Second Church directly, and that was the proposal to merge the Board of Deacons and the Session. Although the matter was tabled in 1973, the decision to reduce both groups from eighteen members to fifteen was a step in that direction. In April 1975, both bodies voted to merge, so Session placed the matter before the congregation, and named a committee to study how to effect the merger if it were to be approved. The congregation gave its approval on May 18, with merger to occur in October[61]

Garbett spoke at length to Session in 1973 of his desire to see Second Church undertake the sponsorship of a foreign missionary. Dr. Mardre Bell donated $1,000 as a memorial to a former member in order to begin a fund to underwrite a missionary. The Witness Committee of Session, under the chairmanship of Elder Earl Flower, undertook to study the project.[62]

Shortly after the congregation undertook the purchase of the former Lexington Presbytery building came the word of a $2 million campaign to expand Sunnyside, the Presbyterian retirement community adjacent to Massanetta. Every church in the new Shenandoah Presbytery was assigned a quota to meet. Second Church was asked to raise $33,000. These two demands, coupled with need for work on the church, led the deacons and Session to endorse a capital campaign for $100,000 over the next three years.[63]

One of the first important contributions that the Centennial Committee made to the church was the request to Session in April 1975 that they be allowed to use the old pastor's study as a museum. Mrs. C. Russell Ramsey and Betty Van Fossen issued a call for memorabilia in a July *Bulletin*, and received many items. The committee kept interest up in the project by publishing in the *Bulletin* each week a description of something donated to the Historical Room. Mrs. Ramsey and Mrs. Wade W. Mitchell arranged the room for the centennial. From this beginning has grown today's handsome history room, where the women of this congregation have done an exemplary job of saving important documents, photographs, and memorabilia that tell the story of Second Church. During the anniversary year, the church also produced a pictorial church directory.

Another important accomplishment of the centennial was the publication of *History of Second Presbyterian Church*,

1875-1975, which was researched and written by Lucille Sanger. The seventy-six-page hardcover book was organized on a topical basis, with sections on such topics as Organization, Manses, Sunday School, Women's Organizations, Music, Scouting Program, Directors and Office Secretaries, and Ministers. The orders were taken in June. Session, in appreciation for her service in writing the history, provided an honorary life membership in the Women of the Church for Mrs. Sanger.

Although the Ladies Auxiliary had held many supper and white sales to raise funds in the years around 1900, it had long been the policy of Second Church that no money-raising events take place at the church. At concerts, for example, a free will offering could be taken, but tickets were not to be sold. The Women of the Church approached the Session in April 1975 asking permission to hold a yard sale. Although the Session agreed, Garbett wanted his negative vote recorded. In addition, the women asked general permission to hold rummage sales, bake sales, and suppers. Session named two elders and a deacon to study this issue. The committee reported back a unanimous decision against such activities.

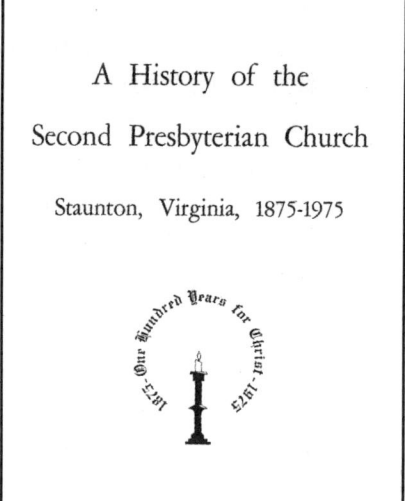

Title page of the 1975 centennial history that Lucille Sanger wrote for the congregation.

One of the ways that the shrinking congregational size affected the Women of the Church was the decline in the number of circles. In the 1950s there were twelve active circles. By 1970 that number had dropped to nine and by the time of the 100th Anniversary celebrations in 1975, there were only eight circles. The majority of the church members were women. The annual reports to presbytery first asked for a gender breakdown in 1974. At that time there were 365 women and 263 men. Of the 600 communicants the next year, 351 were women.

Sunday, November 9, was the day set for the anniversary celebration. The twenty-seven hard-working members of the Centennial Committee had prepared a special day for the congregation. Stanley Thomas had designed a logo for stationery, invitations, programs, and the book. Twenty families donated for memorial flowers so that the sanctuary would be especially beautiful for the occasion. The former pastor, St. Clair, was the guest preacher for the morning worship service. Special guests were the Reverend Donald Neel, Executive Presbyter of Shenandoah Presbytery, Colonel Frank R. Pancake, Mayor of Staunton, and Mrs. Pancake. The service leaflet listed thirty-nine persons in the congregation, ten men and twenty-nine women, who had been members of Second for fifty years or more. On behalf of the congregation, Mrs. Roy A. Sheets presented Garbett a gift in appreciation of his decade of ministry among them.

Some 600 persons attended the service and nearly 500 attended the luncheon that Joseph Vigilione catered following the service. It was a wonderful time of fellowship and fun, remembering loved ones who had been a part of the church family, celebrating the accomplishments of a century, and looking to the future with hope, after experiencing a decade of challenges.[64]

100th Anniversary
November 14, 1875 — November 9, 1975

SECOND PRESBYTERIAN CHURCH
Rev. Julius S. Garbett, M*inister*

STAUNTON, VIRGINIA

1875   1975

Service bulletin for the Centennial service.

At the Centennial ceremony, Pastor Emeritus St. Clair (left) and Pastor Garbett are pictured in the sanctuary.

Chapter Ten Notes

[1]Session Minutes, 29 April, 7 October 1962; Sanger, *History of Second Presbyterian Church*, 17.
[2]Session Minutes, 3 January 1962.
[3]Ibid., 10 October 1962.
[4]Ibid., 10, 20 February, 15 May 1953.
[5]Ibid., 18 September, 16 October, 20 November 1962.
[6]Carolyn Northrup of Flora McDonald College turned down the position offered at $3,300 in February 1960. Martha E. Poarch was interviewed for the job in May, was offered it in July at $4,000, but in September informed the Session that she was no longer interested. Session Minutes, 17 February, 18 May, 20 July, and 21 September 1960.
[7]Ibid., 28 June 1964; Bulletins, 5 July, 19 July 1964.
[8]After this meeting, some raised the question of whether members elected directly from the congregation should also be a part of the selection process. This caused the Session to call another congregational meeting on July 26 to consider rescinding the earlier composition of the committee. The new suggestion was for Session to name two members from each of the three bodies, and then for the congregation to elect three from the floor who were not deacons, elders, or members of the executive committee of the Women of the Church. A small turnout of the congregation voted 96-61 to stay with the original arrangement. Session Minutes, 15, 26 July 1964.
[9]Bulletins, 16 August, 23 August 1964.
[10]*Staunton Leader*, 17 August 1964.
[11]Session Minutes, 11 August 1964, 23 August 1964.
[12]Joint Meeting of Elders and Deacons, 16 September 1964.
[13]Session Minutes, 21 October 1964.
[14]Session Minutes, 13 December 1964, 20 January 1965.

[15] Session Minutes, 20, 31 January, 17 February 1965.
[16] Ibid., 27 December 1964.
[17] Ibid., 28 February 1963; Congregational meeting Minutes, 14 March 1965.
[18] Session Minutes 21 April 1965.
[19] Session Minutes, 17 March 1965.
[20] Ibid., 17 March, 21 April 1965.
[21] Bulletins, January 1965.
[22] Ibid., 5, 9 May 1965; Congregational meeting Minutes, 9 May 1965.
[23] Session Minutes, 16 June 1965.
[24] Ibid., 21 July 1965.
[25] Ibid., 25 July, 1 August, 4 August 1965.
[26] Ibid., 8, 18, 29 August 1965; Congregational meeting Minutes, 29 August 1965.
[27] *Staunton Leader*, 11 October 1965.
[28] *Staunton Leader*, 3[?] October 1965.
[29] Session Minutes, 20 October, 17 November 1965.
[30] Minutes of Joint Elders and Deacons Meeting, Session Minutes, 2 January 1966.
[31] Session Minutes, 19 January 1966.
[32] Ibid., 16 March 1966.
[33] Mrs. Elliott and her husband T.R. Elliott, a district forester for the Virginia Division of Forestry had two grown children and one in junior high school. *Staunton Leader*, 11 July 1966.
[34] Bulletins, September 1966; Joint Meeting Minutes, 25 September 1966.
[35] Session Minutes, 14 August 1966.
[36] Ibid., 15 February, 17 May 1967.
[37] Bulletin, 26 April 1967.
[38] Session Minutes, 14 August 1966.
[39] Ibid., 18 September 1966.
[40] Ibid., 7 January 1968.
[41] Bulletin, 15 January 1967; Session Minutes, 19 May 1968.
[42] Session Minutes, 16 July, 13 August, 11 October, 15 November 1967.
[43] Bulletin, 11 June 1967. This pre-printed Bulletin shell was provided to churches with a summary of the General Assembly that had just completed deliberations in Bristol, Tennessee.
[44] Session Minutes, 16 January, 21 February 1968, 16 January 1969.
[45] Ibid., 8 September 1968; 4 July 1971. Jouette O. Renalds signed the lease on behalf of Dunsmore Business College.
[46] Ibid., 25 September, 30 October 1966.
[47] Ibid., 21 February 1968.
[48] Ibid., 19 June, 18 September 1968
[49] Ibid., 16 July, 17 September 1969.
[50] Ibid., 27 September 1972.
[51] Ibid., 21 October, 9 November, 9 December 1970; 21 March 1971; Congregational Meeting Minutes, 2 May 1971.
[52] Session's Annual Statistical Report to Presbytery, filed with Session Minutes, 7 February 1971.
[53] Session's Annual Statistical Report to Presbytery, filed with Session Minutes, 12 January 1972.

[54] Session Minutes, 12 September 1971; Bulletin, 12 September 1971.
[55] Session Minutes, 22 September 1971, 27 September 1972; Bulletin, 29 September 1971; 12 January 1972.
[56] Session Minutes, 31 May 1972; 1 April, 24 June 1973.
[57] Ibid., May 31, July 26, August 30, 1972.
[58] Ibid., 12 January, 31 May, 26 July, 30 August 1972.
[59] Session Minutes, 28 February, 24 June, 19 September 1973
[60] Annual Statistical Report, filed with Session Minutes, 24 January 1973, 11 January 1976; budget filed with Session Minutes, 2 November 1975.
[61] Ibid., 19 September, 7 October 1973.
[62] Ibid., 24 February, 22 May 1974, 23 April 1975.
[63] Joint Elders and Deacons Meeting Minutes, 4 December 1974, 22 January 1975.
[64] Bulletin, 2 November 1975.

Chapter Eleven
A Time of Testing

Marking the centennial of Second Church was a wonderful occasion and a high point in the history of the congregation. The years that followed this celebration brought new tests for the leadership and called for imagination, dedication, and courage as costs mounted and membership declined.

The bicentennial of American independence came the year after the congregation's centennial and brought with it exceptionally fine programming for Family Night suppers and other special events. The invitations to these events, kept in a scrapbook by Nellie Reeves, show the variety available to all members at Second. Programs ranged from a presentation by an intelligence officer aboard the *USS Pueblo*, the subject of an international incident; to Northern Lights, a musical group of students from a Swedish Bible Institute; to the Covenant Players, an international religious drama group. Missionaries from Korea and Brazil told of their work and the adult and children's choirs gave a Christmas music program to complete the year.[1]

A strong fellowship in the congregation had made Second Church a very loving and caring community from at least the 1920s when the slogan "The Country Church in Town" was adopted. This caring community was evident in the Agape Fellowship that served older men and women in the congregation. There were ninety-seven members in the group in 1976. About fifty members usually attended the monthly luncheon meetings that featured poetry, music, and a guest speaker. Prayer and study groups were also an important part of the Agape Fellowship. Julius Garbett had helped organize the fellowship, so when he accepted a call to another church, the group recognized him for his work in founding and sustaining them.[2]

In 1976, Pastor Garbett was called to the Clifton Forge church and decided to accept the call. The congregation met on May 30 and agreed to ask presbytery to dissolve the pastoral relationship effective July 31. Garbett had helped to steer the congregation through a decade of division and strife in the nation and a decade that brought dissention to many churches, but not really to Second. His leadership style was not dynamic, for longtime deacon and elder, Kenny Sensabaugh, called him "plain old shoe." That same lay leader also noted that Garbett "had a flair — he seemed to have a knack for picking people to do the right job."

The statistics compiled shortly after Garbett arrived showed a membership of 701. When he left at the end of 1976, membership stood at 595, an average loss of ten members a year. In 1967 the total budget for the church was $55,704. Of that amount, $33,719 went to the expenses of operating the church and paying the staff. Budgeted and non-budgeted benevolences amounted to about $10,000. At the time Garbett left, the total contributions to the church were $91,363, of which $66,909 went to the current operating expenses and $24,838 to benevolences. Annual giving averaged eighty dollars a member in 1967, and had nearly doubled to $153 a member in 1977. Furthermore, the giving to benevolences had more than doubled in dollars and had tripled on a per capita basis from fourteen to forty-two dollars.[3]

If the figures for 1967 and 1977 are adjusted for inflation, we learn that members of Second Church increased their individual giving at a greater rate than the rate of inflation, and yet the overall budget of the church did not increase as fast as the rate of inflation. The increase in benevolent giving was even greater. The fourteen dollars per person average in 1967 would have risen to twenty-five based solely on inflation. Instead, it rose to forty-two dollars, considerably above the rate of inflation.[4] This means that those who chose to remain at Second Church demonstrated their commitment with greater financial investment.

After eleven years the congregation had to enter a search mode again. In the meantime, interim supply pastors would fill the pulpit. On June 13, Garbett's final Sunday with them, the congregation met to select a pulpit nominating committee. St. Clair returned to his old pulpit for the Bicentennial service on July 4, 1976 to preach on "Reflections on the 201st Fourth of July." Other summer ministers were A.E. Johnson, A.K. Dudley, Dr. John H. Leith, and Mr. Garth.[5]

In the fall the Session found an interim supply pastor who could remain through the end of the calendar year. This was Dr. Roy K. Patteson, who had begun his ministerial career as a student supply in Goshen and Rocky Spring in southwestern Augusta County around 1960.[6]

On January 2, 1977, Session Clerk A.M. Woodside introduced Dr. James R. Kennedy to fill that post. That same month Shenandoah Presbytery commended Woodside for his excellent service chairing the management team for Homes of the Presbytery. Kennedy, a South Carolinian, had served churches in North and South Carolina and West Virginia before coming to Augusta Stone Church. He was able to remain with the congregation for nearly seven months.[7]

The programs of the congregation moved along at their normal clip even without a full-time pastor. The Women of the Church spearheaded a Blanket Sunday, as they were to do for several years, on behalf of Church World Service. They organized Family Nights, one of which celebrated Pastor St. Clair's birthday, and a Valentine Party for residents at Western State Hospital. Later that year, wedding bells rang for St. Clair, by then several years a widower, when he married Bernice Hoover, a woman long active at Second Church.[9]

The winter of 1977 was another energy crisis season. Session learned that it cost ninety dollars to heat the sanctuary for the Sunday service and after hearing Governor Mills Godwin's proclamation for fuel conservation, the elders voted to hold subsequent services in the Fellowship Hall, which could be heated for only thirty dollars. In addition, Session asked all groups that usually met in the church buildings to meet in private homes in order to conserve fuel.[10]

Several signs of liturgical change were evident in the year that Patteson and Kennedy were at Second. A new kind of Christian music, growing out of the renewal movement, was gradually being introduced into both Protestant and Catholic churches in the 1970s. Bulletins in this period indicate that a number of these praise songs were introduced, for their words and refrains were often printed in the service leaflet for that Sunday. New hymns were similarly introduced, with one example, "Morning has broken" being selected as "Hymn of the Month" in November 1976. Easter, however, was no time for innovation. In addition to traditional Eastern hymns, the choir performed "Hallelujah, what a Savior!" by John Peterson again by popular demand.[11]

The search committee, D.W. Sensabaugh, Betty Van Fossen, E.E. Mullins, Joe Danner, and Lou Ann Burnett, had made progress in finding a new pastor. Dr. Kennedy was moderator of the congregational meeting on Sunday, May 29, 1977, at which the Committee to Nominate a Pastor presented its recommendation of the Reverend T. Dennis Walker of Arlington, Virginia. A graduate of Princeton Seminary, he had been at White Clay Creek Church near Newark, Delaware, before coming to Virginia. National Capital Union Presbytery endorsed Walker in mid-June, and on June 29 he accepted the call. He was to take up his duties on July 31, exactly one year from the time Garbett's pastorate ended.

The Reverend T. Dennis Walker had led congregations in Delaware and Northern Virginia before coming to Second Church.

The terms included four weeks of vacation, two weeks of annual study leave, a $5,000 housing allowance, and all utilities paid by the church.[12]

Walker conducted his first service on July 31, assuring the congregation of his desire to visit in their homes. Walker's installation service took place on September 11, with Charles T. Yerkes delivering the sermon.[13] He met with his Session on August 17 for the first time. It was clear that there were several problems to be addressed. The church was behind in its benevolent payments to presbytery by three months, having chosen that lapse in order to meet operating expenses. The organist and choir director, Edward Van Dyck, had resigned to attend seminary, and Session was having difficulty finding a replacement. The church had to make do with a rotating system of organists for several months. The manse was empty with no prospect of a tenant in sight and thus no rental income. The Weekday Nursery School that the congregation helped sponsor in the education building was having financial difficulties, and Session had been debating whether to continue the school. Once the pastor was in place, Session voted to continue the school one more year.[14]

Every new minister in a congregation brings his own style of leading, pastoring, preaching, and interacting with people. A new pastoral relationship always requires some adjustment on the part of both pastor and congregation as they come to know and understand each other. Often, each side will find aspects of the behavior of the other that they would like to change. The early months of a new pastoral relationship can set the stage for the long term working relationship between pastor and people. Walker and the Session arranged for meetings to be held after church services on September 25 and October 2 to gather "Requests of the People," an effort at widening participation and getting input that could improve the church. The requests went to the chairmen of relevant sessional committees, and were discussed at length by Session in October.[15]

Walker, for his part, had observed some practices that needed change or clarification, or for which clear policy was lacking. He presented a list to Session within his first month as pastor. One of these items was that there seemed to be no policy for the organization and control of Family Night suppers. These were among the most popular and successful longstanding activities at Second Church, so criticism of them might not be taken well.

In addition to the introduction of renewal music, other small changes were taking place in the worship services at Presbyterian churches in the 1970s. One was an increased awareness of the liturgical calendar that had long shaped the worship year for Catholics, Lutherans, and Episcopalians. A more specific recognition of the seasons of Advent and Lent had become common in Presbyterian churches. In 1977, the Presbyterian churches of Staunton had a Lenten schedule of special services at a different one of their churches each Sunday evening, with foreign missions as the focus. Second Church had hosted one of these evenings in March 1977. Another was the introduction at Advent 1977 of a Chrismon tree. This idea was introduced at an October workshop in Fellowship Hall, at which interested members learned about Chrismons, their history, and their purpose.

The service bulletin included illustrations of some of the Christian symbols depicted on Chrismons.[16]

In October, the suggestion was made in Session to change the worship pattern of the congregation for the first time in its 102-year history by giving up the traditional Presbyterian practice of quarterly communion services in favor of monthly communion services. Its first mention was informational only, but Elder Betty Van Fossen told Session that the issue would come up later for a vote. An issue or question that was under debate and consideration in nearly all mainline Protestant churches was that of more frequent communion services. There was recognition by some that the Last Supper was a principal sacramental occasion instituted by Jesus, and a growing sense that it should be the focal point of worship. At this same time, for example, the Episcopal Church, which traditionally had communion on the first Sunday of each month, was moving to weekly celebration of the Eucharist, as were Lutherans. Methodists were moving from quarterly to monthly communion.

Ever since the adoption of a new *Directory of Worship* in 1961 by the United Presbyterian Church in the U.S.A. (Northern) and the 1963 *Directory for the Worship and Work of the Church by the Presbyterian Church in the U.S.* (Southern), there had been a trend toward greater observance of the seasons of the Christian year and toward a linking of preaching of the word and observance of the sacrament.[17] On November 30, the Session of Second Church voted to hold communion the first Sunday of each month for a six-month trial period.[18]

As the end of the six-month period approached, the Worship Committee recommended to Session a process for deciding the frequency of the Lord's Supper. Walker prepared a flyer on the "12 Points for Serving Communion" that would be given to the congregation on April 23. The following Sunday, April 30, Walker would preach a sermon on the communion service. The third week, on May 7,

Session and the congregation would meet after church to discuss their viewpoints, and then at the May Session meeting the elders would make the decision. After this process, Elder E.E. Mullins of the Worship Committee moved that the church return to quarterly communion services. His motion passed, and the question was decided in favor of tradition.[19]

American clergymen of all denominations in the 1970s, especially those who were young-to-middle-age, were much influenced by movements and techniques in the social sciences and education, especially in psychology. It was a time in which many theories about interpersonal relationships, group dynamics, and self-expression circulated. Non-judgmental teaching techniques abounded. Training techniques from the corporate world were routinely adopted by church organizations. Self-help books and popular psychology were best sellers. Buzz groups and brainstorming Sessions became commonplace in church halls.

Walker was familiar with these latest ideas, and had seen many of them employed in the metropolitan Washington area. He believed that Second Church would benefit from these new ways of organizing the routine work of the congregation. With what must have seemed like dizzying speed he introduced many of these ideas.

He saw collaboration between the Women of the Church and the Session as essential and proposed merging Session committees and women's committees into inclusive committees responsible to Session and to Women's Council. That idea was soundly defeated in Session. He experimented with various means of opening and conducting Session meetings, including opening with a fifteen-minute prayer meeting and including in the meeting a half-hour study Session on topics such as the meaning of worship for the church. Another time he suggested that Session break into small groups to discuss the topics on the agenda before meeting in full Session to debate and vote. On another occasion, the meeting began by breaking into three sharing groups, each to discuss three questions: What kind of day it has been for me; my personal need for prayer, and what I want God to help us do tonight.[20] He also suggested the possibility of holding a Session retreat to discuss plans, programs, and goals. This was something that the Session of Second Church had never before done.

The retreat idea appealed to the Session, so in September 1978 they agreed to try it in order "to find real goals as to where we are as a congregation," and to seek ideas about long and short-range priorities. They decided to give the congregation a questionnaire that the Session could interpret at the retreat and present at the January Session meeting. The retreat was to take place at Brethren Woods in Rockingham County on Friday evening, November 17 and all day Saturday.[21]

A major result of the retreat was the decision to develop a questionnaire that would sample the congregation's opinions about many aspects of Second Church and ideas of directions for the future. Walker drafted the document and presented it to Session in January 1979 for its input. In home meetings in April, members discussed "What are the special strengths of Second Church?" and "What are barriers to those strengths?" The questionnaire document was distributed to the congregation in May. Session began to review the results in June, and continued in July. On July 1, Elder Bobby Cook presented the results of questions nine through twelve on church finance and property management. The next Sunday, Elder Woody Wimer presented to the congregation the results of questions thirteen through sixteen about Sunday School and general caring. A total of 102 persons responded, thirty-six men and sixty-six women, out of a membership of 589, or less than twenty percent. The average age of respondents was fifty-two and their average length of time at Second was twenty-six years. On a scale of one to seven, music got the highest rating at 6.1, caring, financial management, and Sunday School each received an average rating of 5.5, and worship had the lowest average at 5.0. Some of the innovations in worship that got minus ratings were children's sermons, participatory prayers, and the "moment of greeting."[22]

In September 1979, as a result of the questionnaires, Walker proposed to Session than an all-church planning event be held in October, with lunch after morning service, and then a division of the congregation into small discussion groups, with a Session member leading each. This meeting provided the basis for Session committees to set goals for the coming year at their November meeting.[23] Something happened in the congregation about this time that caused a strange announcement to appear in the weekly service bulletins for several weeks in October and November. The announcement, called "Rumor Control," noted that "Members receiving questionable information about our pastor or other members may now check the information with a responsible church source." A.M. Woodside and Walter Hodge were the responsible sources to whom members were directed.[24]

The congregation acted on two important measures in 1979. It gave approval by a majority vote to the recommendation of Session to merge the duties of deacons with those of elders and thus dispense with the Board of Deacons. The other measure was to elect St. Clair to the honorary position of Pastor Emeritus by a unanimous vote.[25]

Two issues that troubled the Session in 1979 through 1983 were the visitation program and the weekday nursery school. For many years a regular program of visitation in the congregation on the part of elders had been deemed important. In actuality, the idea had never worked well. The district plan had been the basis for the visitation program for years but everyone agreed that it simply did not work well. By 1983 the Outreach Committee was trying to solve the problem of elders who did no visitation by assigning them households to visit.[26]

At a reception in February 1980, Pastor Emeritus R.L. St. Clair is surrounded by admirers. Front row, left to right: Mrs. Roy Sheets, Elizabeth Grim, Dorothy Scott Thompson, Evelyn Beard. Back row: Hazel Cason, Ashton Critzer, Juanita Mullins, and Richard Beard.

A time to celebrate good fellowship in the past and hope for the future of the congregation was the Homecoming on July 6, 1980. Betty Landes chaired the committee to plan and carry out this event, ably assisted by Richard Beard, the Reverend Mr. Walker and the Reverend Mr. St. Clair. Robert Landes was treasurer for the event. A special program for the Church School hour featured a talk by St. Clair. A coffee hour followed this, prior to the worship service for which the Worship Committee had made special plans for music and liturgy. The Historical Room was open that day for returning and current members to see the impressive memorabilia associated with the congregation's past. The highlight of the day was the picnic on the lawn at nearby Stuart Hall. The school food service staff served a hearty meal to the hundreds of current and former members of Second Church, their families, and friends who gathered for an occasion of happy fellowship.

In January 1980, Session gave the Education Committee permission to hold meetings for the proponents and the

At the 1980 Homecoming at Stuart Hall, the largest family was that of the Mullins. Left to right: Gene Mullins, Jeremy Spitzer, Juanita Mullins, Dana Eastman, Heather Tyree, Pam Snyder holding Kristin, Stephanie, and Michele Nuckols.

opponents of the Weekday Nursery School to present their views at a covered dish meal after church. The committee was to engage a suitable referee for the discussion and pay his expenses. A task force on the nursery that included Richard Robinson and Terry Westhafer reported to Session in March. Once more Session deemed congregational input desirable, following which, Session would vote on the fate of the school. On March 31, by a vote of eleven to seven, Session approved keeping the nursery school. Two elders proposed that the church set up a fund to help operate the nursery for a year, after which time if the school could not support itself, it would be closed. This was also adopted. The school managed to meet the demand and was still operating in 1982 with Charlotte Rankin as teacher to the eleven youngsters. Support of the school was in some ways the principal local outreach of the congregation.[27]

By 1984 the school was on sounder fiscal footing and had a waiting list of twenty children. In addition, students at Mary Baldwin College had been enlisted to assist. Lois Sensabaugh became the teacher in September 1984.[28]

Session meetings themselves became a problem for the church during this period. Agendas were long — one included twenty-six items — so that meetings often lasted more than two-and-one-half hours. Proposals were presented for making the meetings more efficient. Session finally adopted a time limit, but as often as not, this could not be maintained so long as agenda items needed action.

In 1980 and 1981 the Session was much absorbed in the project of making a covenant with the pastor. The issue appeared in April 1980 when Walker reminded the Session that the 1978 edition of the *Book of Order* now called for a covenant between pastor and the church. Because Walker had been called in 1977, a covenant had never been done for him, but needed to be. In June, Walker recommended to Session a plan for a church-wide study of leadership called "The Lord as Servant of All" that included a section on covenant making.[29] Dr. Woody Morriss of Third Presbyterian came six evenings to work with Session in hammering out a draft. By October the document had been drafted and reviewed by Session, with recommendations for future review of the covenant. The document defined the pastor's duties in priority form and told what the Session and congregation could do to support the pastor in performing his duties.[30]

When the Session reviewed Walker's performance in 1981, it concluded that he was working too many hours, that he was overactive and Session underactive, and that Session members felt overwhelmed by the number of new programs he introduced and the number of innovations in worship. Session agreed to assume the responsibility of conceiving any new ideas in the next three months, rather than Walker. For his part, the pastor reported that "he has stopped every impulse to do something new in the service."[31]

One worship innovation that did occur in 1981 was the admission of baptized children to communion. This change from the practice of seeing confirmation as the preparation for communion for children of middle school age was an innovation with roots in the early church. Several denominations were experimenting with this concept at the time, including Lutheran, Episcopal, and Presbyterian. The implementation took place in July, but some criticized the service as poorly planned and confusing. By the following year the Presbyterian Church had developed a Doctrine of Membership regarding the full inclusion of children in the church.[32]

In the spring of 1981, Session studied the idea of employing a Director of Christian Education once more, but concluded instead to work with a consultant. None could be found at the time, but in February 1982, Elder Anita Haessly, chairman of the Christian Education Committee, reported that Margaret "Peggy" Roberson of Swoope, a member of Hebron Church, would become the consultant on a project basis. This arrangement worked well enough to be continued into 1984.[33]

Members of Second Church had to say farewell to a much-loved friend in 1981 when Ray Lawrence St. Clair died on August 7 at the age of eighty-six. The memorial that Session adopted indicated not only his exceptional service to Second Church, but pointed out his remarkable record with Lexington Presbytery and synod.[34] The following year, as a memorial to St. Clair, the church acquired a new white silk damask bookmarker and a pulpit cloth embroidered with a cross and crown.[35]

In 1982 Second Church learned that it was the beneficiary of $5,000 from the will of H. Boswell Jones, Jr., to be used only in local benevolent work. When the final estate payout was made, the fund was $13,195. The pastor was to appoint an administrator for the fund, and named Jean Flower. Nellie Reeves later served in this post. This fund enabled Second Church to help in crisis situations such as sending $500 in 1982 when Valley Mission, which brought bringing services to the troubled and homeless population, was in financial difficulty. Another significant bequest to

Second Church supported the ministry of the Craig Meisner family as missionaries to Bangladesh from 1981 to 1987.

the church was from the estate of Nellie Middleton, who had left 22.5 percent of her estate to Second Church. This amounted to more than $13,000 and made possible the necessary $10,000 to paint the church exterior.[36] In 1984 Nelle Yount left $15,000 to Shenandoah Presbytery Corporation with the stipulation that four-sixths of the income be used for the Glenn E. Yount Memorial Scholarship for youth of Second Church towards higher education.[37]

Shenandoah Presbytery sent representatives to talk with Session about benevolent giving as a result of the revelation that this presbytery was sixtieth, the very bottom, in per capita giving. In 1980 Second Church gave $11,000 to benevolent causes. Presbytery asked $15,260 in 1981 and $20,000 in 1982, significant increases. Session stepped up to the request in the budget it prepared in 1981, but could not reach the 1982 goal. The statistics for the congregation at the end of 1981 were not good. When it realized that the rolls had not been purged of inactive members for several years, a proper review took place, eliminating 114 names. The membership, 598 at the end of 1980, was reduced to 466 at the end of 1981. As a result of the drop below 500 members, Second lost one of the two elders it was entitled to send to presbytery meetings, and thus joined the ranks of the small churches. By 1984 the membership figures had declined further to 438 persons.[38]

For many years the months of January to March at Second Church had been devoted to mission outreach. In the early 1980s the congregation provided partial support to two missionary couples, Bill and Ginny Reinhold in Kinshasa, Zaire, and Craig and Charlene Meisner in Dacca, Bangladesh. Both couples visited Second Church when they were in the states, and reported on the desperate conditions of the people they served with their medical, educational, and agricultural skills. Second Church contributed nearly $700 in 1984 to a fund to purchase a new Toyota for Meisner so that he could reach people in remote villages.[39]

The long-discussed reunion of the United Presbyterian Church U.S.A. and the Presbyterian Church in the U.S. took place in 1983. The question had to be voted at each presbytery in the two denominations, at each synod, and at each general assembly, and had to receive a majority vote at each level. The reunion measure passed by a large majority in every presbytery in the northern church. In the southern church fifty-three presbyteries voted for reunion, but eight voted against it. In Shenandoah Presbytery the vote was 150 for and thirty-six against. When the General Assembly of the southern church met in Atlanta in June to vote, a moving service had been organized in Augusta County for local Presbyterians. Members of a dozen churches including Second gathered at Augusta Stone Church, the oldest in the county, to call the roll of presbyteries and to receive communion at the same hour as the commissioners worshipping at General Assembly.[40]

The new *Book of Order* for the new denomination replaced the former *Book of Church Order* with which the elders were familiar. Although the changes were minor, they did require an annual meeting of the congregation for the

The "Kitchen Angels" represent an important part of the ministry and fellowship of the women of Second Church. Pictured here are Margaret Kesterson, Juanita Mullins, Frances Brown, Gennivee Carey, Leatrice Gibson, Rachel Dull, and Nellie Mitchell.

first time, so that annual reports to the congregation date from 1984.

The Women of the Church at Second distinguished themselves in 1982 and 1983 by sending the President and the Secretary of Shenandoah Presbytery WOC, Betty Van Fossen and Betty Landes. Jane Selph represented the WOC and the congregation as Second's "Key Friend" at Union Theological Seminary, keeping the church informed about the seminary. From time to time since 1960 the WOC at Second had recognized outstanding members for their long record of service and for their leadership by naming them Honorary Life Members. Those honored included Frances Sensabaugh 1960, Ruth Brand 1966, Helen St. Clair, Eunice Wenger, and Elizabeth Kirkpatrick in 1967, Nellie Reeves in 1968, Mary Gardner in 1969, Louise Simpson in 1973, Lucille Sanger in 1975, Anita Haessly in 1981, Frances Brown in 1982, and Juanita Mullins and Mary Virginia Norman in 1983.[41]

The programs of the Women of the Church have a remarkable continuity, durability, and strength. White Cross work is an example of a quiet but important type of outreach that aided mission work by providing bandages, blankets, and newborn clothing. In 1982, for example, the women who met weekly in January and February to roll bandages from clean old sheets rolled 1,100 and in 1982 rolled 2,617. Another quiet work of the women and one that brought great comfort within the congregation was the Dorcas group that Geneva Westhafer organized to meet the needs of bereaving families. The Agape Fellowship, which served the older women in the congregation, met monthly for years from the 1970s for a luncheon, usually served by the "Kitchen Angels", and enjoyed fellowship, Bible study, and crafts.[42]

The Women of the Church sponsored parties for patients at Western State Hospital, gave Christmas baskets to needy families, provided assistance to the Shenandoah Club, especially when it was a tenant of the church, and decorated the church for special events such as Christmas with the poinsettia tree and the Chrismon tree, and at Easter with lilies as memorials. The women also made possible Second's participation in the ROCK program in the summer, an interdenominational summer Bible school and fun program for underprivileged children that the downtown churches operated.[43]

The circles continued to meet, as they had for decades, for monthly fellowship, worship, Bible study, and programs. The twelve circles that flourished when the church had nearly 1,000 members were down to half that number in the 1980s, but it is important to note that Second Church had the largest number of active circles of any church in the Presbytery. To mark the sixtieth anniversary of the Women of the Church in May 1983, the organization sponsored a Mother/Daughter Banquet. Meredith Sanger traveled 200 miles to attend the event with her mother Lucille Sanger.[44]

A significant change took place in the structure of the women's organization. The last person to be president of the Women of the Church was Betty Landes who served in 1988. The next year, the organization became Presbyterian Women, and its elected leader was no longer the president but a moderator. Kitty Sensabaugh was the first moderator of Presbyterian Women at Second Church.

For much of the 1980s there was a significant emphasis at Second Church on the problem of hunger in the world. A program used for a number of years was the two cents a meal plan that came from presbytery and synod. The request here was for each family to reduce its own expenditure on food by two cents per meal per person and to contribute that amount to the fund to aid the hungry around the world. The congregation also operated a food closet for persons in the local community who needed help, and participated in Staunton-Augusta County Relief Association, the interdenominational organization that assisted local poor. The long-standing participation in One Great Hour of Sharing produced an annual offering from the congregation for worldwide relief. In 1987, for example, this was $1,818.

As the 1980s wore on, the membership statistics at Second Church continued to slide downward. The 423 members in 1984 had declined to 390 at the end of 1985, then to 382 at the end of the following year, 365 at the end of 1987, 350 at the close of 1988, and 327 as the decade came to a close. This was a decline of twenty-five percent in just five years, and a reduction of almost fifty percent since 1976. At the same time, the congregation had to shoulder a greater financial burden. The total expenditures were over $130,000. The benevolent budget was over $28,000, and the pastor's salary had passed $22,000 by 1985. This meant an annual contribution of some $333 per member.

In 1985 Second Church honored a man who had devoted most of his adult life to the congregation since coming there in 1934 from North Carolina. The Session elected A.M. "Mack" Woodside as honorary Elder Emeritus in June, one of the few persons so honored in the history of the church. The resolution accompanying the honor reminded that Woodside had become a deacon in 1942 and an elder in 1943. He had served so long as Clerk of Session that he was known in presbytery as "the most knowledgeable clerk." In September, the congregation presented him a plaque at the morning service, and the entire congregation honored him at a "roast" that brought a great sense of community camaraderie over shared memories of half a century.[45]

Another celebratory occasion was the banquet marking the 110th anniversary of the church in November 1985. This came after the Session had talked for some months of ways to "jazz up" the activities of the church to get more involvement of youth and children. But in the midst of the celebration, there was grave concern about the future of the church. The Session was just then preparing the budget for 1986 and struggling with motions to eliminate the consultant services of a Director of Christian Education, to reduce the custodian's wages, not to give the minister a raise, to eliminate the *Presbyterian Survey* magazine for members, to end the athletic program, and cancel funding for the Agape fellowship. The question of costly asbestos removal, at possibly $60,000, was also a worry.[46] Financial worries continued into 1988 and 1989. Although the audit showed that the books were properly kept, many questions surfaced about financial oversight, especially in the light of several thousand dollars that could not be accounted for, and plans were laid for improved reporting and management.[47]

By January 1986, Session had decided that a task force on the future of Second Presbyterian was needed. Steve Landes, one of the new, young members of Session, presented a plan for the task force. The group was to comprise two members of Outreach and Membership Committee, two from Women of the Church, five elected from the congregation, and the pastor as ex-officio. Teams would be organized to visit all members of Second Church to survey their ideas, and report back in June 1986 with recommendations. David Miller and Jo Peduto would represent Session, Mary Rainey and Kitty Sensabaugh from Women, Albert Gibson and Patsy Easley from Outreach and Membership, and from the congregation John Burner, Lucille Sanger, Terry Westhafer, Steve Landes, Terry Harmon, and Gennivee Carey.[48]

The task force worked all year in 1986, and presented its report to the congregational meeting in January 1987 with survey results and recommendations. The report indicated a strong desire to make Second a "more inviting" church, and to reach out to new people. In his annual report, Walker challenged the congregation asking if they were ready to be inviting to persons who are different, whose values are different. What, for example, if an unmarried couple living together wanted to join? Would they be accepted? He noted that some of these questions go to the core of the church, but that he would make a new commitment to the congregation, and that if Second really wanted to reach out, he would drop what he was doing to answer any need. The task force recommended a regular planning committee be established to continue to plan for the future of the church.[49]

Walker addressed the theme again in May 1988, recommending a book called *The Inviting Church*. He reminded the congregation of the old motto "The Country Church in the City" as he noted that most Americans now wanted to be in the country away from downtown. "For those who see the downtown as dying, perhaps it says Second Church is poorly placed and out of step with the trends. Maybe. But I like to view it differently: Let's invite our country cousins downtown."[50]

There were high points in the midst of questioning the future of the church. In May 1987 the Cathedral Chimes were dedicated, an addition to the organ made possible by the Memorial Fund at Second Church.[51] The following year the needs of the organ were obvious, and nearly $12,000 was allocated for a major rebuilding of parts. These improvements made possible the beginning of a concert series, starting with an organ concert on May 31, 1989, at which organists from several area Presbyterian churches performed. Eugene Mullins, in commenting on this concert, reminded members of the great organist Marcel DuPré who performed on the organ when it was installed.[52]

One important development that came out of the task force survey and subsequent planning committee work was the establishment of Church Night. This occasion combined some of the features of the old Family Night, but an inexpensive catered dinner replaced the covered dish dinner, added a nursery for children with a special musical Bible study program, and provided the opportunity for all the principal church meetings to take place that evening. The fellowship and the convenience made this a successful new way to do the Lord's work at Second Church.

As the final decade of the twentieth century opened, an important project at Second Church was the complete renovation of the Historical Room under the auspices of the Presbyterian Women. Kitty Sensabaugh chaired this important work. Her committee included Evelyn Beard, Betty Landes, Nellie Reeves, and Beckie Sherwood. They worked with Joseph Johnson of Staunton's T.J. Collins and Son architectural firm. J.B. Wine was the contractor and Robert S. Landes was overseer for the project. The work included design and installation of storage cabinets for archives and exhibit cases for artifacts telling the story of the congregation, its ministers, its missionaries, and its outreach.

The congregation remained hopeful, but the desired growth was not taking place. Many people did not agree with all of the changes that Walker proposed. Some left the church, others were very outspoken. In 1993, Walker resigned his pastorate, and the congregation was prepared to enter the next stage of its development as it looked for a new pastor to lead them into the new millennium.

Chapter Eleven Notes

[1] Scrapbook compiled by Nellie Reeves, 1975-1976.
[2] Miscellaneous articles from *Staunton Leader* throughout 1976 about Agape Fellowship meetings, grouped in Nellie Reeves Scrapbook.
[3] Annual Statistical Report for Presbytery, filed with Session Minutes, February 1967 and January 1977.
[4] The basis for the calculations is The Inflation Calculator at www.westegg.com, a website that uses *Historical Statistics of the United States* (USGPO, 1975) for statistics prior to 1975, and the annual *Statistical Abstracts of the United States* for figures from 1975-2000. The eighty-dollar average per capita donation to the operating expenses in 1967 would have risen to $140 if giving were based only on inflation. That the average increased to $153 shows that the individual donors were exceeding the rate of inflation in their giving to the operating costs of their local church.
[5] Bulletins, 27 June, 4, 18, 25 July, 1, 8, 15, 22 August 1976.
[6] Ibid., 5, 12 September 1976; Howard M. Wilson, *Lexington Presbytery Heritage*, 225, 365.
[7] Session Minutes, 30 January 1977.
[8] Bulletin, 15 December 1976.
[9] Ibid., 23, 20 January, 6 February 1977. The wedding took place on 21 July 1977 and was noted in the Bulletin, 31 July 1977.
[10] Ibid., 30 January, 13 February 1977; Bulletin, 6 February 1977.
[11] Bulletin, 27 June, November 1976.
[12] "Endorsements for the Call" filed with Session Minutes, 15 May 1977.
[13] Bulletin, 11 September 1977.
[14] Session Minutes, 13 July, 17 August, 14 September 1977.
[15] Ibid., 9 October 1977.
[16] Bulletin, 11 September, 2 October 1977.
[17] Julius Melton, *Presbyterian Worship in American: Changing Patterns since 1787* (Richmond: John Knox Press, 1973), 140-148.
[18] Session Minutes, 19 October, 30 November 1977.
[19] Ibid., 19 April, 17 May 1978.
[20] Ibid., 7 December 1977, 18 January, 15 March, 28 June 1978.
[21] Ibid., 28 June, 20 September 1978.
[22] Ibid., 30 May, 27 June, 1, 8, 18 July 1979.
[23] Ibid., 5 September, 21 November 1979.
[24] Bulletin, 28 October, 4, 11 November 1979.
[25] Congregational meetings, 10 June, 30 December 1979.
[26] Session Minutes, 20 July 1983.
[27] Session Minutes, 23 January, 19, 31 March 1979; WOC Activities Scrapbook, 1982-1983, March.
[28] Ibid., 19 Sept. 1984.
[29] Ibid., 16 April, 25 June 1980.
[30] Ibid., 22 October 1980.
[31] Ibid., 18 February, 18 March 1981.
[32] Ibid., 18 March, 22 July 1981, 24 February 1982.

[33] Ibid., 24 February 1982, 18 April 1984.
[34] Memorial to Ray Lawrence St. Clair, Session Minutes, 19 August 1981.
[35] WOC Activities Scrapbook, 1982-1982.
[36] Session Minutes, 18 February 1981, 20 January, 21 April, 18 August 1982, 23 February 1983.
[37] Ibid., 25 January 1984.
[38] Ibid., 18 October, 16 December 1981, 20 January 1982.
[39] WOC Activities Scrapbook, 1982-1983, January.
[40] Ibid., June.
[41] Ibid., March 1982, September 1983.
[42] Ibid., March 1982, January 1983.
[43] Bulletin, 26 July 1987.
[44] WOC Activities Scrapbook, May 1983.
[45] Session Minutes, 26 June, 29 September 1985.
[46] Ibid., 20 February, 15 May, 20 November 1985.
[47] Ibid., December 1989.
[48] Ibid., 17 December 1985, 5, 26 January, 21 May 1986.
[49] WOC Activities Scrapbook, 1987-1988, Annual report 1987
[50] Ibid., Newsletter for May 1988, Pastor's Letter.
[51] Bulletin, 24 May 1987
[52] Bulletin, 15 April 1988; Newsletter for May 1989.

Chapter Twelve
Living in the Present, Looking to the Future

A congregation that has experienced the turmoil of a pastor's resignation under pressure, the divisions among members over difficult issues such as the personality and the integrity of the choir director, and the closing of the congregation-sponsored weekday nursery school after twenty years is a congregation in need of healing.

The procedures and mechanisms of the presbytery came into play in assisting Second Church over its difficult times. The Commission on Ministry worked carefully with the Session and the congregation throughout the process of termination of the pastoral relationship with Dennis Walker. Both the committee chair, the Reverend Tom Biggs, and the executive secretary of the Shenandoah Presbytery, Homer Pfifer, Jr., assisted, as did a retired local minister, the Reverend Clifford Douglas "Kip" Caldwell, who moderated several meetings.[1] As often happens in times of turmoil and strong emotion such as these were, several members of Session resigned and one of them even transferred membership to another denomination.[2]

A schedule of supply ministers was established for July and August 1993, including Millard Stevens, Roy Patteson, and Lundy Barkley. Shenandoah Presbytery delegated Beth Smith, an elder and Vice Chairperson of the Commission on Ministry as the commission's liaison with Second Church. Her function was to help Session assess where they were as a church, to explain the qualities they needed in an interim minister, and to clarify the responsibilities of a Pulpit Nominating Committee. Session was to select the interim, but the congregation, as usual, would elect the pastor. Phifer strongly recommended that Session opt for a full-time interim, considering the circumstances of the congregation. Session chose the Reverend Frank Preston as full-time interim for a term of twelve months.[3]

Preston began his work in September 1993. Early in 1994, the Session approved several important expenditures for improving the comfort of worship and the preservation of the building. One was upholstering the seats and backs of the pews, a project that Anita Haessly headed. Associated Church Furnishings installed the attached cushions and backs in July 1994. Another improvement was the air conditioning of the sanctuary, and the third was placing Flexon protection on the stained glass windows on the lower side of the building on Lewis Street.[4]

In the area of church music, two important steps were taken at that same time. One was to engage a new organist and choir director to replace Roger Sethman, who had served in that capacity from January 1993. Ted Grudzinski was chosen for the post of Director of Music at a starting salary of $8,700 on a six-month trial basis. Linda Lickliter presented the other proposal to Session in March 1994 when she reported that a twenty-five handbell starter set would cost $4,000. Grudzinski indicated willingness to work with the hand bell committee to integrate the bells with the choir and music program. Session voted in May 1994 to purchase Schulmerich handbells, using a gift of $1,500 from the Presbyterian Women and up to $3,000 from the Memorial Fund. With improvements in the music program, the choir needed to look its best, so Session voted another $3,000 from the Memorial Fund to purchase new choir robes.[5]

By the time Preston's year was half over, Session voted to ask the Commission on Ministry for permission to form a

Pastor Nominating Committee. Biggs and Smith returned to Staunton to review the nomination process that was in place in the churches of Shenandoah Presbytery, and the special provisions for a church such as Second to work with its COM liaison. The new search process required a self-study of the congregation, which Preston agreed to assist in preparing, and could generally be expected to cost the church $4,000 – $5,000. The congregation met in May to elect a Pastor Nominating Committee. Those elected to the committee were Evelyn Beard, Betty Clemmer, Alan Minnick, Kay Moyer, Mary Rainey, and D.W. Sensabaugh. The elected committee chose Mary Rainey as its chairperson, and then set about its slow and deliberate task. Meanwhile, Session voted to extend Frank Preston's contract for another twelve months.[6]

A fortunate windfall for the congregation occurred in June 1994 when Session received word that the Emma Ramsey estate bequest to Second Church amounted to $115,000. Session sought the advice of an investment specialist on how to make the most of its investments. Session decided to place this and another smaller bequest from Lola Sites with the Shenandoah Presbyterian Corporation at 8.1 percent return.[7]

When Grudzinski's six-month review took place, the Session decided to renew his contract and to raise his salary to $9,200. He played an important role in organizing the Reformation Festival Chorus Concert on October 30, 1994, with eleven churches participating and a chorus of 125 voices, including the choir of Second Church. Music for the event cost $916, but Session felt sure that some reimbursement would come from the freewill offering at the concert and from the other participating churches. However, when Grudzinski requested another $750 to engage a small orchestra to assist for the occasion, Session balked and refused the funding. Session spent some time discussing where to donate the offering funds from the fall concert series. The

December concert proceeds were designated for the Augusta Free Clinic.[8]

The Student Loan Fund, which had served the young folk of Second Church so well since the 1920s, was nearly depleted by July 1994. Its balance was a mere $100, so that Session had to borrow from the Contingency Fund in order to make a $500 loan to a deserving student. Part of the problem lay with the fact that so many students in the past had failed to repay their loans. By March 1995, some $8,000 in past due loans had accumulated, with neither students nor their co-signing parents responding to requests for payment.[9]

Preston was unable to remain until a new pastor was chosen. He resigned effective the end of April 1995. The congregation gave a reception for Dr. and Mrs. Preston on April 30, and for Violet Ralston who was leaving the post of church secretary. Session had to decide whether to engage a short-term interim minister or be contented with supply preachers. Consultation with the Commission on Ministry was required, so once more Beth Smith worked with the elders, both in their decision, and in reviewing the exit interview with Preston. The Session determined to use supply ministers, as the Pastor Nominating Committee appeared to be near the end of its work. The Reverend Messrs. Ralph Bucy, J. Hoge Smith, Jr., John Timberlake, Thomas E. Henderson, and Chalmers Goshorn helped until late August. Before the end of June, Mary Rainey reported that the PNC had a candidate and requested that Session call a congregational meeting. The candidate would meet with the Commission on Ministry on June 29 to be examined.[10]

Session met on July 2 to approve the term of call to be offered to Dr. Daniel Steven Williams if he were voted the next pastor. At the congregational meeting on July 9, there were 111 votes for and none opposed to Williams as pastor. At Presbytery meeting on July 25, Commissioner Pete Lindamood led a delegation of forty from Second Church to support Williams.[11]

Daniel Steven Williams, D.D., was installed as pastor in 1995.

Williams had wisely requested that the Pastor Nominating Committee remain active for a year as an advisory body in helping to forge a successful relationship between the congregation and the new pastor. The congregation turned out with great joy to welcome the Williams family to Staunton and to Second Church. He arrived on August 15 and stayed with Bill and Maxine Robertson for a week until the house he and Sharon had selected in Stuarts Draft was ready for them and their two sons, Timothy and Jonathan.[12]

The installation service for the new pastor took place the evening of September 10, 1995, with the Reverend Chalmers Goshorn as the preacher. Participants in the service included the Reverend Joseph Condro, pastor at Bethany Church; Elder Beth Smith from the Commission on Ministry; and Mary Rainey, Kay Moyer, and Mark Robertson from the Pastor Nominating Committee.[13]

At the very first meeting that Williams moderated, he and the Session had to face a difficult personnel situation. The new covenant between the church and the Director of Music had been approved by Session in June. Meanwhile,

Session had received complaints about selections the choir was singing and about the failure to incorporate the chimes into service music. The Director of Music tendered a letter of resignation to the Personnel Committee on June 28, but Session took no action on it. When the Personnel Committee presented the approved covenant to the music director, he had stipulations to present that contrasted with portions of the covenant. When Session voted in July to hold firm on the terms of the covenant, they also decided to accept the letter of resignation, effective September 1, but to give a month's compensation. A representative of the choir thanked Session for its support in the difficult matter.[14]

Charlotte Ralston joined the church staff as secretary the same week that Williams took the helm as pastor. Another personnel change occurred the following month when Doris Miller resigned as Director of Christian Education. Session accepted her decision with regret and referred the matter of whether to fill the post to the Christian Education Committee. The congregation honored Ms. Miller for her work along with Sue Lindamood for her efforts with the *Newsletter* at a reception after Christmas. The Christian Education Committee decided it was important to seek a replacement for Miller.[15]

Meanwhile, the Personnel Committee recommended the employment of Debbie O'Neil as Director of Music at a salary of $8,500 plus $500 for conferences and in-service training. She was pleased to work out an arrangement so that the handbells and the chimes would be used alternately in the Sunday morning worship services, and formed a handbell ensemble for teens. She also used her training opportunities to good advantage, attending conferences of Presbyterian music leaders in Albuquerque and in Winchester.[16]

Three other women received special recognition for their contributions to the life of Second Church in the late 1990s. Inez Coffey and Dot Cason were honored for their

Former Session member and Delegate from Augusta County to the Virginia legislature, Steve Landes presents a certificate to Lucille Sanger in recognition of her service.

faithful keeping of the nursery during the Sunday worship service through the donation of a rocking chair for the nursery bearing a plaque with their names. Lucille Sanger's sixty-three years teaching Sunday School were recognized when one of the adult classrooms was named the "Lucille Sanger Classroom" and a plaque and photograph of her placed in the room.[17]

Session, at a called meeting in December 1995, engaged Kay Mader as the new Education Consultant. The report in *Second's Chronicles* the next month indicated to the congregation that her areas of responsibility were the training of teachers and providing them resources, assisting the Christian Education Committee to plan special programs such as the Vacation Bible School, and the general support of the Sunday School.[18]

Williams brought a greater sense of organization to the operation of the church than had been the case for some time. The weekly *Bulletin,* which had taken a haphazard look in recent years, got a facelift. Session minutes were kept in a neater, better organized form. New computers and upgraded software were obtained for the secretary and the pastor to enable them to keep up with the times in those aspects of the church's ministry. The conference room in the educational building was converted into a more attractive and commodious office in which the pastor could work and meet with small committees and persons he was counseling. Careful attendance statistics were kept Sunday by Sunday, and the church roll carefully reviewed in order to have an accurate understanding of who were active members and contributors to the work of Second Church. Attendance at the Sunday service in spring and fall averaged around 145, with dips in winter and summer, then peaks approaching 200 for special occasions such as Mother's Day, Christmas, and Easter. The new pastor planned ahead, and presented his schedule for eight communion services a year in advance for Session's approval. He was also conscientious about seeing that communion was taken regularly to members who were homebound.[19]

The new pastor started his regular series of Bible studies right away, and has continued every year with a Bible course on a specific theme. Another method he employed to teach his flock has been through his monthly letter in *Second's Chronicles*. This offered him the opportunity to comment, instruct, admonish, and guide as the occasion warranted on such diverse topics as congregational government, the destructive power of rumors and gossip, the role of music in contemporary worship, issues facing the General Assembly, fiscal worries of the Session, and options for the organ, along with a host of other topics. The pastor could relax and have fun too. The congregation enjoyed the Christmas Open House that Dan and Sharon Williams shared with them. It was Pastor Williams who started the annual trip to see the Baltimore Orioles play too.

The officers of Second Church have a long tradition of outstanding care of the church property. Their attention to these details was no less committed in the 1990s. In addition to the creation of a new pastor's study after Williams's arrival, and the work in the sanctuary just prior to that, a memorial gift from the Katherine Wimer estate made it possible to have a "bride's room," later called the Hospitality

Room. Steeple repair was another necessity, and the paint job that topped it off, with painters delivered by crane, captured the attention of the local press.[20] Another property matter seemed to crop up with regularity. That was the destruction of the church sign at the corner of Lewis and Frederick as out-of-control automobiles plowed into it. This occurred in October 1995, causing the Session's property committee to seek bids on repair. When the problem occurred again in the spring of 1996, the property committee installed three steel posts filled with concrete, angled outward to the street to protect the sign, and hid the posts behind a picket fence. The church sign has not been destroyed since. The painting of the exterior of the church in 1999 for $27,000 was an important job completed not only for routine upkeep, but also to have the church looking its best for the 125th anniversary in 2000.[21]

It could be fairly said that the 1990s was a decade in which Second Church gave exceptional and consistent attention to the problem of hunger, both on a worldwide scale and right in their own back yard in the Staunton-Augusta community. The "2 cents a meal plan" in which the congregation had participated for many years changed its name to Hunger Offering and urged participation at the four cents a meal level. This project was a responsibility of the Mission Committee, which was eager to produce greater participation in the offering, collected the last Sunday of each month. One of the most faithful and stalwart members of Second Church, Nellie Reeves, received special recognition in the March/April 1995, issue of *Shenandoah Seeds* for her contributions to the relief of hunger. Year after year, the annual offering for One Great Hour of Sharing, often taken on Maundy Thursday and Good Friday, went in part to the relief of hunger. The ecumenical offering, collected annually in many Protestant churches since its founding in 1949, enabled Second Church to participate in projects around the world.[22]

Not only did the emphasis on hunger relief remain high, but also several other types of outreach in the local community characterized the congregation of Second Church. Session approved the use of church facilities for a regular Alcoholics Anonymous meeting, to the Pregnancy Help Center for Parent Training classes, and by the First Night of Augusta program for a community-wide, alcohol-free New Year's Eve celebration.[23] The Mission Committee undertook in 1996 to make the congregation more aware of need in the world by focusing Family Night programs on local work. Family Night programs included the weekday religious education program that Second Church had supported for sixty years, Valley Mission, and hunger in the Valley.

Another local outreach project in which Second Church participated in the mid-1990s was the "Bucket of Nails" for Habitat for Humanity. Members could buy a nail for just fifty cents or buy three for a dollar from fellow members stationed at the church doors. In this way, funds were raised to help build a Habitat house. Members of Second Church helped Habitat in several other ways. In 1997, the pastor answered phones for the WTON Habitat for Humanity radiothon. In 1999, several Staunton area churches banded together to build four houses in a large area cleared on W. Johnson and Green Streets. One was the Presbyterian house, and when the call went out for forty to sixty workers to frame and roof the houses, members of Second were among those who answered.[24]

When a serious flood swept through the Windy Cove area in Bath County and damaged the church and its furnishings severely in July 1997, the Mission Committee invited the Windy Cove pastor, Rob Sherrard, to speak about the damage at a Church Night supper. The Mission Committee challenged the members of Second Church to raise $3,000 to $5,000 for Windy Cove. While the members did not meet that goal, they rallied and collected $1,800 for the beleaguered church.[25]

Another area in which the congregation reached out to the world's needy has been through the programs and special offerings of the Presbyterian Women. Many of these, such as the Blanket Offering, taken annually in February, and the Birthday Offering, have a long tradition. The women often raised nearly a thousand dollars for Blanket Offering, at five dollars a blanket. The Birthday Offering celebrates the founding of the women's organization throughout Presbyterian churches by selecting four or five major projects to support. In 1997, for example, the Birthday Offering was divided among the Duvall Home in Glenwood, Florida, the Rural Ministry Project on Johns Island, South Carolina, Villa International in Atlanta, and the Animal Husbandry Project in Cameroon. In 1999, the beneficiaries of the Birthday Offering were a women's resource shelter in State College, Pennsylvania, First Light in Birmingham, Alabama, the Fort Thompson Reservation in South Dakota, and a conference and training center for Presbyterian women in East Africa at Mombasa, Kenya.[26]

The women of the congregation, through their formal organization called Presbyterian Women, have traditionally contributed much that the members of the congregation recall as the warmth and love and caring that makes Second Church so special to them. The Agape Fellowship, which was reorganized and revitalized in 1998 is one example of this caring. Another is the project that Linda Lickliter started in 1995 to prepare boxes of "goodies" — cookies, nuts, and candy — to send to the college students in the congregation as they entered exam week each December.

As spring arrives each year, the Presbyterian Women really come into their own. The "Burst Into Spring" Luncheon with its hat show was a feature for most of the 1990s and attracted nearly 100 attendees for fun, fellowship, fashion, and fine food. Palm Sunday brings the annual Palm Sunday luncheon after the service, at which the famous lamb cake is the favorite feature. The flowers on the communion table for Palm Sunday are always given by the Presbyterian Women in memory of those members who have died since the previous Palm Sunday. Among those remembered in 1997 was "our dear friend Sue Walker," wife of former pastor Dennis Walker, who died of cancer in June 1996. Her many friends at Second remembered her for snapping and sharing photos of all the church's social events and fellowship gatherings and for starting the Advent booklet, among many other activities. The annual show of red geraniums decorating the church for Pentecost is another evidence of the thoughtfulness of the women. The red geraniums are then planted outside to provide a brilliant touch of color on a busy corner and a constant reminder of the gift of the Spirit.[27]

The women continued to honor special members of their group with Honorary Life Memberships for their exceptional service over many years. Gennivee Carey, honored in 1996, had been a member for fifty-nine years and leader of Circle 1 for many years. Eileen Brown was another so honored. In 1996 the women obtained a plaque to which each name plate could be affixed, and which offered public display as a reminder of the honorees. Another woman in the congregation honored in 1996 was Martha Wilkerson who stepped down from the coordinator's job for Meals on Wheels after ten years in that demanding position helping so many other volunteers to fill a need for area elderly. In the late 1990s, two women in the congregation, one a lifelong active member and the other a late teen, had the opportunity to participate in service projects abroad.

Betty Landes took part in the Windy Cove project in Haiti, and collected tee shirts, toys, books, and school supplies to take with her. Her vivid account helped members understand something of the lives of the people in one of the world's poorest nations. In 1999 Kristin Hagerstrom was chosen to participate in the presbytery youth mission trip to Puerto Rico, and on her return told of her experiences at a church night supper.[28]

Nonetheless, membership statistics were still low, income not as good as desired, and budget problems substantial. Membership held steady at 257 in 1996 and 258 in 1997. By the end of 1996 the Stewardship Committee reported that pledges amounted to $118,619. Committees were ordered to trim their budget requests by fifteen percent. By January 1997, Session concluded to let the custodian go, with a one-month separation package, and to engage Paul and Shirley Wolfe to handle that work in exchange for the amount that they would have pledged.[29]

In April 1997, the Commission on Ministry of Shenandoah Presbytery made its regular triennial visit to Second Church and met with Session. The discussion focused on the questions, "What are we presently celebrating about Second Church?" What are the areas that need the most attention, what are the church and weekday programs, and finally, what is the mission of Second Church and where will it be in ten years? At the next Session meeting, elders received a copy of *The Inviting Church: A Study of New Members Assimilation* for review and discussion. Session decided, starting in June of 1997, to open meetings for several months with a discussion of one or two chapters of the book *How to Build a Magnetic Church* by Herb Miller.[30]

There was little about the 1998 statistics to cheer. The number of active members continued to decline, from 258 in 1997 and 205 in 1999. At the same time, in spite of efforts to freeze spending, costs continued to rise. The individual contributions amounted to $148,223 out of a total budget of $198,505. The church looked to receiving $17,600 in rental income. However, when the district office of the United Methodist Church left its longtime quarters at Second, the loss of this principal tenant was a budgetary blow.[31]

An issue that pulled the congregation together, but not without considerable explanation and education, was the condition of the organ as the twentieth century drew to a close. In April 1997 the Session learned of the immediate need for organ repairs. After considerable discussion, the problem was referred to the Property Committee to investigate and make recommendations. That group understood its duty to look at the problem broadly and consider whether repair alone would suffice, or whether a much more substantial project — rebuilding the organ — was needed, or whether an entirely new instrument was required. When word got out that the committee and pastor were going to Pennsylvania to see a digital organ, the rumor flew around that the church was going to get rid of its Möller organ and install a new digital instrument. The pastor had to employ his skilled pen in *Second's Chronicles* to remind that the committee was fulfilling its responsibility to gather all the necessary facts so that Session could make a responsible decision.[32]

Session voted in November 1997 to rebuild the Möller organ. The next step was to solicit bids from several companies. These were on hand by the January 1998 meeting. At the annual congregational meeting on February 22, the pastor reported that Session had chosen Shenandoah Organ Studio for the work. The project would last ten months and cost $56,900. Already the Session had $19,000 in hand, but the congregation would be invited to pledge toward the remainder. By mid-June 1998, some sixty-one persons had pledged $19,000. Robert Lent was the principal for the company. Session engaged Robert Moody as an overseer to work with the committee of Jo Peduto, Pam Snyder, Dick Hippeard, Danny O'Neil, Debbie O'Neil as Director of Music, and Dorothy Kiger. Hippeard dropped out and was replaced by Elder Marion Samuels. The right hand chamber was done first, then the left-hand chamber, and then the console was fitted. The first stage was to be finished by mid-September.[33]

The completion of the organ restoration was a clear statement of the significance that a high quality music ministry has had at Second Church for at least seventy-five years. Although the choir, like the congregation, had decreased in size by the close of the twentieth century, it maintained its excellence. D.W. Sensabaugh and Kenneth Sensabaugh are lifelong choir members and others have sung with the choir for more than forty years. Louis Van Fossen's special solos have brought inspiration to hundreds of members.

By the time the year 2000 rolled around, the congregation, with its beautifully painted exterior and completely rebuilt organ, was ready to celebrate its 125th anniversary. The motto for the celebration year, "Doorkeepers of the Millennium: Reflecting on the Past . . . Preparing for the Future," was the work of Evelyn Beard and Mary Rainey. An active 125th Anniversary Committee was named and charged with planning and carrying out all aspects of the celebration. Its co-chairpersons were Pam Snyder, who had special oversight of worship and music and Evelyn Beard as historian. Other committee members were Susan Johnson, bulletin; Betty Clemmer and Betty Landes, decorations; Dick Robinson, property issues; Martha Wilkerson, invitations; Don Cobble, meal and public relations; Beckie Sherwood, finance; Linda Lickliter and Nancy Swisher, hostesses and hosts.

Two mementos of the church were available to mark the occasion, a brass Christmas tree ornament featuring a cut-out shape of the church and pictures of the church in two sizes. In addition, Session voted to have a complete history of the church written, although it could not be researched, written, and printed in time for the anniversary date in November.

More than thirty-one individuals and families made outright contributions or gave them in memory or in honor of loved ones toward the costs of the anniversary celebration. The Historical Room, which had been extensively renovated in 1992, received additional gifts at the time of the 125th anniversary, making possible re-painting, improvements to the cabinets, and new draperies. A portrait of founding member, longtime Elder and Sunday School Superintendent, Jed Hotchkiss was given by Sharon and George Goodrow in honor of her parents, Kenneth and Lois Sensabaugh. Betty Wall's bronzed organ slippers were given by her daughter Peggy Barbour.

Two special dates were set aside to mark the occasion. On Saturday, November 11 at 3 p.m., there was an organ re-

The Historical Room was renovated as part of the 125th anniversary celebration.

cital and rededication of the rebuilt organ. The organists who played were Robert Lent of Shenandoah Organ Studio that rebuilt the organ, David Shue, Robert Moody, and Howard Hanson, acting music director for Second Church. A reception followed the recital. On Sunday, November 12, at the 11 a.m. festive worship service, the pastor officiated and the former pastor, Julius Garbett, preached. A catered luncheon followed the service at which time dozens of persons who came home to Second Church reminisced about the fellowship and fun they shared in the past.

The members of Second Church look to the future with courage and optimism as they enter the new millennium. They are under no illusion that growth is a goal easily attained. Like other downtown churches in Staunton, especially First Church, Central United Methodist, and Emmanuel Episcopal, they take great pleasure in the warm and caring community that they are. The members give more generously of their time and their treasure than is often the case at larger churches. They are a

125TH Anniversary

1875-2000

Doorkeepers of the Millennium

Reflecting on the Past...Preparing for the Future

Second Presbyterian Church

Lewis and Frederick Streets
P.O. Box 175
Staunton, Virginia 24402-0175
(540) 885-8159

The Reverend Dr. Daniel S. Williams
Pastor

The program for the 125th Anniversary worship service.

faith community and they live in the belief that they are trying to respond to God's call and live out the lives to which their Creator has called them.

Chapter Twelve Notes

[1] Session Minutes carefully record the details of this difficult situation. Beginning in July 1992 until at least April 1994, nearly every monthly meeting of that elected governing body deals with some aspect of the issues over the integrity of the choir director, the ineffectiveness of the minister, declining membership and giving, transfer of elders out of the church, a petition circulated in the congregation, and how to face the future once Walker had resigned.
[2] Session minutes, 16 June, 22 September 1993.
[3] Ibid., 21 July, 25 August 1993.
[4] Ibid., 23 February, 22 March 1994.
[5] Ibid., 22 February, 6 and 22 March, 27 April, 25 May, 22 June 1994.
[6] Ibid., 27 April, 22 June 1994.
[7] Ibid., 22 June 1994, 19 February 1995.
[8] Ibid., 25 September, 28 October, 28 December 1994.
[9] Ibid., 27 July 1994, 22 March 1995.
[10] Ibid., 22 March, 26 April, 24 May, 21 June 1995; *Bulletin,* 23 April, 7, 14 May, 4 June, 16 July 1995, 13 August 1995.
[11] Ibid., 2, 26 July 1995; Congregational Meeting Minutes, 9 July 1995; *Bulletin,* 30 July 1995.
[12] *Bulletin,* 6, 20 August 1995.
[13] Ibid., 10 September 1995.
[14] Session Minutes, 21 June, 26 July, 30 August, 1995.
[15] Ibid., 27 September, 25 October 1995.
[16] Session Minutes, 29 November 1995; *Bulletin,* 26 November 1995; and *Second's Chronicles,* September 1996.
[17] Session Minutes, 23 October 1996, 23 April 1997.
[18] *Second's Chronicles,* January 1966.
[19] Session Minutes, passim.
[20] Ibid., 19 June, 20 November 1996.
[21] Ibid., 25 October, 29 November 1995; *Second's Chronicles,* April 1996, May 1999.
[22] Session Minutes, 19 February, 22 March 1995.
[23] Ibid., 26 April, 25 October 1995, 24 January 1996
[24] *Bulletin,* 16 March 1997; Presbyterian Women, notebook, 1999.
[25] Ibid., 22 March, 29 November 1995, 26 March, 23 April, 24 September, 21 October 1997; *Second's Chronicles,* September 1997.
[26] *Bulletin,* 18 May 1997, May 1999.
[27] Presbyterian Women notebook, 1996 (April, May), 1997 (April), 1999 (April).
[28] Ibid., 1996 (June), 1999 (April).
[29] Session Minutes, 18 December 1996, 22 January 1997.
[30] Ibid., 23 April, 18 June, 27 August, 24 September, 21 October 1997.
[31] Statistics for year ending 31 December 1998, filed with Session Minutes, 4 January 1998; Presbyterian Women notebook, 1999.
[32] *Second's Chronicles,* September, October, December 1997.
[33] Session Minutes, 4 January, 1 February, 22 February 1998; Congregational Meeting Minutes, 22 February 1997.

SECOND PRESBYTERIAN CHURCH
P.O. BOX 175
STAUNTON, VIRGINIA 24402
(540) 885-8159

CHURCH ROSTER
July, 2002

Adkison, Mr. & Mrs. Herman G.(Irene)
Armstrong, Mr. & Mrs. Randall W.(Linda)
Atkinson, Mrs. L. E. (Tillie)
Baber, Mrs. Sheldon E. (Helen)
Bahrs, Mr. Ken B., Jr.
Baylor, Mrs. Claudia
Beard, Mr. & Mrs. Richard T. (Evelyn)
Bell, Mr. Dwight Joseph
Brand, Mrs. William F. (Virginia)
Brooks, Mrs. Nancy T.
Brown, Mr. Larry A.
Cain, Mr. & Mrs. Homer (Evelyn)
Carey, Jr., Mr. & Mrs. H. Maitland (Gennivee)
Casiday, Mrs. Trenton B.(Betty)
Cason, Ms. Dorothy
Cason, Mrs. H. R. (Hazel)
Clemmer, Mrs. Burness C. (Loretta)
Clemmer, Mr. & Mrs. Willis (Betty)
Cobble, Mr. & Mrs. Donald (Sarah)
Coffey, Miss Inez
Cook, Mrs. Donna
Craig, Jr., Mrs. John H. (Virginia)
Crickard, Mrs. Stanley A.(Frances)
Crosby, Mr. C. M.
Culpen, Mrs. Richard (Ruby)
Dale, Mr. & Mrs. Bobby E.(Charlotte)
Dale, Mr. Cory
Dale, Mr. Randy
Davies, Mrs J. B. (Elizabeth)
Dice, Mr. Harry B., III
Dice, Mr. Larry M.
Dice, Jr., Mr. & Mrs. Harry B. (Shirley)
Duken, Mrs. Elaine

Dull, Mrs. Rachel
Easley, Mr. Andrew
Easley, Mr. & Mrs. Brannock (Patsy)
Edney, Mrs. Felecia
Farrar, Mrs. Bland W. (Aurelia)
Fields, Mrs. Jo C.
Flower, Mr. & Mrs. Earl G. (Jean)
Flower, Mr. Frederick C.
Folk, Miss Lori
Folk, Mr. Muzon
Fulk, Mrs. Patty Arner
Gardner, Mary
Gaunce, Mrs. Robert C. (Mary Margaret)
Gibson, Mr. & Mrs. Albert M.(Leatrice)
Gilbert, Mrs. Louise
Gregory, Miss Margaret C.
Grover, Mrs. Ruth
Haessly, Mr. & Mrs. William J.(Anita)
Hagerstrom, Kristen
Hermanson, Mrs. Kim Kelley
Herold, Mr. & Mrs. Warren G. (Mamie)
Hicklin, Miss Shirley
Hippeard, Mr. & Mrs. Preston C.(Talitha)
Hippeard, Scott Dr. & Mrs. (Lisa)
Hippeard, Miss Shari Lynn
Hite, Mrs. J. G. (Virginia)
Hodge, Jr., Mr. J. Walter
Holsinger, Kathryn
Hutchens, Mrs. A. P. (Sarah)
Hutchens, Mr. & Mrs. Harry E. (Katherine)
Jack, Mrs. Hattie H.
Jack, Mr. & Mrs. William E. (Evelyn)
Jenkins, Linda
Johnson, Mr. & Mrs. Richard (Susan)
Jones, Mrs. Lillian
Julian, Mrs. Edith
Kelley, Mrs. Francis W. (Helen)
Kelly, Sgt. M. Scott
Kesterson, Mrs. Margaret C.
Kiger, Mrs. L. J. (Dorothy)
Kincheloe, Chris

Kincheloe, Mrs. Jack (Edith)
Kincheloe, Mr. Stephen R. (Linda)
King, Andrea Miss
King, Mr. & Mrs. David R. (Teresa W.)
King, Rachel Miss
Knibbs, Mrs.George (Ruby)
Lamb, Mr. Ernest D.
Landes, Mr. & Mrs. Robert (Betty)
Lickliter, Miss Ashley
Lickliter, Mrs. Howard C. (Linda)
Lightner, Mr. & Mrs. Robert (Lelia)
Lindamood, Mr. & Mrs. Howard (Sue)
Long, Mrs. Karen Kincheloe
Lyle, Mrs. Florence J.
Lynn, Mrs. William T. (Mary)
Mader, Mr. & Mrs. James E. (Kay)
Mader, Mr. & Mrs. Louis F. (Lucille)
Marcum, Mr. & Mrs. James
Martin, Mrs. Hilda
Mason, Mrs. Darlene
McCarthy, Mrs. Aileen F.
McDearmon, Mr. Chad
McNamara, Mrs. Mary
Miller, Mr. & Mrs. David F. (Carolyn)
Miller, Mrs. Frederick (Doris P.)
Minnick, Mr. Alan
Minnick, Mrs. Brenda
Minnick, Mr. Heath
Mitchell, Mr. Wade
Moore, Mr. Brannen
Moore, Mr. & Mrs. Harry (Sondra)
Morris, Mr. & Mrs. Robert L. (Barbara)
Moyer, Mr. & Mrs. Macon (Kay)
Moyer, Mr. Matthew
Moyer II, Mr. & Mrs. Macon A. (Beth)
Mullenax, Miss Amy
Mulllenax, Mrs. Eugene E. (Doris)
Mullins, Mrs. E. E. (Juanita)
O'Neil, Dr. & Mrs. Danny (Debbie)
Patterson, Mr. Thomas P.
Paul, Mrs. Jane

Pfeiffer, Jr., Mr. & Mrs. Curtis E., Jr.(Florence)
Phillips, Mrs. William (Catherine)
Rainey, Mrs. Clark (Mary)
Rainey, Mr. Carson
Ramsey, Miss Betty F.
Ramsey, Mr. & Mrs. Marshall (Beth)
Ramsey, Mr. Matthew Ellis (Angie)
Ramsey, Mrs. Roy W. (Wreatha)
Rasmussen, Mrs. Harriet
Ridle, Bob & Ann
Robertson, Mr. Mark
Robertson, Mr. Matthew
Robertson, Mr. & Mrs. William H. (Maxine)
Robinson, Mr. & Mrs. R. R. (Sherrill) (Dick)
Roby, Miss Jane
Rohrer Sr., Mrs. Robert W. (Phyllis)
Routt III, Mr. & Mrs. William K. (Marcette)
Rush, Mrs. Carolyn
Rusmisel, Justin
Rusmisel, Mrs. Melissa
Rusmisel, Mr. Randall A.
Samuels, Mrs. J. Paul (Marion)
Sandidge, Mrs. Laquitta H.
Sanger, Mrs. Lloyd S. (Lucille)
Schaefer, Mr. & Mrs. Jonathan (Stephanie)
Scott, Tanya W.
Sedr, Billy
Sedr, Jr., Mrs. William W. (Debbie)
Selph, Mrs. Jane R.
Selph, Mr. John
Sensabaugh, Mr. D. W.
Sensabaugh, Mr. & Mrs. Kenneth (Lois)
Sheets, Mrs. Paul (Joanna)
Sherwood, Mr. & Mrs. Stewart (Beckie)
Shiflett, Mrs. Lois Ann
Shifflett, Mr. & Mrs. L. V. (Jayne)
Shiflett, Mrs. Patricia E.
Shover, Mr. Carl
Silling, Mr. Richard
Simpson, Mrs. Charles (Louise)
Smiley, Mrs. Charles E. (Geneva)

Smiley, Mrs. Kelly W.
Snyder, Mrs. Patricia (Pam)
Staton, Mrs. Lucille P.
Supringer, Mrs. Brian (Bethany)
Swisher, Mrs. Calvin (Ileen)
Swisher, Mr. Glenn
Swisher, Mr. & Mrs. Hugh (Nancy)
Swisher, Mr. Olen
Swisher, Mrs. Roy C. (Beulah)
Tuttle, Mrs. Robert (Katherine)
Tyree, Mr. & Mrs. Dan (Mary)
Tyree, Mrs. Heather
Updike, Mr. & Mrs. O. Kenneth (Sue)
Van Fossen, Mr. & Mrs. Louis (Betty)
Wagner, Mrs. Albert C. (Frances)
Wallace, Jr., Mr. & Mrs. Joseph L. (Sarah)
Weller, Mr. & Mrs. Ralph W. (Ruth)
Wenger, Mrs. Tracy (Eunice)
Wilhelm, Dr. & Mrs. Howard (Jane)
Wilhelm, Mr. Thomas
Wilkerson, Mrs. Carlyle E. (Martha)
Williams, Mrs. Alma (Polly)
Williams, Dan & Sharon
Williams, Jonatha
Wilson, Henry & Jean
Wimer, Mr. & Mrs. Gary W. (Nita)
Wimer, Mr. Kevin
Wiseman, Mrs. Forrest (Marie)
Woebke, Mr. & Mrs. John (Carolyn)
Wolfe, Mr. & Mrs. Paul H. (Shirley)
Wright, Mr. & Mrs. James E. (Brenda)
Young, Mrs. W. Durwood (Mabel)

Deceased (2002) Members:
Baber, Mrs. Harry (Marie)
Kiger, Mrs. L. J. (Dorothy)
Mullins, Mr. Eugene
Swisher, Mr. Calvin
Valo, Mrs. Sterling

Name Index

A

Adkinson, Herman G. 133, 147
Allen, Mary S. 61
Allen, S. Brown 48, 55, 61, 78, 82, 84
Anderson, James 12
Anderson, Stephen 181
Anne, Queen of England 8
Argenbright, Mrs. Heiskell 67
Argenbright, Newton 60
Augsberger, Myron 180

B

Baker, William E. 18, 23, 24, 25, 26, 27, 30
Baldwin, John B. 31
Baldwin, Mary Julia 28, 49
Baldwin, Susan M. 31
Barbour, Peggy 229
Barger, Baxter 147
Barkley, Lundy 215
Baylor, Howard 134
Beard, Evelyn 201, 212, 217, 229
Beard, Richard T. 162, 163, 166, 201
Bell, David S. 22, 27
Bell, Mardre 180, 182, 184
Bell, Mrs. Mardre 182
Bell, Richard 78, 91
Bell, Richard H. 74
Bell, Richard Henry 74
Bell, Thomas Addison 60, 74, 94, 96, 109
Beltz, William F. 105
Biggs, Tom 215, 217
Bisceglia, J.B. 119
Blair, John 15
Blair, Robert 5
Blakemore, Rumsey S. 82
Bodie, Mrs. W.J. 116
Booker, James Edward 34, 36, 47, 65
Bosserman, L.B. 105
Bosserman, L.B., Jr. 129, 131
Bowen, Margaret 106
Bowman, Gilbert 151
Bowman, J. Rice 30
Bowman, Mrs. O.P. 118
Bradford, Robert C. 168
Brand, Alice 126
Brand, Christian 77

Brand, Louis C. 89, 119, 120, 121
Brand, Martha 126
Brand, Mrs. F.W. 112
Brand, Mrs. W.A. 117, 140
Brand, Ruth 98, 102, 175, 207
Brand, Virginia 121
Brand, W.A. 132, 134
Breitenhirt, B.B. 161
Brice, Edward 5
Bridges, R.W. 147
Bright, Bill 180
Broman, Carl 137
Brown, Frances 207
Brown, Frank 147
Brown, John F. 105, 132, 139, 145, 155, 161, 176, 179, 182
Brown, Mrs. John F. (Eileen) 154, 160, 175, 179, 182, 226
Bucy, Ralph 218
Budge, Ronald H.G. 153
Bumgardner, James 22
Bundy, Helen 104
Burner, John 211
Burnett, Lou Ann 194
Burton, Cecil 98
Burwell, H.W. 66

C

Caldwell, Clifford Douglas "Kip" 215
Calhoun, William 17
Calvin, John 2, 3
Campbell, W.C. 66
Carey, Gennivee 207, 211, 226
Carson, C.C. 108
Cash, Jim 147
Cason, Dick, 147
Cason, Dot 220
Cason, Hazel 201
Cason, Walter 147
Charles I, King of England 5
Charles II, King of England 7
Chester, Saul H. 34
Chittum, Earl 147, 154
Chittum, William McClanahan 93
Christian, Ellen Howison 97
Christian, Robert Elmore 93, 97

238

Clemmer, A.L. 147
Clemmer, Betty 217, 229
Clemmer, W.N. 85
Clemmer, Willis 147
Clinedinst, Charles Gates 93
Cobble, Don 229
Coffey, Inez 220
Coiner, Ronnie 147
Collins, Evelyn 128
Collins, T.J. and Son 132, 212
Condro, Joseph, 219
Cook, Bobby 199
Cox, Delmar Ross 93
Craig, John 13, 16
Craig, John Howard 147
Craig, Mrs. T.C. 117
Crawford, William Anderson 61, 70, 71
Critzer, Ashton 201
Cromwell, Oliver 7
Cullum, A. Douglass 116
Culpin, Richard 147
Culpin, Ricky 147
Cumming, William 41, 42, 45, 46
Cunningham, Robert 5

D

Dabney, Eugene H. 132
Danner, Joe 194
Davis, Watson Emmet 94, 95, 96, 98, 99, 141
Deaver, Guy 133, 176
DeJarnette, Joseph Spencer 67, 77, 78, 93
DeJarnette, Mrs. Joseph Spencer 67, 98
Dennison, John 124
Dice, Harry 133
Dice, Mrs. Frank W. (Irene) 132, 141
Dice, Mrs. Harry 139
Donald, Walter 154
Doyle, Thomas S. 22, 24, 27
Driver, Jesse 70
Driver, Laura 70
Driver, Leta 70
Dubose, Dr. 65
Dudley, A.K. 193
Dudley, Alberta 89
Dull, Augusta N. 143

Dull, Frank 61
Dull, Gus 102
Dull, Mrs. Frank A., Jr. 175
Dull, Rachel 207
Dull, W.D. 74
Dull, William Frank 60, 73
Dunsmore, J.G. 120
DuPré, Marcel 137, 138, 212
Dyer, Donnie 127

E

Easley, Patsy 211
East, William H. 92
Echols, John 24
Edgar, Marguerite 105
Edgar, Morrison McClurkin 90, 93, 94, 102, 105, 120, 137
Edgar, Mrs. M.M. 112
Effinger, J. Frederick 27, 35
Effinger, M. Harvey 22, 24, 26
Effinger, Mrs. Margaret 22, 27
Eggleston, Dr. 77
Elizabeth I, Queen of England 5
Elliott, Mrs. T.R. 173, 178, 189
Elliott, T.R. 189
Ellis, I.M. 108
Erwin, Benjamin 17
Erwin, Holmes 22, 27
Everett, G.D. 22

F

Fauver, Eliza 118
Fix, Mrs. J.W. 118
Flower, Earl 184
Francis, Captain 87
Franck, Cesar 138
Fraser, A.M. 47, 57, 60, 82, 91, 109, 110
Frazier, Charles 74
Frazier, William 25
Freeman, David R. 170
Fretwell, George W. 60, 61, 75

G

Garbett, Julius S. 169, 170, 171, 172, 178, 179, 185, 188, 192, 230
Gardner, J. Carson 134
Gardner, Mary 207
Geiger, William C. 27

Gibson, Albert 211
Gibson, Harold C. 82, 85, 87
Gibson, Leatrice 207
Gilmore, R.C. 58
Glasgow, F.T. 72
Glendy, John 16
Godwin, Mills 194
Gooch, William 12
Goodman, Frank L. 153
Goodrow, George 229
Goodrow, Sharon 229
Goodwin, Susan Hill 106
Goshorn, Chalmers 218, 219
Graham, Billy 180
Grattan, George G. 22
Greene, Mrs. Joe M. 160
Grim, Elizabeth Morrison 106, 201
Grove, W.I. 153
Grudzinski, Ted 216, 217
Guerrant, Dr. 45

H

Haessly, Anita 204, 207, 216
Hagerstrom, Kristin 226
Haines, William Atwell 109
Halderman, Roy 104
Hamilton family 4
Hamilton, James 5
Hamilton, Patrick 2
Hanger, Walter 105
Hanson, Howard 230
Harlowe, Mrs. Carl 160
Harman, Mrs. H.M. 69
Harmon, Terry 211
Harris, Lewis Valentine 94
Harris, Mrs. Dell 118
Harris, Mrs. L.V. 112
Hawes, Alice 37
Hawes, Hattie 37
Hawes, Herbert B. 38
Hawes, Herbert Henry 37, 38, 39, 41, 44
Hawes, Louise 37
Hawes, Mary Virginia 37
Hawes, Samuel 37
Hemp, Mrs. O.C. 118
Hemp, Omri C. 98
Henderson, Thomas E. 218
Henry, Hugh W. 32, 46, 50

Herndon, John 132
Hippeard, Dick 228
Hodge, J. Walter, Jr. 166, 169, 200
Hodge, Walter 147
Hoge, Moses D. 48
Holt, C.A. 35
Holt, Charles A. 55
Holt, Frank Thomas 55, 74, 82, 93
Homerton, J.R. 71
Hoon, Manira 105
Hoover, Bernice 194
Hoover, Herbert 105
Hotchkiss, Jedediah 22, 23, 26, 27, 28, 29, 33, 35, 37, 43, 50, 52. 61, 69, 71, 78, 97, 115, 229
Hotchkiss, Nellie 22, 27, 33
Hotchkiss, Sarah 22, 27
Houser, Ray 141
Howard, Luther 89
Howison, Allan Moore 55, 78
Howison, Ellen Moore 61, 71
Howison, Mrs. A.M. 69, 71, 97
Howison, Robert 17
Hudson, W.E. 109
Hudson, William A. 22, 27
Huffman, Nelson 108
Hughes, Benjamin Franklin 38, 44, 55, 78, 86, 93, 109
Hullihen, W.Q. 61
Hurt, Fleming 152, 157, 159
Hyde, Hal 149
Hyde, W.C.H. 70

I

Irvine, Mrs. John 140
Irwin, David C. 26

J

Jackson, Gen. Thomas "Stonewall" 22, 28
James II, King of England 7
James VI, King (of Scotland, I of England) 5
Jamison, W. Chalmers 167, 169
Jefferson, Thomas 16
Jenkins, Larry 147
Johnson, A.E. 193
Johnson, Joseph 212
Johnson, Susan 229

Jones, H. Boswell, Jr. 204
Jones, John 147
Jones, Owen Gilliam "Buddy" 124
Jordan, Hezekiah 48
Jordan, Mrs. William 31
Jumper, Andrew 179
Junkin, Ebenezer D. 22

K

Keller, Mrs. R.C. 118
Keller, Randolph C. 127, 132
Kelley, J. Luther 132, 134, 170
Kelly, J. Luther 70
Kennedy, Frank Bartley 93, 98, 123, 136
Kennedy, Isa Bishop 123, 136
Kennedy, James R. 193
Ker, James 73
Kerr, Robert 65
Kesterson, Margaret 207
Keyser, Dallas 147
Kiger, Dorothy 152, 228
Kirkpatrick, Elizabeth 175, 207
Kirtland, Lelia G. 89, 119, 121
Knopp, Phillip 147
Knox, John 2, 3, 4

L

Landes, Betty 175, 201, 207, 209, 212, 226, 229
Landes, Robert S. 147, 152, 154, 161, 201, 212
Landes, Steve 211, 221
Lawrence, Alton A. 100
Lawrence, Charles 83, 84, 85, 88, 91, 100
Lee, J.M. 76
Lee, Robert E. 28, 56, 65
Leith, John H. 193
Lent, Robert 228, 230
Lessley, Byron 147
Lessley, John 147
Lewis, Dr. and Mrs. Z.E. 119
Lewis, Frank Bell 140
Lewis, Harry Miles 42, 46, 70, 74, 82, 88, 90, 93, 95
Lewis, John 12, 95
Lickliter, J.M. 35, 37
Lickliter, Linda 216, 225, 229

Lindamood, Pete 218
Lindamood, Sue 220
Link, Mrs. Winfred C. 152, 154, 161
Link, Winfred C. 147, 152, 160, 161
Lohr, Lucille 118
Lotts, James Stuart 93
Louis XIV, King of France 8
Lovegrove, John W. 48
Lucas, Mrs. W.E. 117, 132
Luther, Martin 2
Lynn, Elizabeth 106

M

Mader, Joe 147
Mader, Kay 221
Mader, Lewis 147
Makemie, Francis 10
Marcus, Mrs. Turner 118
Marcus, Virginia 118, 123, 132
Martin, T.J. 49
Mary, Queen of England 8
Masincupp, Elwood 147, 154
Maxwell, C.W. 66
McClure, S. Finley 92
McCorkle, E.W. 58, 95
McCormick, William F. 160
McCoy, Charles D. 22, 23, 27, 30, 31
McCoy, Mrs. M.M. 31
McCue, John 16
McCue, William A. 73
McCullough, Nellie Hotchkiss 44, 48
McCullough, S.T., 48
McCutchan, H. Newton 93, 94
McDonough, Mary 22
McGuffin, Charles Robert 82, 93, 94
McLaurin, Alma 90
Meisner, Charlene 206
Meisner, Craig 205, 206
Messiaen, Olivier, 138
Middlekauf, R.L. 89
Middleton, Nellie 205
Miller, David 147, 211
Miller, Doris 220
Miller, Fred 145, 147
Miller, Herb 227
Miller, Mrs. Marvin 128
Minnick, Alan 217

Mitchell, Nellie 184, 207
Mitchell, Wade 129, 131
Montgomery family 4
Montgomery, John 17
Moody, Robert 228, 230
Morris, R.D. 116
Morris, Robert 147
Morrison, C.K. 105, 116, 121
Morrison, Mrs. C.K. (Rose) 117, 118, 140, 141
Morriss, Woody 203
Morton, Arthur Sydnor 78, 85, 93
Morton, Mrs. T.C. 69
Morton, Thomas Colgate 33, 35, 41, 46, 55, 56, 62, 73
Mosely, Randolph Talcott 85, 88
Moyer, Kay 217, 219
Mullins, Eugene E. "Gene" 165, 182, 194, 198, 212
Mullins, Juanita 129, 182, 201, 207
Munro, Robert 7
Murray, J.J. 165, 166
Murray, James 22, 26

N

Neel, Donald 186
Norman, Mary Virginia 207
Northrup, Carolyn 188

O

Olivero, Peter 180
O'Neil, Danny 228
O'Neil, Debbie 220, 228

P

Palmer, A. Mitchell 85
Pancake, Frank R. 186
Pancake, Mrs. Frank R. 186
Parker, Freeman 135
Parker, Freeman B. 151
Parrish, Calvin 147
Patterson, B. Craig 52
Patteson, Roy K. 193, 215
Peduto, Jo 211, 228
Penn, William 11
Pfifer, Homer, Jr. 215
Piland, Ralph Malcolm 166, 167
Poarch, Martha E. 188

Potter, Richard 151
Pratt, John W. 39
Pratt, Maria 51, 68
Preston, Frank 216, 218
Prestwood, Mrs. Cecil 118
Pruitt, Hortense 122
Putney, Mrs. L.L. 98

R

Rainey, Mary 211, 217, 219, 229
Ralston, Charlotte 220
Ralston, Violet 218
Ralston, Walter 147
Ramkey, William H. 161, 162
Ramsey, Elsie 167
Ramsey, Emma 217
Ramsey, Francis M. 133, 52, 165
Ramsey, Mrs. C. Russell 175, 184
Ramsey, Mrs. J.G.M. 166
Ramsey, Russell 147
Rankin, Charlotte 202
Reeves, Nellie 175, 191, 204, 207, 212
Reid, Donnie 147
Reid, Floyd 147
Reid, Marshall 147
Reinhold, Bill 206
Reinhold, Ginny 206
Renalds, Jouette O. 189
Reubush, Mrs. Ward 180
Richardson, W.T. 34
Roberson, Margaret "Peggy" 204
Robertson, Bill 219
Robertson, Emmett G. 93
Robertson family 100
Robertson, Mark 219
Robertson, Maxine 219
Robertson, Mrs. Oliver W. 86, 87, 100
Robertson, Oliver Walker 87, 93
Robertson, Reta 100
Robinson, Richard 202, 229
Roosevelt, Franklin D. 115, 122
Rosebro, John R. 92
Rosebro, John W. 27
Ross, Preston A. 49
Rowan, Helen 134
Ruffner, William Henry 28

S

Sadler, Mrs. B.S. 117
Samuels, Marion 228
Sanger, Lloyd 147
Sanger, Lucille 152, 175, 185, 207, 208, 211, 221
Sanger, Meredith 208
Sanger, Mrs. Lloyd A. 152
Sanger, Sammy 147
Scott, Agnes Morton 56, 66, 71
Scott, Annie Brook 56
Scott, Charles C. 71
Scott, John A. 56
Scott, John A., Jr. 66
Scott, Littleton E. 65
Scott, Nannie 66
Scott, William N. 55, 56, 57, 60, 62, 66, 71, 74, 77, 78, 82, 83, 84, 112
Scrogham, J.L. 105
Scrogham, Mrs. Hugh 118
Sears, Barnas 28
Seaton, Butch 147
Selph, Jane 207
Sensabaugh, Charles 145, 147
Sensabaugh, D.C. 147, 166, 169, 173
Sensabaugh, D.W. 152, 160, 168, 194, 217, 229
Sensabaugh, Dickie 147
Sensabaugh, Frances 207
Sensabaugh, Kenneth 147, 158, 192, 229
Sensabaugh, Kitty 209, 211, 212
Sensabaugh, Lewis 147
Sensabaugh, Lois 202, 229
Sensabaugh, Mrs. D.C. 118
Sethman, Roger 216
Sheahan, Paul 156
Sheets, J.K. 104
Sheets, Mrs. Roy A. 186, 201
Sheffer, Forrest 147
Sheffer, Larry 147
Sherrard, Rob 224
Sherwood, Beckie 212, 229
Shiflett, Gerald 147
Shipp, Gordon 180
Shue, David 230
Silling, David 137
Silling, Stuart Preston 93, 94, 120
Silling, Meredith 160
Simantel, Mrs. W.A. 156

Simmons, Harry 147
Simpson, Louise 175, 207
Simpson, MacDuff 21, 33, 62
Sites, Lola 217
Smiley, Mrs. R.S. 118
Smith, Benjamin Mosby 17
Smith, Beth 215, 217, 218, 219
Smith, J. Hoge, Jr 218
Smith, Joseph 17
Snyder, Pam 228, 229
Speck, Mabel 105
Sprouse, W.W. 83, 109
Sprunt, James 153
St. Clair, David 104
St. Clair family 168
St. Clair, Harvey 104
St. Clair, Helen 207
St. Clair, Ray Lawrence 102, 103, 104, 107, 109, 110, 111, 127, 132, 136, 141, 145, 153, 158, 161, 164, 183, 186, 188, 193, 194, 200, 201, 204
Steagall, Virginia 122
Steele, John 17
Stevens, Millard 215
Stevenson, Paul 17
Stokes, Agnes 106
Strickler, Givens B. 22, 25, 62
Stump, W.H. 133
Sunday, Billy 104
Swarzel, Harry 147
Swisher, Nancy 175, 229

T

Tate, Major 34
Tate, William 26
Tate, William M. 22
Thomas, Jim 147
Thompson, Dorothy Scott 201
Timberlake, John, 218
Timberlake, Wayt 143
Tinsley, H.C. 73
Tom Thumb 140, 141
Tomes, Mrs. J.W. 118
Trimble, Francis Marion 120
Trimble, Isaac Henry 93, 109
Trimble, Martha Cline 112
Trimble, Mrs. I.H. 112
Truman, Harry S 142
Tudor, Mary 2, 3
Turner, Charles W.S. 22, 27

Turner, Herbert S. 166, 167

U

Ussher, James 5

V

Van Dyck, Edward 195
Van Fossen, Betty 104, 182, 184, 194, 197, 207
Van Fossen, Louis 229
Vance, Joseph Al 45
Vaughan, Harry 142
Vigilione, Joseph 186

W

Waddell, James 16
Wade, Mrs. Clyde A. 151
Walker, Henry 31
Walker, Henry A. 27, 37
Walker, J.W. 30
Walker, Robert C. 27
Walker, Sue 226
Walker, T. Dennis 194, 195, 196, 197, 198, 200, 203, 211, 212, 215, 226
Wall, Mrs. R.P. (Betty) 116, 118, 133, 137, 138, 145, 176, 229
Waller, C.D. 91
Waller, Charles DeVries 92
Walthall, D.K. 83, 91
Walthall, David B. Kirby 92
Walton, Howard 124
Wampler, Jeffrey 169
Ware, A.S. 151
Washington, George 16
Wayland, J.E. 109
Weller, Bessie 156
Wells family 51
Wells, John Miller 46, 47, 50, 52
Wells, Thomas 51
Wenger, Eunice 207
Wenger, W. Tracy 133, 152, 160
Wentworth, Thomas 5
Westhafer, Geneva 182, 208
Westhafer, Terry 202, 211
Wetzel, Robert 152, 160
Whaling, Thornton 65
Whitbeck, Donald V. 105
White, R.W. 49
White, William C. 95

Wilkerson, Carlyle 147
Wilkerson, Martha 166, 226, 229
William of Orange 7
Williams, Daniel Steven 218, 219, 221, 222
Williams family 219
Williams, Jonathan 219
Williams, Sharon 222
Williams, Timothy 219
Willson, Mrs. Gilpin, Jr. 130
Wilson, Arthur 61
Wilson, D.B. 93, 112
Wilson, Dorsey 52
Wilson, Howard Craig 93
Wilson, Howard M. 153
Wilson, Joseph Ruggles 17, 52
Wilson, Mrs. D.B. 112
Wilson, Thomas Woodrow 18, 52, 78, 84
Wilson, W.A. 60
Wimer, Katherine 222
Wimer, Woody 199
Wine, J.B. and Son 158, 212
Wine, Joseph 139
Wiseman, C. Wallace 70
Wolfe, Paul 227
Wolfe, Shirley 227
Wood, Calvin 147
Wood, David 147
Wood, Eddie, 147
Woodhouse, Mrs. A.S. 48
Woodrum, Mrs. Ronald 118
Woodrum, Ronald 105, 133, 165
Woods, Lucy D. 27
Woodside, A.M. "Mack" 128, 140, 142, 161, 164, 165, 166, 167, 174, 183, 193, 200, 210
Wren, Christopher 149
Wymer, Raymond Charles 93

Y

Yenem, Y.N. 45
Yerkes, Charles T. 195
Yount, Glenn E. 132, 152, 161, 205
Yount, Mrs. Glenn E. (Nelle) 117, 161, 205